Rhode Island

A History

William G. McLoughlin

**With a Historical Guide
Prepared by the editors of
the American Association for
State and Local History**

W. W. Norton & Company
New York · London

American Association for State and Local History
Nashville

Author and publishers make grateful acknowledgment to Patrick T. Conley, for permission to quote from "Rhode Island Constitutional Development, 1616–1841" (Ph.D. dissertation, University of Notre Dame, 1970).

Published and distributed by
W. W. Norton & Company, Inc.
500 Fifth Avenue
New York, New York 10110

Library of Congress in Publication Data

McLoughlin, William Gerald
    Rhode Island: A history
    (The States and the nation series)
    Bibliography: p.
    Includes index.
    1. Rhode Island—History. I. Series.
F79.M32   974.5   78-2911

ISBN 978-0-393-30271-4

Printed in the United States of America
5 6 7 8 9 0

This book is affectionately dedicated to
Jack and Patty Thomas
Bill and Sal Jordy
John and Pamela Strom,
friends who make Rhode Island home

Contents

Original Maps by Harold Faye

An Historical Guide

TO RHODE ISLAND

Colonial Newport

Newport

★ From the late seventeenth century until the American Revolution, Newport reigned as one of the leading ports in colonial America. The city's flourishing coastwise trade and highly profitable international commerce stimulated the Rhode Island economy and inspired an urban elegance rivaled only by Boston in the mid-eighteenth century. Beautiful homes constructed in the lat-

Hunter House

est styles and filled with elegant furnishings testified to the affluence of Newport's entrepreneurs, and the erection of equally fine public buildings further demonstrated pride in the city's wealth and power. Newport's golden age of commerce came to a close with the War for Independence, but an amazing number of the structures from that period survive today in the Newport Historic District, a National Historic Landmark. The district preserves Newport's colonial past and commemorates Rhode Island's emergence as a major commercial center in the British empire.

Roger Williams' insistence on religious tolerance made colonial Rhode Island a haven for dissenters. One such group from the Massachusetts Bay Colony established the town of Newport in 1639 on the south coast of Aquidneck Island. From the first, activity centered around the deepwater harbor. Newport's first street, Thames, was laid out parallel to the harbor, and a dock was constructed at the end of Marlborough Street later that first year. Over the next decades the community developed in a rather haphazard fashion that reflected immediate needs rather than any formal plan. By 1680, over four hundred structures stood along the narrow streets around Washington Square, a commons area that became the heart of the colonial settlement. By that time entrepreneurs had also constructed the Long Wharf at the foot of the square, and a burgeoning maritime industry assured the settlement's success.

Although shipbuilding began at Newport as early as 1646 and remained an important industry throughout the period, shipping and commerce provided the catalyst for the settlement's growth prior to the Revolution. Before the close of the seventeenth century, Newport's commercial activity expanded from coastwise trade with other colonies to trade with the West Indies and Europe. Ships arrived at the Newport harbor with manufactured goods from Britain, whale oil from New Bedford and Boston, and spices, sugar, molasses, and slaves from the West Indies. Exports ranged from such local products as rum, spermacetti candles, and hemp to finely crafted furniture, clocks, and silver. The most profitable commercial activity was the triangular trade in molasses, rum, and slaves. By the beginning of the eighteenth century, fifty to sixty Newport-based ships were engaged in this activity, and Newport had become the center for the New England slave trade. Much of the city's growing wealth and influence was due to this highly profitable but notorious activity. In fact, an import tax on the slaves between 1707 and 1732 financed the construction of bridges and the paving of Newport streets.

Maritime activity provided a solid economic base for the city's growth and development. By the mid-eighteenth century, Newport flourished as one of the most prosperous ports in the colonies and the economic center of Rhode Island. Affluent merchants and sea captains erected stylish new homes and filled them with finely crafted furnishings. Craftsmen and small tradesmen built more modest homes and shops along the streets that lined the bustling harbor. Churches and civic buildings incorporated the best of Georgian style and stood as symbols of the town's wealth and power. Only Boston equaled the stylish grace and urban sophistication of Newport in the decades prior to the Revolution.

This golden age of Newport's prosperity ended with the war. Newport never fully recovered from wartime cessation of commerce, and economic leadership shifted to Providence in the 1780s. Although the city did not regain its position as a commercial center, its popularity as a resort for the wealthy brought economic revival by the mid-nineteenth century. Summer visitors largely avoided the old colonial city, however, and consequently many of the historic structures escaped significant alteration and demolition. Indeed, no comparable collection of colonial buildings exists today in the state or perhaps in the nation. The Newport Historic District constitutes a unique historical and architectural legacy.

Few buildings survive in Newport from the seventeenth century. The best example of housing that remains from that era is the Wanton-Lyman-Hazard House at 17 Broadway. Build by Stephen Mumford about 1695, the two-and-a-half-story frame structure uses medieval construction techniques but details and ornamentation are suggestive of the later Georgian style. The White Horse Tavern at 26 Marlborough Street dates from at least two decades earlier. William Mayes began operating a tavern in this two story frame building in 1687, and it now boasts of being the oldest such business in continuous operation in the United States. Across Farewell Street stands an early symbol of Newport's tradition of religious diversity—the Meetinghouse of the Society of Friends at 30 Marlborough Street. The original portion was erected in 1699 by Quakers from Connecticut and Massachusetts. Subsequent enlargements in the eighteenth and nineteenth centuries marked the growth of the Quaker community and its growing influence in Newport commerce.

Eighteenth-century structures clearly predominate in the district. The most distinctive are the Georgian civic buildings and churches designed by Richard Munday and Peter Harrison. Munday, a local master carpenter, designed the Colony House, the center of early Rhode Island government. Erected in 1739 at the east end of Washington Square, this structure housed the colonial and early state governments and was the scene of numerous historic occasions, including Rhode Island's ratification of both the Declaration of Independence and the Constitution. At the west end of Washington Square at the head of the Long Wharf stands the Brick Market, a market house constructed in 1726 at the peak of Newport's commercial development. Designed by noted amateur architect Peter Harrison, this structure and the Colony House reflect the commercial and civic activity that made Washington Square the heart of colonial Newport. Harrison also designed the Redwood Library at 50 Bellevue Avenue and Touro Synagogue at 72 Touro Street, two important edifices whose histories reflect Newport's tradition of religious tolerance.

The basic fabric of the district, however, is residential. Whether of grand design or the simplest plan, most houses in eighteenth-century

Newport were constructed of wood. As late as 1793, only six brick structures stood in the city, including the Colony House and the Brick Market. Small frame houses give the district much of its charm and distinctiveness today, and several particularly interesting examples stand west of Thames Street in an area known as Easton's Point. There tradesmen and craftsmen erected houses and shops accessible to the harbor and shipping facilities. Among the craftsmen were the Townsend and Goddard families, leading Newport cabinetmakers known for their exceptionally fine furniture. The Townsends had several shops and residences along Bridge Street, including a house-workshop complex built for Christopher Townsend in 1725 at 74–76 Bridge Street and another erected before 1758 at 68–70–72 Bridge by Job Townsend. John Goddard, an apprentice to Job Townsend, later became an accomplished cabinetmaker himself and resided in the house at 81 Second Street.

As Newport prospered in the mid-eighteenth century, wealthy merchants and sea captains built larger and more elegant homes alongside these modest residences. The Jonathan Nichols-Hunter at 54 Washington Street is typical of the houses erected along the harbor for wealthy shipping entrepreneurs. Like many other waterside residences, the Hunter House originally had adjoining wharves and shops in order to take full advantage of the location. Erected in 1748, it has a pineapple-crowned pediment above the entrance, a symbol of Newport hospitality and a reflection of the city's West Indies trade. Once called Shipwrights Street because so many ships' carpenters lived and worked there, Bridge Street later became known for the sea captains that resided there at the close of the eighteenth century. The Captain Peter Simon House at 25 Bridge Street, a sea captain's residence erected before 1727 and altered prior to the Revolution, is typical.

These are but a few examples of the many fine colonial structures that line the streets of the Newport Historic District. Their preservation and restoration reflects the efforts of the Newport Historical Society, the Preservation Society of Newport County, the Newport Restoration Foundation, Operation Clapboard, the Oldport Association, and numerous other individuals and groups. Now carefully restored through their efforts to its eighteenth-century elegance, the colonial city of Newport recaptures an era of commercial wealth and maritime power unequalled in modern Rhode Island history.

Slater Mill Historic Site

Pawtucket

★ Industrialization, the factory system, and mass-production technology shaped the history of Rhode Island and indeed of the nation in the nineteenth and twentieth centuries. The turning point in the transition from cottage hand-

Mill complex on the Blackstone River

crafts to factory machine production came in 1790, when Samuel Slater and his associates at Pawtucket successfully produced machine-spun cotton thread for the first time in the United States. Three years later, they opened what came to be known as the Old Slater Mill, the nation's first successful cotton factory and the progenitor of the modern industrial plant. The Slater Mill Historic Site preserves this historic building and commemorates both the beginnings of textile manufacturing and industrialization in Rhode Island and the birth of the American Industrial Revolution.

The example of British industrialization inspired numerous attempts at establishing manufacturing in the United States in the decades after the American Revolution. These efforts failed at first because of lack of capital and inadequate knowledge of the machinery and the production process. In the late 1780s, however, Moses Brown, a wealthy Quaker merchant from Providence, decided to try his hand at textile manufacturing. Brown had the necessary capital, but none of the machines he acquired matched the reputed performance of the spinning machinery developed by Richard Arkwright in England in the 1760s. Brown, his son-in-law William Alvey, and his nephew Smith Brown sought someone with firsthand knowledge of the Arkwright mills, but they had little success because of British restrictions on the emigration of skilled mechanics. At about this same time, Samuel Slater came to the United States from England. As a former apprentice to Jedediah Strutt, one of Arkwright's partners, Slater had the expertise that Smith and his associates needed to make their enterprise a success. After an exchange of correspondence, Slater and Brown met in 1790 and agreed to join forces.

Slater was far from impressed by the assortment of machinery Brown had assembled in a fulling plant at Pawtucket. Brown's spinning machines did not measure up to the Arkwright equipment Slater was familiar with, and the Americans clearly had no perception of the requirements of the production process. With the help of local mechanics like Oziel and David Wilkinson and Sylvanus Brown, Slater rebuilt the spinning frames, constructed drawing and roving frames, and completed work on a carding machine. While these improvements in the machinery were important, Slater's most significant contribution was his understanding of the whole production process. Because he had been apprenticed as an overseer, he was familiar not just with individual machines but with how they functioned as a system. He knew how to set up a mill and maintain continuous production flow without bottlenecks and waste. Although historians have long emphasized Slater's role in duplicating the Arkwright machines, his expertise in organizing and managing machines proved more significant to the development of the modern system of factory organization and production.

In December 1790, Slater and his associates finally completed installation of the machinery and began production of the first machine-spun cotton thread. Located in rented space in a Pawtucket fulling mill, this first textile factory clearly demonstrated the profitability of spinning yarn and convinced Slater, Almy, and Moses' son Obadiah Brown to construct a new mill building to house an expanded textile factory. In 1793 they erected a simple two-and-a-half-story, timber-framed structure. Although constructed of wood rather than stone, as Slater was accustomed to in England, the mill was solidly built to withstand the wear and tear of factory use. Well-scaled Neoclassical details enhanced the exterior and made the edifice more acceptable at a time when manufacturing was still viewed with suspicion by the public. Innovations included a trap-door monitor on the gabled roof and open interior spaces. The former provided a source of light in the attic and became a distinguishing feature of early American factories. The open interior on each floor provided flexibility in organizing the mill. With the machinery from their rented quarters installed in the new building, Almy, Brown, and Slater began operating in 1793 the nation's first successful water-powered cotton manufactory.

In 1797, Slater established a partnership with his father-in-law Oziel Wilkinson and several brothers-in-law and erected a new, larger mill across the Blackstone River. His former associates also established new mills, and until 1803 the three entrepreneurs together owned all the spinning factories in the United States. Competitors entered the field after 1803, and by 1815 Rhode Island had over one hundred mills in operation.

Although mechanized spinning had become commonplace, weaving remained a cottage industry at Pawtucket until 1815, when David Wilkinson constructed a workable power loom based on a design by William Gilmore. By that time Francis Cabot Lowell and the Boston Associates had taken the lead in the textile industry by integrating the production process from raw cotton to finished cloth. Although Rhode Island remained a strong competitor in the textile industry for some time to come, Pawtucket's era ended in 1829 when the major companies folded in the wake of a national economic collapse.

Over the next decades, the various owners of the Old Slater Mill used it for different purposes. When demolition threatened the historic structure in 1921, the Old Slater Mill Association was established to preserve it. The structure was restored in 1924 and 1925, but not until 1955 was it opened as a museum of technology and industry. The present mill includes the original 1793 building as well as additions made in 1801 and 1812 through 1817. Although much altered over the years, the building has been restored to its 1835 appearance. Exhibits focus on the evolution of the textile industry and the transition from cottage handcrafts to machine production.

In 1973 two additional historic structures, the Wilkinson Mill and the Sylvanus Brown House, were also opened to the public. At the Wilkinson Mill, erected in 1810, visitors can see a recreated nineteenth-century machine shop and the restored power system. The Sylvanus Brown House, which dates from 1758, has been restored and furnished as an example of a skilled artisan's home in an early urban-industrial community.

Public programs at the Slater Mill Historic Site include guided tours, exhibits, craft demonstrations, and a variety of educational programs. The visitor to the site learns not just about machines, technology, and water power but also about factory life, the workplace, and living conditions in an early industrial village. No other site is so historically important or offers such valuable insight into the industrial experience in Rhode Island at the dawn of the Industrial Revolution.

Aldrich House

Providence

★ The zenith of Rhode Island economic development and political power came in the decades between 1860 and 1910. The dominant figure of this golden age was Nelson W. Aldrich, United States Senator from Rhode Island from 1881 to 1911 and a symbol of the integral relationship between business and politics in this period. His Providence home still stands as a reminder of his impressive career. In light of his

Aldrich House

impact on the state's history, it is fitting that the structure now houses the Museum of Rhode Island History of the Rhode Island Historical Society.

Nelson Aldrich was fully committed to the conservative, pro-business philosophy that guided the Republican party in the last half of the nineteenth century. He was convinced that establishing a favorable climate for business growth and development was the essential function of the government, and his career reflected this single purpose. He refused to become simply a spokesman for Rhode Island business and insisted that his constituents' interests would best be served if he focused his attentions on harmonizing the needs of American business broadly. In this broker role, Aldrich became one of the most powerful men in the nation and amassed a fortune consistent with his intimate relationship with the American business and industrial community.

Aldrich's political career began in 1869, when he won election to the Providence Common Council. Although initially an Independent Republican, he soon aligned himself with the party faction headed by Henry Anthony, the "boss" of Rhode Island politics until his death in 1884. After five years on the city council, Aldrich advanced (with Anthony's assistance) to the state legislature in 1875 and to the United States House of Representatives in 1878. Then in 1881, the Anthony-controlled state legislature selected Aldrich to succeed the late General Ambrose Burnside in the United States Senate. After Anthony's death his successor, Charles R. Brayton, continued the tight political operation that kept Aldrich in the Senate for three decades.

Appointed to the Senate Finance Committee, Aldrich became a leading Republican strategist on economic policy. From 1883 to 1909, he played a major role in every tariff bill that came before the Senate. Basically he tried to mediate between conflicting interests and work out compromises within the context of the protectionism he and his colleagues were convinced was essential to continued economic growth. In 1888 he took the lead in Senate opposition to a Democratic-sponsored proposal for tariff reduction. Aldrich's counterproposal became a cornerstone of the Republican platform in the presidential race that fall and two years later served as a model for the highly protective McKinley tariff. Aldrich guided the latter through the Senate in 1890. Public reaction against high tariffs gave the Democrats a temporary majority in Congress in the mid-1890s, but Aldrich still managed to hold off significant downward tariff revisions in the Wilson-Gorman act of 1894. He remained an unyielding advocate of high tariffs and in 1909 co-sponsored the controversial Payne-Aldrich tariff. Insurgent Republicans had secured party endorsement of tariff reform in the 1908 platform, but the 1909 act did not deviate from traditional Republican protectionism and clearly indicated Aldrich's unassailable power. Public reaction against Payne-Aldrich contributed to the erosion of party support in 1910 and 1912 elections, but Aldrich refused to compromise his position and remained an ardent protectionist and spokesman for powerful Old Guard Republicanism.

After the Panic of 1907, the Rhode Island senator became concerned with the inflexibility of the currency. In 1908 he sponsored the Aldrich-Vreeland Act, which provided emergency currency during financial crises such as that in 1907. More important, the act created the National Monetary Commission. With Aldrich as chairman, the commission studied the currency problem and in 1909 proposed the "Aldrich plan" for a strong central bank. The senator retired before Congress took action, but his plan did provide the basis for the current Federal Reserve System.

During his three decades there, Aldrich became in many ways the "boss" of the Senate. His leadership on central economic issues explains part of this, but the rest of the explanation rests with his skills as a politician. He manipulated his colleagues not through speeches but through persuasion, trade-offs, and the like. With seniority, his influence expanded, and his chairmanship of both the Senate Finance Committee and the Steering Committee placed him in a position to discipline party members. He worked closely with an inner circle that included William B. Allison of Iowa, John C. Spooner of Wisconsin, and Orville H. Platt of Connecticut. Together these men dominated the major Senate committees and maintained tight control over their Republican colleagues. In an era of weak presidents, this legislative power was crucial. When Theodore Roosevelt attempted to restore the power of the presidency after the turn of the century, even he had to make concessions to the boss of the Senate.

Aldrich had been a successful businessman prior to entering politics, but as a public servant he became a multimillionaire. His political power and business contacts gave him access to profitable investments in sugar, tobacco, rubber, banking, street railways, gas, and electricity. In the 1890s his wealth enabled him to purchase an impressive house on Benevolent Street in Providence and to develop an estate at Warwick Neck. He retained both until his death in 1915 at the age of 73. Ownership of the Providence residence remained with the family until 1974, when they deeded it to the Rhode Island Historical Society.

The house at 110 Benevolent Street dates from 1821–1872. John Holden Green designed the Federal-style mansion for Robert S. Burroughs, and several others owned it prior to Aldrich's purchase in the 1890s. The three-story structure has a clapboard exterior, a low-pitched hipped roof and cupola, and a small portico supported by Doric columns and pilasters at the main entrance. Interior features have been retained whenever possible, but the house does not contain period rooms. Instead, this historic structure provides a handsome setting for the Museum of Rhode Island History, the state's first comprehensive history museum. The structure houses both exhibits and a variety of educational and interpretive programs. Other facilities of the Rhode Island Historical Society include the John Brown House, an eighteenth-century historic-house museum, and the Rhode Island Historical Society Library on Hope Street.

Other Places of Interest

*The following suggest other places of
historical interest to visit. We recommend
that you check hours of operation in advance.*

THE ARCADE, *130 Westminster Street, Providence.* Three-story shopping
arcade in the Greek Revival style, built in 1827 and recently renovated; one
of the earliest enclosed arcades in America.

ELEAZER ARNOLD HOUSE, *449 Great Road, Lincoln.* Seventeenth-century stone-end house, typical of Rhode Island vernacular architecture.

BABCOCK-SMITH HOUSE, *124 Granite Street, Westerly.* A mansion built
in 1832 for Dr. Joshua Babcock, town postmaster and physician, active in
state politics.

BRICK SCHOOL HOUSE, *24 Meeting Street, Providence.* One of Providence's first schools, and an early school for black children; now the headquarters of the Providence Preservation Society.

BRISTOL HISTORICAL AND PRESERVATION SOCIETY, *48 Court Street,
Bristol.* Museum in the 1828 town jail, including costumes, toys, furniture,
Indian artifacts, military items, and other collections.

COGGESHALL FARM MUSEUM, *Colt State Park, Bristol.* A working
eighteenth-century farm with restored buildings and demonstrations of crafts
and agricultural practices.

COLLEGE HILL HISTORIC DISTRICT, *Providence.* The heart of the original town settlement, including many well-preserved public buildings and
private homes from the eighteenth and nineteenth centuries.

FIRST BAPTIST CHURCH IN AMERICA, *North Main Street, Providence.*
Built in 1774 and 1775 by the congregation founded by Roger Williams;
restored colonial church was also the site of Brown University's commence-
ment ceremonies.

FORT ADAMS, *Fort Adams State Park, Newport.* The second-largest bas-
tioned fort in the United States, covering twenty-one acres, begun in 1799.

GOV. STEPHEN HOPKINS HOUSE, *Hopkins Street, Providence.* Home of
an early governor and signer of the Declaration of Independence, and one
of the oldest homes surviving in Providence; period herb gardens.

INTERNATIONAL TENNIS HALL OF FAME AND TENNIS MUSEUM, *Newport Casino, Bellevue Avenue, Newport.* Center of public life during Newport's gilded age and site of the first national tennis tournaments.

JOHN BROWN HOUSE, *52 Power Street, Providence.* Georgian mansion built in 1786 by one of Providence's most prominent merchants; headquarters of the Rhode Island Historical Society and noted for collection of Rhode Island furniture.

NAVAL WAR COLLEGE MUSEUM, *Coasters Island, Newport.* In Founders Hall, location of the world's first naval war college (1884); exhibits on naval warfare and the Navy in Narragansett Bay.

NEWPORT HISTORICAL SOCIETY, *82 Touro Street, Newport.* Exhibits on Newport and Rhode Island history, including decorative arts, maritime collection, toys, and textiles.

OLD STATE HOUSE, *150 Benefit Street, Providence.* Site of the renunciation of Rhode Island's allegiance to King George III, May 4, 1776.

PRESCOTT FARM, *Route 114, Middletown.* Collection of colonial farm buildings, including a working windmill and post-and-beam house with seventeenth-century furnishings.

PRESERVATION SOCIETY OF NEWPORT COUNTY, *Mill Street, Newport.* Maintains and operates seven historic properties in Newport and one in Portsmouth, spanning over 150 years of the county's history.

PROVIDENCE CITY HALL, *Kennedy Plaza, Providence.* Beaux Arts-style building (1875–1878), recently restored; elaborate interior stenciling.

RHODE ISLAND BLACK HERITAGE SOCIETY, *1 Hilton Street, Providence.* Archive and museum collection documenting the life of blacks in the state from the earliest slaves to recent immigrants.

ROGER WILLIAMS NATIONAL MEMORIAL, *North Main Street, Providence.* Site of the original (1636) settlement of the town.

SMITH'S CASTLE, *U.S. 1, N. Kingstown.* Early trading outpost, enlarged during the era of Rhode Island plantation system in the eighteenth century.

SOUTH COUNTY MUSEUM, *State 2, N. Kingstown.* Exhibits of early Rhode Island rural life and industry, including tools, farming implements, and vehicles.

UNIVERSITY HALL, *Brown University, Providence.* Built 1770–1771, the oldest building at Brown; used as a hospital and barracks during the Revolutionary War.

JAMES MITCHELL VARNUM HOUSE, *57 Pierce Street, E. Greenwich.* Carefully restored Georgian house built in 1773 for General Varnum, Revolutionary War commander, lawyer, and congressman.

WHITEHALL, *311 Berkeley Avenue, Middletown*. Home of George Berkeley, philosopher and minister, his family, and others sent from England in 1729 to prepare to found a college in Bermuda.

WHITEHORN HOUSE, *416 Thames Street, Newport*. Federal-period home that houses the collections of the Newport Restoration Foundation.

WILBOR HOUSE AND BARN, *West Main Road, Little Compton*. Decorative arts and agricultural collections from three centuries of Little Compton's history, including artifacts from the development of commercial poultry production.

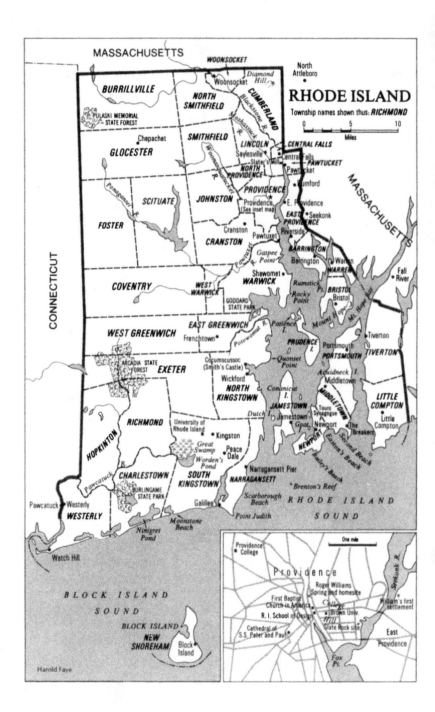

MASSACHUSETTS

WOONSOCKET

North
Attleboro

RHODE ISLAND

Township names shown thus: *RICHMOND*

0   5   10
Miles

Diamond
Hill
Woonsocket

BURRILLVILLE

Blackstone R.

CUMBERLAND

*NORTH
SMITHFIELD*

PULASKI MEMORIAL
STATE FOREST

Mohassuck R.

SMITHFIELD

Chepachet

LINCOLN   *CENTRAL FALLS*

GLOCESTER

Saylesville
Slater's Mill

Central Falls   *PAWTUCKET*

Pawtucket

Woonasquatucket R.

*NORTH
PROVIDENCE*

Ponaganset R.

SCITUATE

Rumford

JOHNSTON   *PROVIDENCE*

Providence
(See inset map)

E. Providence

Seekonk

FOSTER

*EAST
PROVIDENCE*

Cranston

Riverside

Pawtuxet

CRANSTON

BARRINGTON

Barrington   Warren

Gaspee
Point

WARREN

Pawtuxet R.

Shawomet

WARWICK

Rumstick
Pt.   *BRISTOL*

COVENTRY

*WEST
WARWICK*

Rocky
Point

Bristol

Fall
River

GODDARD
STATE PARK

Mount Hope   Mt. Hope Bay

EAST GREENWICH

Patience
I.

WEST GREENWICH

Frenchtown

Pottowomut R.

PRUDENCE

Portsmouth

Tiverton

Prudence
I.

PORTSMOUTH   *TIVERTON*

Quonset
Point

Cocumscussoc
(Smith's Castle)

EXETER

Wickford

Aquidneck I.

Middletown

ARCADIA STATE
FOREST

*LITTLE
COMPTON*

Conanicut
I.

*NORTH
KINGSTOWN*

JAMESTOWN   *MIDDLETOWN*

RICHMOND

University of
Rhode Island

Kingston

Dutch I.

Touro
Synagogue

Jamestown
Goat I.

Newport

Little
Compton

HOPKINTON

Great
Swamp

Peace
Dale

The
Breakers

Worden's
Pond

Second
Beach

NEWPORT

Easton's Beach

CHARLESTOWN

*SOUTH
KINGSTOWN*

Bailey's Beach

BURLINGAME
STATE PARK

Narragansett Pier

NARRAGANSETT

Brenton's Reef

Galilee

Scarborough
Beach

RHODE ISLAND

Pawcatuck R.

Pawcatuck   Westerly

WESTERLY

Point Judith

SOUND

Moonstone
Beach

Ninigret
Pond

Watch Hill

BLOCK ISLAND

SOUND

BLOCK ISLAND

*NEW
SHOREHAM*

Block
Island

Harold Faye

CONNECTICUT

MASSACHUSETTS

One mile

Providence
College

P r o v i d e n c e

Roger Williams
Spring and homesite

First Baptist
Church in America

College

William's first
settlement

R. I. School of Design

Brown Univ.

Slate Rock site

Cathedral of
S.S. Peter and Paul

East
Providence

Seekonk R.

Fox
Pt.

Invitation to the Reader

IN 1807, former President John Adams argued that a complete history of the American Revolution could not be written until the history of change in each state was known, because the principles of the Revolution were as various as the states that went through it. Two hundred years after the Declaration of Independence, the American nation has spread over a continent and beyond. The states have grown in number from thirteen to fifty. And democratic principles have been interpreted differently in every one of them.

We therefore invite you to consider that the history of your state may have more to do with the bicentennial review of the American Revolution than does the story of Bunker Hill or Valley Forge. The Revolution has continued as Americans extended liberty and democracy over a vast territory. John Adams was right: the states are part of that story, and the story is incomplete without an account of their diversity.

The Declaration of Independence stressed life, liberty, and the pursuit of happiness; accordingly, it shattered the notion of holding new territories in the subordinate status of colonies. The Northwest Ordinance of 1787 set forth a procedure for new states to enter the Union on an equal footing with the old. The Federal Constitution shortly confirmed this novel means of building a nation out of equal states. The step-by-step process through which territories have achieved self-government and national representation is among the most important of the Founding Fathers' legacies.

The method of state-making reconciled the ancient conflict between liberty and empire, resulting in what Thomas Jefferson called an empire for liberty. The system has worked and remains unaltered, despite enormous changes that have taken

place in the nation. The country's extent and variety now surpass anything the patriots of '76 could likely have imagined.
The United States has changed from an agrarian republic into a
highly industrial and urban democracy, from a fledgling nation
into a major world power. As Oliver Wendell Holmes remarked
in 1920, the creators of the nation could not have seen completely how it and its constitution and its states would develop.
Any meaningful review in the bicentennial era must consider
what the country has become, as well as what it was.

The new nation of equal states took as its motto *E Pluribus
Unum*—"out of many, one." But just as many peoples have
become Americans without complete loss of ethnic and cultural
identities, so have the states retained differences of character.
Some have been superficial, expressed in stereotyped images—
big, boastful Texas, "sophisticated" New York, "hillbilly"
Arkansas. Other differences have been more real, sometimes instructively, sometimes amusingly; democracy has embraced
Huey Long's Louisiana, bilingual New Mexico, unicameral Ne-
braska, and a Texas that once taxed fortunetellers and spawned
politicians called "Woodpecker Republicans" and "Skunk
Democrats." Some differences have been profound, as when
South Carolina secessionists led other states out of the Union in
opposition to abolitionists in Massachusetts and Ohio. The result was a bitter Civil War.

The Revolution's first shots may have sounded in Lexington
and Concord; but fights over what democracy should mean and
who should have independence have erupted from Pennsylvania's Gettysburg to the "Bleeding Kansas" of John Brown,
from the Alamo in Texas to the Indian battles at Montana's
Little Bighorn. Utah Mormons have known the strain of isolation; Hawaiians at Pearl Harbor, the terror of attack; Georgians
during Sherman's march, the sadness of defeat and devastation.
Each state's experience differs instructively; each adds understanding to the whole.

The purpose of this series of books is to make that kind of understanding accessible, in a way that will last in value far
beyond the bicentennial fireworks. The series offers a volume
on every state, plus the District of Columbia—fifty-one, in all.

Each book contains, besides the text, a view of the state through eyes other than the author's—a "photographer's essay," in which a skilled photographer presents his own personal perceptions of the state's contemporary flavor.

We have asked authors not for comprehensive chronicles, nor for research monographs or new data for scholars. Bibliographies and footnotes are minimal. We have asked each author for a summing up—interpretive, sensitive, thoughtful, individual, even personal—of what seems significant about his or her state's history. What distinguishes it? What has mattered about it, to its own people and to the rest of the nation? What has it come to now?

To interpret the states in all their variety, we have sought a variety of backgrounds in authors themselves and have encouraged variety in the approaches they take. They have in common only these things: historical knowledge, writing skill, and strong personal feelings about a particular state. Each has wide latitude for the use of the short space. And if each succeeds, it will be by offering you, in your capacity as a *citizen* of a state *and* of a nation, stimulating insights to test against your own.

James Morton Smith
General Editor

Preface

WHEN Cotton Mather called Rhode Island and Providence Plantations "the fag end of creation" and "the sewer of New England," he did not mean that the beautiful harbor and fertile fields of the area were not highly desirable real estate. The Puritans who surrounded the colony used fair means and foul to get control of it. They just didn't like the people who lived here. But I have found them fascinating—from the ultra-Puritans who started an experiment in freedom to the rebellious smugglers who burned the King's naval cutter, from the textile manufacturers who started the country on its industrial revolution to the twentieth-century immigrants and children of immigrants who waged a bloodless revolution to take control of the state from the waspish Yankees. They are an intriguing assortment of idealists, patriots, entrepreneurs, politicians, rogues, and rascals. For those who still think of it as "Rogue's Island," this is a rogues' gallery. But it also delineates many gallant souls—champions of religious liberty, valiant Indian chiefs, black patriots, antislavery reformers, resolute feminists, and fiery trade unionists.

Yet, amid all this diversity and perversity, there are central themes. Rhode Island's genius has been to survive against the odds. Its self-made, strong-willed, resilient people have not minded going against the mainstream—or with it. Rugged individualists, they believed in experimentation, believed in trying something and, if that didn't work, trying something else. They have been in all periods ingenious, imaginative, forthright. Born in freedom, adaptable and enterprising, Rhode Island epitomizes all the ambiguities of the American dream.

When Roger Williams founded the colony as a refuge for the oppressed, he was setting the main theme for America. But he might be surprised to find that its diverse ethnic population has become predominantly Roman Catholic.

It would take, they say, two hundred states of Rhode Island's size to fill Texas, but a tremendous amount of American history has been packed into this small, inviting spot. I hope I have done it justice.

ACKNOWLEDGMENTS

I wish to thank Professor Patrick T. Conley of Providence College; Mr. Albert T. Klyberg, Ms. Nancy Chudacoff, and Michael J. Probert of the Rhode Island Historical Society; Professor Howard Chudacoff of Brown University; Professor Sydney V. James of the Department of History, University of Iowa, and others who read this book in manuscript form and offered many helpful suggestions. I have benefited greatly from their comments and corrections. I am indebted also to Kathleen Dunnigan and Amy Printz, who provided much of the basic research and data for the book. The staffs of the Brown University Library, of the Providence Public Library, and of the Rhode Island Historical Society gave generously of their time and skills. And my wife, Virginia Ward McLoughlin, as usual helped, both with the menial chores of typing and proofreading and also in copy editing and suggestions for clarity, direction, and emphasis. The mistakes that remain and the interpretations are mine alone. The above did their best to save me from too many errors.

Rhode Island
A History

1

Religious Freedom and Local Self-Government

$\mathcal{R}$HODE ISLAND's beginning involved five different settlements: Roger Williams's in Providence; Anne Hutchinson's in Pocasset; William Coddington's in Newport; William Arnold's in Pawtuxet; and Samuel Gorton's in Shawomet. Its formative years, 1636 to 1690, were marked by two simultaneous struggles: the search for unity among these diverse settlements around Narragansett Bay and the resistance of settlers there to efforts by the neighboring colonies to assume authority over their land. At first the threatened encroachment of the neighbors exacerbated internal confusion. Ultimately it forged a sense of common cause. The self-willed, stubborn, religious zeal that motivated, or forced, emigrants to leave the rigid, established churches of Massachusetts, Connecticut, Plymouth, or England for the liberal heterodoxy of Rhode Island kept them from working harmoniously together after they arrived. Fiercely jealous of the local independence of their various settlements, Rhode Islanders often proved their own worst enemies. They lacked that communal sense of purpose and the unity of church and state that gave stability and order to the other colonies. Furthermore, the absence of clearly defined leadership or an upperclass to whom deference was due, plus the availability of so much free land for the taking, gave a very egalitarian and individualistic cast to Rhode Island's infant plantations. Indeed, they were at first almost anarchic. Hard experience rather than ideological consensus finally forced Rhode Islanders toward unity, just as it did the thirteen colonies.

Being come-outers from strict Puritanism was not the only reason Rhode Islanders were treated so scornfully by their English neighbors. They had no charter—no official sanction from the king for their settlements. What right, therefore, had these settlements to make and enforce laws? What validity had their purchases of land? Some who came here assumed that by settling on the frontier they were free from all government. Even those who accepted majority rule questioned the extent of the authority their fellow settlers had over them. Could they collect taxes? Levy fines? Whip, banish, or imprison dissidents? Could they call to arms people who preferred pacifism?

Roger Williams's settlement in Providence in 1636 witnessed two secessions from its self-constituted government within its first five years, and Anne Hutchinson's settlement at Pocasset (on Aquidneck Island) in 1638 had a schism within two years. Dissenters who had "come out" once from a social system they disliked did not hesitate to do so again. Eventually, experience taught the folly of perpetual secession. But where, precisely, did legitimate law and order originate? That remained a central question for Americans for many years to come.

Because Williams's settlement at the northern end of Narragansett Bay was so small and disorganized during the seventeenth century, some historians have dated the birth of the colony from the founding of Newport in 1639. After all, Newport was the dominant town in the bay until the Revolution, and Williams was not the first white settler in the area. He had been preceded in 1634 by the eccentric loner the Reverend William Blackstone, in what is now Cumberland. But that interpretation ignores the fact that Williams's friendship with the Indians was the key to opening this region to English settlement. Williams did not, as he said, purchase the land: the Indians gave it to him. And so did they give Aquidneck to the Hutchinsonians as a favor to Williams. "The truth is," Williams wrote, "not a penny was demanded" by the Narragansett Indians. "It was not price nor money that could have purchased Rhode Island. Rhode Island was purchased by love." [1] The wampum beads and other goods given to the chiefs who made three grants were merely tokens of esteem, "only a gratuity," not a measure of the land's worth to Indians or whites.

Still, the Indians may have had other purposes in mind. It was convenient to have friendly white settlements between them and the more aggressive Puritan colonies. The lands granted first were in a disputed Indian zone, a no man's land separating the Narragansetts west of the bay from the Wampanoags on the east. While the Narragansetts had, previous to the landing of the Pilgrims, won hegemony over the Wampanoags, the Wampanoags, by allying themselves to the English after 1620, had hopes of reasserting their autonomy. Neither tribe, of course, ever expected the white population to increase and expand as rapidly as it did.

But if the Indians miscalculated in their dealings with the Pilgrims and Puritans, they were right in treating Williams as an honest friend. Rhode Islanders did not join in the annihilation of their Indian neighbors, and Williams constantly sought to maintain the peace. "I have," he said in his old age, "not spared purse nor hazards (very many times) that the whole land, English and natives, might sleep in peace and security." [2] Until 1675 he succeeded in keeping Providence and Aquidneck Island free from Indian warfare, though they were in the very heart of Indian territory.

Williams's friendship with the Indians, and their respect for him, derived from his firm belief that "Nature knows no difference between European and American [Indian] in blood, birth, bodies, etc." [3] He did not share the contempt of the English for the "savage." For most of his first three years in New England, Williams traded and preached with the Indians, taking the trouble (which few English did) to learn their language. He

1. Ola E. Winslow, *Master Roger Williams* (New York: MacMillan Co., 1957), pp. 133–134.

2. Winslow, *Master Roger Williams*, p. 157.

3. Cited in Perry Miller, *Roger Williams* (Indianapolis: Bobbs-Merrill Co., 1953), p. 64.

was the first New England apostle to the Indians, though he admitted making few conversions. He thought the English, being superior in certain civilized skills, should teach and help the Indians to improve their lot. The conquest of them by force was not something to be applauded, he said in one poem:

> Boast not proud English of thy birth and blood,
> Thy brother Indian is by birth as good;
> Of one blood God made
> Him and thee and all,
> As wise, as fair, as strong, as personal [human].[4]

The result of Williams's careful study of the Indian way of life and the Indians' trust in him resulted not only in friendship between them but in the publication of one of the first American works of anthropology and linguistics, Williams's famous *Key into the Language of America* in 1643.

Williams was born sometime between 1599 and 1603, the son of a merchant tailor in London. Educated at Pembroke College in Cambridge University, he graduated in 1627. Though ordained a clergyman in the Church of England, he thought its bishops had not gone far enough in the reformation of Roman Catholic errors. He therefore joined the Puritan movement, which was no help to the advancement of his career. He was present in 1629 when a group of Puritans under John Winthrop decided to escape the harassment of King Charles I by moving to Massachusetts Bay. But he did not follow them there until 1631.

Williams found a warm welcome upon his arrival in Boston because he was a devout, dedicated Puritan, thoroughly orthodox in his Calvinism. He was also a warmhearted, generous, earnest man of considerable charm, despite his perfectionist temperament. Modest, yet frank, he was unafraid of hardship, danger, or authority. Honored by being asked to accept the pastorship of the first Puritan church in Boston, he astonished everyone by rejecting the offer because he thought the Puritans should openly break with the Church of England instead of try-

---

4. Cited in Miller, *Roger Williams*, p. 64.

ing to purify it from within. He therefore departed to the Pilgrim colony of New Plymouth, a few miles south of Boston, where William Bradford and his followers had frankly declared themselves to be "Separatists" from Anglicanism.

Williams spent almost three years in Plymouth; there, in addition to farming, trading, and preaching to the Indians, he assisted in the Pilgrim church. In his diary, Governor Bradford described Williams as "a man godly and zealous, having many precious parts but very unsettled in judgment." [5] What was unsettling was Williams's gradually increasing critique of Puritanism. When he returned to Massachusetts Bay in 1633 he was forced by the authorities to burn a manuscript in which he had made slighting remarks about King James I and denied the right of the King to grant to English colonists a patent expropriating land from the Indians without paying them for it.

However, Williams was so obviously devout and sincere in his quest for the absolute truth of God's word that he was invited to be pastor of the church in Salem. He accepted and in 1634 built a house that is still standing, though it is now known as the Corwin House or "the Witch House," because of its connection with the witchcraft trials of 1692. His soul-searching next led him to conclude that civil magistrates did not have the right to compel adherence to the first four of the Ten Commandments ("the first Table" of God's law). Only God's spiritual power could enforce spiritual commands over men's consciences. To compel people to honor the Sabbath was "forced worship." Williams declared that "Forced worship stinks in God's nostrils." [6] God wants only voluntary allegiance. He also argued that it was "false swearing" to force an unconverted person to take an oath in God's name, a position that created difficulty in compelling honest testimony or obtaining oaths of allegiance.

These new views were deemed dangerous to the peace and

5. Clifton E. Olmstead, *History of Religion in the United States* (Englewood Cliffs: Prentice Hall, Inc., 1960), p. 68.
6. Anson Phelps Stokes, *Church and State in the United States,* 3 vols. (New York: Harper and Bros., 1950), 1:199.

good order of the Bible Commonwealth. Williams was ordered
to recant them. John Winthrop reported in his diary that Williams had then "broached and divulged divers new and dangerous opinions against the authority of magistrates," [7] when he
persuaded his church in Salem to write letters to the other
churches in Massachusetts urging them to rebuke members of
the colony's legislature for denying a grant of land to the people
of Salem in an effort to punish the Salem church for following
Williams's views. Williams was put on trial for these opinions
in the fall of 1635 and found guilty. The verdict was banishment.

His departure was postponed until spring, but when the magistrates in Boston heard that he was planning to move to the
Narragansett Bay area to found a settlement with some twenty
of his more dedicated friends in Salem, they sent officers to arrest him in January. Being forewarned that he would be shipped
back to England (where his views would certainly have got him
in trouble with King Charles I), Williams left his ailing wife and
his children, to depart alone into the snow-filled woods. He en-
dured great hardship for many weeks before he found his way
by compass to what is now Bristol, Rhode Island. Here, on
Mount Hope, Williams's friend Ousamequin (Massasoit), chief
of the Wampanoags, had his winter headquarters.

Ousamequin not only gave him hospitality for the winter, but,
the following spring, deeded him a piece of land in what is now
Rumford, Rhode Island, about ten miles north of Mount Hope,
on the east bank of the Seekonk River. Here, in March 1636,
Williams was joined by five or six families from Salem who
began to build homes and plant the ground. However, Governor
Edward Winslow of Plymouth informed Williams that that land
belonged to Plymouth and he had better cross over the Seekonk
to the west if he wished to be beyond the long arm of Massachusetts. No sign of that first settlement remains except the
spring from which the settlers took their water. Not until 1746

7. Samuel Greene Arnold, *History of the State of Rhode Island and Providence Plantations*, 2 vols. (New York: D. Appleton and Co., 1859), 1:37.

did Rumford, as part of East Providence, become officially part of Rhode Island.

Williams obtained from Ousamequin another deed to land west of the Seekonk, but that area was also claimed by the Narragansett Indians. Williams and his friends explored the region in a dugout canoe and were greeted at Slate Rock (the Plymouth Rock of Rhode Island) in May or June of 1636 by several Narragansetts who called out to him the famous words that are still on the seal of the city of Providence, "What cheer, Netop? ('What news, friend?')." After consulting these Indians, Williams and his friends paddled to the mouth of the Seekonk, where it enters the Providence River, then around Fox Point and up the Providence River to where the Moshassuck River enters it. There he found a good spring on the eastern bank of the Moshassuck and replanted his settlement. He called it Providence, later explaining why he gave the striking name to his "plantation": "I, having made covenantes of peaceable neighborhood with all the sachems and natives round about us, and having in a sense of God's merciful providence unto me in my distresse, called the place Providence; I desired it might be for a shelter for persons distressed of conscience." [8]

A few weeks later the sachems, or chiefs, of the Narragansetts, Miantonomi and Canonicus, also good friends of Williams, gave him a large grant of land extending from the Pawtucket River on the east to the Pawtuxet River on the west. It was not clear how far inland this grant extended, but the white men were given the right to graze their sheep and cattle as far up the streams as they wished. The Narragansetts, who numbered perhaps five thousand, continued to roam over the whole western side of the bay just as the fifteen hundred Wampanoags did on the eastern side until King Philip's War in 1675. Had these tribes joined forces with the Pequots in 1637, they could easily have driven the English far back from the bay, perhaps

8. *Records of the Colony of Rhode Island and Providence Plantations in New England*, 10 vols., edited by John R. Bartlett (Providence: A. C. Greene and Bro., 1856), 1:22.

eliminating the Puritan settlements. But Williams persuaded the Narragansetts to ally themselves with Massachusetts against the Pequots, who were old enemies, and thus saved the English from a terrible slaughter.

Providence grew very slowly. In 1638 there were only twenty families—about 100 persons; in 1645, about fifty families or 250 persons; in 1675, perhaps 350 to 400 persons. This slow growth resulted in part from fear of the Indians; in part from the instability produced by internal quarrels among the settlers; and in part from the fact that the radical principles upon which Providence was founded appealed only to the ultra-Puritans or the more eccentric and bold Englishmen and Englishwomen of that day. Williams said frankly that his purpose in founding the colony was to create a free community of seekers after Truth and a haven for those persecuted elsewhere for their conscientious beliefs. Expecting those who came to accept a system of majority rule and mutual responsibility for the general welfare, he described his community as a "town fellowship." Unfortunately, many who came were stiff-necked individualists, while others were more eager to engross as much land for themselves and their posterity as they could. Accepting the fact that he was only one among equals, Williams often found himself bound by majority decisions he did not fully agree with.

Although Williams wrote no constitution or civil compact for his settlement, he did get his friends to agree "that no man should be molested for his conscience." They also signed a simple statement saying "we do promise to subject ourselves . . . to all such orders or agreements as shall be made for public good of the body in an orderly way by the major consent," but "only in civil things." [9] However, town meeting majorities can govern effectively only if there is a fundamental consensus to begin with. Providence people soon discovered that religious liberty, while good in itself, often came into conflict with many accepted social beliefs and practices difficult to reconcile with social order. The case of Joshua Verin, one of

9. Arnold, *History of Rhode Island and Providence*, 1:103.

the first Salem men to settle in Providence, is typical of the civil difficulties surrounding the effort to separate church and state. Verin built his home next door to Williams, across from the town spring, in 1636. His wife, Ann, was a pious woman who faithfully attended the religious services Williams held in his home. The early settlers met for prayer, Bible reading, and prophesying (or giving testimony) not only on the Sabbath but frequently during the week as well. In 1637 Verin became annoyed that his wife was so often away from home at these services. When she insisted on going, he began to beat her so vehemently that the neighbors heard her screams. The pious majority told Verin he was infringing upon his wife's freedom of conscience. Verin replied that in disobeying him she was breaking God's commandment requiring "the subjection of wives to their husbands." The pious said that "if they should restrain their wives [servants, children] etc. all the women in the country would cry out of [against] them" for being hypocrites. A few of the more radical held that if Verin continued to abuse the soul liberty of his wife, "the church should dispose her to some other man who would use her better." Thus individualistic perfectionism threatened even the bonds of matrimony.[10]

The more conservative argued that Verin was only acting "out of conscience" and that he must not "be censured for his conscience" in demanding Ann's obedience. The matter came at last before the town meeting, the only source of authority. The issue was put to a vote and "It was agreed that Joshua Verin, upon the breach of a covenant for restraining libertie of conscience, shall be witheld from the liberty of voting till he shall declare the contrarie." [11] Verin did not take kindly to his disfranchisement nor the weakening of his patriarchal authority. Consequently he took his wife and goods and returned to the more traditional life of Salem.

The problem lay not in belief or opinion but in practice.

10. Arnold, *History of Rhode Island and Providence,* 1:104.
11. Arnold, *History of Rhode Island and Providence,* 1:105.

Williams remained throughout his life an orthodox Calvinist in theology and at the age of seventy-two rowed eighteen miles down Narragansett Bay in his boat to debate the obnoxious views of a new sect called the Society of Friends (or Quakers) who entered Rhode Island as a refuge from Puritan intolerance. Of course Williams did not say that Quaker opinions were so dangerous to civil order as to justify civil persecution. He merely thought them theologically wrong-headed and tried to argue them out of their errors. Punishment for what he called their "ignorance and boisterousness" he left to God.

Still, people in Rhode Island wished to form churches for worship and it was extremely important to discover what the Bible had to say about the proper way to organize totally purified churches. Since 1627 Williams had believed that a congregational polity, in which the church members regulated all church affairs, was preferable to any form of hierarchy. But after 1638 he became confused as to who should be considered a voting church member. Specifically, he wondered whether children baptized in infancy automatically became church members at adulthood. In 1639 Catherine Marbury Scott, the sister of Anne Hutchinson and wife of Richard Scott of Providence, convinced Williams that infant baptism was not commanded in Scripture and that only those capable of confessing their faith and experience of grace should be baptized. That fall or winter, Williams and ten others in Providence recanted their infant baptism and baptized each other by total immersion.

This was the first Baptist Church in America and the church thus founded and led by Williams still bears that name, though Williams, characteristically, left the church after four months because he began to have doubts about the validity of baptism by immersion as the true basis of church order. Thereafter he called himself a "Seeker" and never joined any church. At first the theology of the First Baptist Church was Calvinistic, but in 1652 the church divided over the doctrine of predestination. Those who held that Christ died so that all could be saved, not just the elect, thereupon became Arminian Baptists. At the same time, they adopted the ritual of "laying on of hands" upon all new members, which made them "Six Principle" Baptists as

opposed to the old "Five Principle" (or Particular, predesti-
narian) Baptists. Two decades later, another group of Baptists
in the colony adopted Saturday as the rightful day of worship
and split off to form the first Seventh Day Baptist churches in
America. This perfectionist (and literalist) search for the most
pure form of faith and worship produced as much confusion and
fragmentation in Rhode Island's religious life as the principles
of democracy and religious liberty produced in the colony's
civil affairs.

Until 1640 Providence functioned politically through its ad
hoc town meeting democracy. In July of that year, the freemen
(those admitted to the privilege of holding land and voting)
adopted a covenant of twelve articles that may be considered the
town's first constitution. Under that system, town meetings assembled quarterly, and, in between meetings, five men were
selected to act as the town's executive officers (the selectmen).
However, the power of the selectmen was limited by the fact
that any freeman who disliked any of their decisions could challenge it at the next town meeting. There were no magistrates,
however, no courts, nor constables. The police power after
1640 was similar to that of the "Wild West" in later years—
posse comitatus. Whenever there was trouble, a posse of citizens was formed to pursue and apprehend the criminal. It was a
rough and unstable form of justice, and many resented it. Williams struggled in vain to maintain a sense of brotherliness and
community among these individualists. He ran into difficulty
with both religious fanatics, who objected to any authority over
them except God's, and with those whose desire to get rich led
them to worship not the God Jehovah but what Williams called
"the God land."

In 1638 twelve of the first settlers argued that those who had
come first to Rhode Island deserved more land than those who
came later because they had borne the heavy burdens of original
settlement. They insisted that Williams's grant from the Narragansetts be shared (what had not already been parcelled out to
latecomers) by them and Williams. Led by William Arnold,
William Harris, William Carpenter, and Robert Cole, these
twelve persuaded Williams to include them as joint owners or

"proprietors" of the original Indian deed. Reluctantly, Williams agreed. The thirteen proprietors voted to reserve for themselves a large tract of land along the Pawtuxet River, planning to increase this area by further purchases from the Indians. The Arnold-Harris faction sought to fix a boundary line between Pawtuxet and Providence, which would, in effect, divide the original grant into two separate towns.

But there was disagreement about the borders of "the Pawtuxet Purchase." The Arnold-Harris group read the original deed to include a far greater gift from the Narragansetts than Williams believed was intended. The rough draft of the original oral grant was ambiguous, and there was no way to judge the correct interpretation. The result was a bitter quarrel that extended long after Williams's death. Some of the Pawtuxet group, whom Williams called "the monopolizers," finally became so exasperated by their inability to obtain a favorable resolution for their scheme that they asked the magistrates of Massachusetts Bay to settle it. Massachusetts said it could only act if the Pawtuxet people would acknowledge its authority. In September 1642, four of the monopolizers who had moved to Pawtuxet from Providence (led by William Arnold and his son Benedict) sent a written statement of their allegiance to Massachusetts.

John Winthrop and the Puritans jumped at this opportunity to annex a valuable piece of land along the coast of Narragansett Bay (though technically it was outside their charter boundaries). As Winthrop said in his diary, the annexation gave Massachusetts the opportunity "to draw the rest of those parts either under ourselves or Plimouth, who now lived under no government but grew offensive, and the place was likely to be of use to us. . . . and seeing it came without our seeking and would be no charge to us, we thought it not wisdom to let it slip." [12] Pawtuxet, in effect, had seceded from Providence, leaving its

12. John Winthrop, *Winthrop's Journal, History of New England: Sixteen Thirty to Sixteen Forty-Nine,* 2 vols., edited by James K. Hosmer (New York: Barnes and Noble, 1908), 2:81.

border and indeed its autonomy at the mercy of the powerful forces of Massachusetts.

This controversy over Pawtuxet had been exacerbated by the arrival in Providence of Samuel Gorton in 1640. Gorton, a man of considerable personal magnetism, preached a creed unlike any yet heard in New England. Born near Manchester, England, in 1592, he learned Greek and Latin but never attended college. He also appears to have taken considerable interest in theology and law. A clothier by trade and an ultra-Puritan in religion, he emigrated to Boston in 1637 with his wife and children "to enjoy liberty of conscience." [13] Arriving in the midst of the controversy over Anne Hutchinson's doctrines, he found so much bitterness and authoritarianism that he moved to Plymouth. In Plymouth he refused to attend the parish church and conducted services in his own home for those who shared his views.

Today it is difficult to know precisely what his views were, since he left no formal church organization nor clear statement of his theology. He called himself "a professor of the mysteries of Christ" and seems, like the Antinomians and Quakers, to have believed that God's spirit communed directly with man through an "inner light." Among his more radical beliefs were those stressing the equality of all believers to preach, including women; an opposition to baptism, communion, and other church ordinances; a belief in the overpowering goodness and mercy of God; and a denial of the claim that heaven and hell were states of the soul following death. God, he said, rewards or punishes us daily by his spiritual presence or absence from our hearts. Contemporary accounts by Puritan authorities describe him as "a man whose spirit was stark drunk with blasphemies" and a "most prodigious minter of exorbitant novelties." But he was also an ardent champion of religious freedom and the separation of church and state.[14]

---

13. Adelos Gorton, *The Life and Times of Samuel Gorton* (Philadelphia: George S. Ferguson, Co., 1907), p. 13.
14. Arnold, *History of Rhode Island and Providence,* 1:163.

According to all accounts, Gorton was a good husband, a good farmer, and a faithful friend. But when he felt that injustice was being done, he fought back with a tongue so sharp that it nearly cost him his life. His political theory was rooted in a firm belief in the constitutional rights of Englishmen and the sanctity of the common law. Convinced that neither the Puritan courts nor those in Rhode Island were free to act contrary to these fundamental principles, he did not hesitate to criticize the legal systems of the New England colonies. In November 1638, Gorton appeared in Plymouth court to defend his maidservant against charge of "offensive speech and carriage" (she is said to have smiled in a church service and angered the pastor). He objected so strenuously to the injustice of the charge and the unfair proceedings of the court—while quoting many strange interpretations of Scripture in her defense—that the authorities banished him from Plymouth. Some accounts say he was whipped for contempt of court.

From Plymouth, Gorton moved to Pocasset Plantation on Aquidneck, where the Hutchinsonians had settled in the spring of 1638. Here, too, he exhibited truculence toward authority, and once again the cause of his banishment arose over his behavior in court defending a female servant. She was accused of assaulting a woman caught trespassing on Gorton's property. Gorton refused to acknowledge the legitimacy of the judges because the colony had no patent from the king, and the court did not follow the prescribed rules of English jurisprudence. He further angered the justices by calling them "just asses"; he urged the spectators to ignore them. The authorities put him in jail, along with his servant, gave him a public whipping, and then banished him in March 1641.

When he arrived in Providence a few weeks later, he challenged the authority of its political system, coming to the aid of one of his friends, Francis Weston, when the town sought to distrain Weston of some cattle in payment for a fine. Gorton also confuted the religious views of Williams and the Baptist church. "Master Gorton," Williams wrote, "having foully abused high and low at Aquidneck, is now bewitching and bemaddening poor Providence, both with his unclean and foul

censures of all the ministers of this country . . . and also denying all visible and external ordinances.'' When Gorton applied
to the town for admission as a voter and landholder (or freeman)
in May 1641, the town denied his request, calling him ''an
insolent, ra[i]ling and turbulent person.'' They also excluded from
town fellowship Gorton's followers, John Wickes and Randall
Holden.[15]

Denied any standing in Providence, Gorton and six of his
friends bought land in Pawtuxet from Robert Cole. But there
they ran afoul of William Arnold. When Pawtuxet put itself
under Massachusetts's jurisdiction, Gorton decided to move
again. He purchased a tract of land south of the Pawtuxet from
Miantonomi in October 1642. The tract was called Shawomet
and was inhabited by a group of Narragansetts under two local
sachems, Pomham and Socononoco. Though Pomham signed
the deed along with Miantonomi for the sale of Shawomet, he
later told the Pawtuxet and Massachusetts authorities that he had
done so out of fear, that he really did not acknowledge Miantonomi as his chief. Socononoco agreed with Pomham that
Miantonomi did not have the right to sell their land to the Gortonists. The Pawtuxet people, who expected to get this land for
themselves, appealed to Massachusetts along with the two local
sachems for help in getting rid of Gorton.

The Providence plantations (Providence, Pawtuxet, and Shawomet) were now in a hopelessly confused situation. The only
way to clear it up was to appeal to the king. ''Upon the frequent
exception taken by Massachusetts that we had no authority for
civil government,'' Williams said, ''I went purposely to England [to secure a patent or charter].'' [16] The people of Providence
who commissioned Williams to present their case in London
placed all their hopes on his diplomacy. In the fall of 1643,
after Williams had left for England, the Massachusetts authorities sent soldiers to Shawomet to force the Gortonists to stand
trial in Boston. Gorton and his followers barricaded themselves

---

15. Samuel H. Brockunier, *The Irrepressible Democrat: Roger Williams* (New York: Ronald Press Co., 1940), p. 130.

16. Gorton, *The Life and Times of Samuel Gorton*, p. 134.

in a house and for two days exchanged shots with the soldiers. Then they surrendered. Nine were taken away in chains. At the trial, Gorton was vituperative and "blasphemous," as usual, and narrowly escaped hanging. Six of the nine, including Gorton, were imprisoned at hard labor for six months. Released in 1644, they were forbidden to return to Shawomet or Providence.

Meanwhile, to the southward on Aquidneck Island, two very different settlements of ultra-Puritans were trying to establish their own claims to independence. Like Williams's plantation, the Aquidneck settlements originated in a theological dispute over the true meaning of Puritanism. In fact, the group that gathered around the remarkable Anne Hutchinson in Boston between 1634 and 1637 was considered far more dangerous by John Winthrop than Williams or Gorton had ever been.

Born Anne Marbury in Alfred, England, in 1591, she married a London merchant, William Hutchinson, in 1612. Over the next thirty years, the couple had fifteen children. This "American Jezebel," (as Cotton Mather called her), was no ordinary woman. Her husband strongly supported her teaching, and he was a man of sufficient wealth and influence in the colony to carry some weight. But Anne seems to have derived her strong will and argumentative faculties from her father, Thomas Marbury, a devout and strict Anglican minister who criticized his fellow Anglicans for their spiritual and moral laxity but never became a Puritan.

Anne and William Hutchinson lived near the town of old Boston in Lincolnshire after their marriage and went there often in the 1620s to hear the Reverend John Cotton preach. Cotton was a non-Separatist Puritan trying to reform the Anglican Church from within. Threatened with imprisonment, he departed for Boston in New England in 1633. A year later the Hutchinsons followed him. In Boston Anne's experience as a mother and her skill in nursing and midwifery made her a host of friends among the women. She also began to expound theology to these women at Monday morning meetings in her home. They discussed the fine points of the preceding day's sermons by the Reverend John Wilson and the Reverend John Cotton, co-pastors of the Boston church. A person of strong intelligence, tremendous energy, and intense moral zeal, Anne Hutchinson was described by John Winthrop as "a woman of ready wit and bold spirit." [17] John Cotton spoke of her "sharpe apprehension" and "ready utterance." [18] One of her opponents, the Reverend Thomas Weld, portrayed her as "a woman of haughty and fierce carriage, of a nimble wit, and active spirit and a very voluable tongue, more bold than a man." [19]

The theological position she expounded was later labeled "Antinomianism"—which meant "against law"—by her enemies. Actually it was simply Calvinism with an emphasis upon the mystical side of spiritual communion with God, rather than upon the legalistic or doctrinal side. She believed that "the person of the Holy Ghost dwells in a justified [spiritually saved or converted] person" and was highly critical of the prevailing view in Massachusetts pulpits that men and women could "prepare" their hearts to receive God's saving grace by means of constant prayer, Bible reading, church attendance, and soul-searching. In her view, that smacked of "salvation by works"—through human effort. A century later, Jonathan Edwards was to revive Anne's mystical emphasis in Calvinism and to denounce the Boston clergy of his day for the same theological error she found—Arminianism. But when a woman said that, in 1634, she was deemed out of her place. Her teaching became particularly dangerous when some very influential men in the colony came to hear and believe her.[20]

With the full support of the Hutchinsonians in 1636, Sir Henry Vane ousted John Winthrop (Anne's foremost opponent) from the governorship. Anne stepped up the temper of her criticism, encouraging her followers to attend various churches throughout the colony and to walk out when they heard the min-

17. Winthrop, *Winthrop's Journal*, 1:195.

18. Emery Battis, *Saints and Sectaries* (Chapel Hill: University of North Carolina Press, 1962), p. 6.

19. Thomas Welde, *A Short History of the Rise, Reign, and Ruine of the Antinomians* (London: Ralph Smith, Printer, 1644), p. 31.

20. Edmund S. Morgan, *The Puritan Dilemma* (Boston: Little, Brown and Co., 1957), p. 139.

ister preaching false doctrine. She herself and her friend Mary
Dyer led a walkout, much to his chagrin, from one of John Wilson's sermons in Boston. Her friends then urged that John
Wheelwright, her brother-in-law, be made a co-pastor with Cotton and Wilson. That was supported by leading magistrates like
Vane and William Coddington. When Winthrop opposed it,
Wheelwright stood up in church and threatened that God's
wrath would fall upon the colony unless it changed its ways.
By implication, that seemed to urge the people to throw the Arminians out of office in church and state and choose only Hutchinsonians to lead the colony.

The authorities took that as a political threat. Wheelwright's
speech was declared seditious, and he was placed on trial. Sir
Henry Vane was defeated for governor in 1637 through the
votes outside of Boston, and he returned to England. When
seventy-five people signed a petition opposing Wheelwright's
conviction, they were forced to give up their weapons in November 1637 and threatened with banishment if they continued
to support Wheelwright. That same month, Anne Hutchinson
was put on trial for publicly "traducing the ministers" [21] of the
colony.

She successfully held her prosecutors at bay until she let it
slip that she had in the past guided her actions by direct revelations from God. She said that even now she had a revelation
that the whole of Massachusetts Bay Colony would be destroyed
if its leaders continued to persecute her for speaking the truth:
"Take heed what ye go to do unto me . . . for I know that for
this you go about to do to me God will ruin you and your posterity and this whole State." [22] At this outburst even the ambiguous support of John Cotton waned and she stood publicly condemned of preaching that God spoke directly to believers
—"Antinomianism." If people obeyed voices and revelations,
how could law and order ever prevail?

She was imprisoned. Her church tried her and cast her out for

21. Winnifred K. Rugg, *Unafraid: A Life of Anne Hutchinson* (Boston: Houghton,
Mifflin Co., 1930), p. 183.
22. Morgan, *Puritan Dilemma*, p. 152.

heresy. A dozen of her foremost adherents were banished from the colony in the spring of 1638, and many more were threatened with banishment. Before leaving Boston, on March 7, 1638, nineteen heads of families, led by William Coddington, allegedly the richest merchant in Boston, signed the following compact as the basis for a new plantation in Rhode Island:

> We, whose names are underwritten, do here solemnly, in the presence of Jehovah, incorporate ourselves into a Bodie Politick, and as he shall help, will submit ourselves, lives and estates unto our Lord Jesus Christ, the King of Kings and Lord of Lords, and to all those perfect and most absolute laws of his given to us in his holy word of truth, to be guided and judged thereby.[23]

A few weeks later, this new body politic moved to Aquidneck Island, where they sought the aid of Roger Williams in obtaining a grant from the Narragansetts. True to his principles (though he did not share their Antinomianism), Williams welcomed these new dissenters and used his good auspices to persuade Miantonomi to remove twenty Narragansetts from the island and deed it to William Coddington, whom the dissenters had chosen as their leader or "judge."

The Hutchinsonians settled near a small harbor at the northeastern corner of the island known as Pocasset. They changed the name to Portsmouth in 1643 and a year later changed Aquidneck to Rhode Island. This group of settlers was, on the whole, wealthier, better-educated, more cohesive than those in Providence, and (despite their Antinomianism) more eager to establish a carefully structured, paternalistic, socially-stratified political system very much like that they had known in Massachusetts. Unlike Williams's group, who tried to give equal plots of land to all respectable settlers, Coddington's government allocated land in proportion to the wealth and social rank of each settler. "Gentlemen" received larger grants than millers or coopers; and they, in turn, had larger shares than common laborers. Moreover, land was given sparingly to newcomers, at first; hence, only a minority of the inhabitants were entitled to vote.

23. Arnold, *History of Rhode Island and Providence*, 1:124.

The Hutchinsonians differed from the Bostonians, however, in their dislike for the restrictions upon profits and speculation that Massachusetts laws sustained in the interest of the general welfare. Antinomianism, by placing more authority in the individual through direct communion with God, allowed for a more aggressive, profit-oriented, and individualistic form of business enterprise than was possible in Boston. The settlers on Rhode Island, particuarly those who followed Coddington to Newport in 1639, fully carried out this enterprising behavior in later years. Prospering merchants took their business success as a sign that God was pleased with their piety and concluded that the state should not meddle in business or regulate trade. It was the other side of the coin of religious liberty. Together, they added up to the principle of laissez-faire that has ever since been so congenial to American entrepreneurs.

It should be noted that Coddington had been part of the Boston court that banished Roger Williams; he never had much use for Williams or the people at Providence. Coddington sought to keep the island a distinct political entity from the wayward Providence plantations and later espoused the Quaker views that Williams found so appalling. Politically and socially, Coddington was very conservative, though he had risked much to side with the Antinomians. Williams later wrote that Coddington was always more concerned with his private profit and power than with the general welfare—"a worldly man," Williams called him, "a selfish man, nothing for public but all for himself and private." [24] Nevertheless, Coddington for many years loomed as the most important rival to Williams's leadership in the bay area, and for two decades he thwarted all efforts to unite the northern and southern settlements. From 1645 to 1655, he even sought the support of Plymouth, Connecticut, Massachusetts, and the Dutch in his effort to keep Rhode Island independent from the Providence plantations.

In addition to Coddington, the leading members of the Aquidneck group were William Hutchinson, William Dyer, John Coggeshall, Nicholas Easton, William Brenton, and John

24. Gorton, *Life and Times of Samuel Gorton*, p. 33.

Clarke. For some Rhode Island historians, Clarke has been undeservedly overshadowed by Williams, both as a defender of religious liberty, an upholder of democracy, a founder of the Baptist faith, and a guiding force toward unification of the bay settlements. It was Clarke who obtained the important charter from King Charles II in 1663. It is Clarke's definition of religious liberty, not Williams's, that is engraved in letters a foot high under the marble dome of the state capitol today. Some even claim that Clarke's Baptist church in Newport is the oldest Baptist church in America, since the Providence church "warped off" into Arminianism and Six Principle views. Clarke wrote the first tract by an American defending the Baptist persuasion and was the first Baptist to take a missionary trip into Massachusetts Bay (in 1652) to spread that persuasion (for which he narrowly escaped whipping).

Born in Westhorpe, Suffolk, England, in 1609, Clarke was educated at Cambridge and probably went to the University of Leyden in Holland to study medicine. Arriving in Boston in November 1637, with his wife, Clarke had already adopted the principle of religious liberty. Finding himself in the midst of the Antinomian crisis, he identified with the Hutchinsonians and was disarmed with the others in that faction. He wrote later, of that incident, "I thought it not strange to see men differ about matters of Heaven, for I expect no less upon Earth. But to see that they were not able so to bear with each other in their different understandings and consciences as in those utmost parts of the world to live peaceably together [led me to move elsewhere]." [25] He joined that group of Hutchinsonians who thought New Hampshire would be a better spot to move to than Rhode Island or Delaware, but the winter of 1637–38 proved so cold there that most of the group decided to move to Aquidneck instead. (Wheelwright, however, made peace with the Bostonians and did not join his admirers in Rhode Island.)

Because of its conservatism, its more experienced leadership, and its commercial success as a seaport, Aquidneck received far

---

25. Thomas W. Bicknell, *The Story of Dr. John Clarke* (Providence: Published by the author, 1915), p. 77.

more immigrants in the early years than Providence. One hundred settlers came to Pocasset during its first year. But the little harbor there proved too shallow for large ships. In 1639, after some political factionalism, William Coddington, John Clarke, Nicholas Easton, and six other prominent leaders moved farther down the island to establish a new plantation. William Hutchinson remained behind and was elected leader in Pocasset. When he died in 1642, his wife, who had continued to conduct religious meetings in her home, feared that the Boston authorities would gain control of Rhode Island and try to apprehend her. Anne Hutchinson had scornfully denounced the Boston church when it sent a delegation to Pocasset to try to persuade her to admit her errors and seek their forgiveness: "What, from the Church at Boston?" she asked the delegation mockingly. "I know of no such Church neither will I own it; call it the Whore and Strumpet of Boston [but] not a Church of Christ!" [26]

In 1643 she took the younger of her children and, with one of her sons-in-law, moved to the Dutch Colony at Pelham Bay, now part of the Bronx near the Hutchinson River. Unfortunately, that very year the Dutch so antagonized the Indians on Long Island that they rose up and destroyed all the outlying settlements. Anne and all but one of her children were tomahawked to death. The unharmed child was adopted by the Indians.

The precise reasons for the schism from the settlement at Pocasset and the founding of Newport have never been clear. The inadequacy of Pocasset Harbor was only one reason. Some of the ordinary folk apparently disliked the efforts of the wealthy to lord it over them. "At Aquidneck," wrote John Winthrop in 1639, "the people grew very tumultuous and put out Mr. Coddington and the other magistrates and chose Mr. William Hutchinson [as governor] only a man of very mild temper and weak parts and wholly guided by his wife, who had been the beginner of all the former troubles in the country and

26. Bertram Lippincott, *Indians, Privateers and High Society* (Philadelphia: J. B. Lippincott Co., 1961), p. 60.

still continued to breed disturbance." [27] How much Anne had to do with the election of her husband over Coddington is not known. Some historians blame—or credit—Samuel Gorton, who appeared that year in Pocasset, as the real cause of this democratic uprising. Gorton appears to have raised questions about the rightful power of the leaders and to have advocated greater popular participation in the governing process.

In any case, Coddington and the nine who left with him found at the southwest end of the island a perfect harbor, one of the best on the whole east coast. They called it Newport, and by the end of 1639 there were ninety-three persons residing there. Lacking a large hinterland, Rhode Islanders had to make their living chiefly by the sea—by trade, more than by fishing. Coddington, who was much interested in merchandizing, was one of the first in Rhode Island to build ships large enough to engage in coastal trade. He also led the way in farming and in raising sheep, cattle, and horses, all of which were to become prime items of export from the colony. Before Coddington's death in 1678, he was regularly shipping sheep, cattle, horses, corn, peas, butter, cheese, wool, and mutton as far as the West Indies. The first official seal of Newport contained a picture of a long-tailed sheep, the equivalent of Boston's famous codfish.

By 1690 the population of the seaport was 2,600, half of them engaged in some aspect of maritime trade. By 1776 Newport, along with Boston, New York, Philadelphia, and Charleston, was one of the five major seaports of the British colonies. Coddington and his friends had a good eye for the main chance. It was a basic ingredient of the colony's prosperity, once the political problems of unification were settled. With this trading instinct came the readiness to accept black slaves as a prime article of trade. Some accounts claim that as early as 1649 a Newport ship engaged in the "Guinney trade"—the name for a slaving voyage. At first, however, the principle slaves transported in Rhode Island ships were New England Indians (Pequots, Wampanoags, Narragansetts) captured in "just

27. Arnold, *History of Rhode Island and Providence*, 1:134, n. 1.

wars.'' Shipping slaves to the West Indies or southern colonies was a different matter from importing them into Rhode Island. When that was first tried, in the 1650s, a law was passed by the towns of Warwick and Providence (during a period when Aquidneck towns were trying to remain independent) outlawing hereditary black slavery. Some accounts claim this to be the first antislavery law in the British colonies:

> Whereas there is a common course practised amongst Englishmen to buy negers to the end that they may have them for service or slaves forever, for the preventing of such practices among us, let it be ordered that no blacke mankinde or white being forced by covenant bond or otherwise to serve any man or his assigns longer than ten years . . . And at the end or terme of ten years to sett them free as the manner is with English [bond]servants.[28]

Regrettably, the law became a dead letter soon afterward, when the Narragansett Bay settlements were united, and the Aquidneck communities refused to acknowledge the law as binding on them. In the eighteenth century, Newport became the largest slaveholding community in New England and one of the major slave-trading depots in the British Empire.

For a time, the religious situation on Aquidneck (now Rhode Island) was almost as confused as that in Providence. No church appears to have been formed in Pocasset, though John Clarke preached there, and Anne Hutchinson had conducted meetings. Some say this congregation broke up over quarrels between Clarke and Nicholas Easton as to whether God was the author of sin. When Anne Hutchinson's sister and brother-in-law, Catherine and Richard Scott, began arguing against infant baptism in 1639, they may have been influenced by recent Baptist immigrants from England. The belief in adult baptism by immersion was adopted by John Clarke in 1644, when he founded a church on Calvinistic Baptist principles in Newport. He presided over it till his death in 1676, though it went through various schisms led by Six-Principle and Seventh-Day Baptists.

---

28. John R. Bartlett, editor, *Records of the Colony of Rhode Island and Providence Plantations in New England,* 10 vols. (Providence: A. C. Greene and Bro., 1856), 1:243.

In the 1650s, the new Quaker doctrines were imported into Newport from Boston. They seemed compatible with much of what Anne Hutchinson had taught, and Quakerism quickly became the most important denomination on Aquidneck. In fact, Newport became the center for Quakerism throughout southeastern Massachusetts during the colonial era.

Meanwhile, the political difficulties that had led to the founding of Newport continued to cause trouble. In 1640 the towns of Pocasset and Newport tried to unite into one jurisdiction under the governorship of Coddington. Perhaps as part of that reunion and as a concession to the Pocasset democrats, a law was passed in 1640 defining the political system of the two towns as "a democracie or popular government; that is to say, it is in the power of the freemen, orderly assembled, or the major part of them, to make or constitute just laws by which they shall be regulated and to depute from among themselves such ministers [of government] as shall see them faithfully executed between man and man." [29] Another law that same year asserted the basic right of freedom of conscience, proclaiming "that none be accounted a delinquent for doctrine, provided it be not directly repugnant to the government or laws established." [30] Then, in 1644, the island found itself threatened by Plymouth Colony, just as the Providence plantations were threatened by Massachusetts. Plymouth sent one of its magistrates to the island to assert that it considered those settlements within the jurisdiction of Plymouth, probably on the basis of its possession by the Wampanoags in the past.

In 1643 the four New England colonies of Massachusetts, Plymouth, Connecticut, and New Haven had formed a federation that pointedly excluded the otherwise-minded heretics of the Narragansett area. These four colonies argued that the Rhode Island and Providence plantations lacked legal title to any land. Claims by the larger colonies over that area were based upon the conquest of the Pequots, treaties with the Wampanoags, alliances with the Narragansetts, and the submission of

29. Arnold, *History of Rhode Island and Providence*, 1:148.
30. Arnold, *History of Rhode Island and Providence*, 1:149.

the Pawtuxet settlers to Massachusetts's authority. In order to fend off the imperialistic ambitions of these aggressive neighbors, Rhode Islanders began to see the necessity of some form of union. And that required a charter from the king.

Roger Williams obtained the first legal or official patent for the political sovereignty of the Narragansett settlements in 1644, but in that he seemed once again favored by divine Providence. The Puritan leaders in Parliament had forced King Charles I to flee from London in 1642, and Parliament was ruling without the king when Williams arrived. Being himself a Puritan (though a radical one), a friend of Oliver Cromwell, Sir Henry Vane, John Milton, and other leaders of the Puritan movement, Williams had immediate access to power that he would have lacked had the king been in charge. Furthermore, by publishing his book on the Algonquin language soon after he arrived, he impressed the pious leaders of the new government with his concern for saving the souls of the heathen. In the spring of 1644, his request for a charter was granted by the Parliamentary Commissioners for Plantations, presided over by Robert Rich, Earl of Warwick. The king did not sign it, but it bore the seal of the highest power short of the king and was, under the circumstances, the best he could get.

The patent seemed to provide at last the political authority that would ensure the good order and political independence of the colony. Furthermore, it was based upon principles that Williams had long espoused and that he published while in London in his famous tract, *The Bloody Tenent of Persecution.*

> . . . a civil government is an ordinance of God to conserve the civil peace of people so far as concerns their bodies and goods . . . But the sovereign, original, and foundation of civil power lies in the People. . . . And if so that a people may erect and establish what forms of Government seems to them most meet for their civil condition, it is evident that such governments as are by them erected and established have no more power, nor for longer time, than the civil power, or people consenting and agreeing, shall betrust them with.[31]

---

31. Miller, *Williams*, p. 147.

Although Williams's words and the charter's implications appear democratic and egalitarian, it has to be remembered that not everyone who came to Rhode Island automatically became a freeman or voter. Each had to be separately granted land and the franchise by vote of the town meeting where he settled. Democracy evolved, in the end, from the absence of any clear standards of social difference on the frontier, rather than from any theoretical commitment to the later Jacksonian concept of universal manhood suffrage. Like other frontiers, Rhode Island worked toward egalitarianism pragmatically, rather than ideologically.

In addition, Williams's patent contained nothing specific regarding religious liberty—except by intentional omission. Most colonial charters contained specific requirements regarding the establishment of a religious system conforming to the principles of the Church of England. Williams's patent spoke only of "civil power." Like the constitution that the American people were to write for their new government in 1787, it was a secular document. All unspecified power (including religious freedom) was retained by the people. Rhode Island forecast the future.

Williams's patent specifically united the mainland and the island communities around the bay for the first time in a single body politic. It granted to the "inhabitants of the Towns of Providence, Portsmouth, and Newport a free and absolute Charter of Incorporation. . . . together with full Power and Authority to rule themselves and such others as shall hereafter inhabit within part of the said Tract of land, by such form of civil government as by voluntary consent of all or the greater part of them they shall find most suitable to their estate and condition. . . ." [32] The great weakness of the charter was that it gave no clear geographical boundaries for the new colony, beyond stating that they included such lands as the inhabitants had purchased from the Indians and "bounding on" the colonies of Massachusetts, Plymouth, and Connecticut. Since the charter

32. Irving B. Richman, *Rhode Island, A Study in Separatism* (Boston: Houghton, Mifflin Co., 1905), p. 34.

did not say whether Providence included the area claimed by the Pawtuxet proprietors or the area of the Gortonists in Shawomet, there was still plenty of room for controversy.

Moreover, the people of Newport and Portsmouth had not asked Williams to obtain a charter including them. To some of them, Coddington in particular, it seemed as if Williams were being as imperialistic as Massachusetts or Plymouth. Coddington and some of his wealthy merchant friends had no intention of allowing their thriving plantation at Newport to come under the domination of a majority which included the poor and eccentric people of the mainland. Majority rule might well lay the heaviest burdens of taxation upon the Newport rich to support the incompetent Providence poor. Coddington immediately made clear his unwillingness to accept the patent and set about negotiating with the surrounding colonies to gain their support for his continued control of the Aquidneck settlements.

Meanwhile, the Gortonists, afraid to return to Shawomet, concluded that they too must send a delegation to London. In May 1645, Gorton and Randall Holden sailed for England to secure their rights as an independent settlement. Before they left, Gorton persuaded the Narragansett Indians, then under pressure to accept the domination of Massachusetts, to sign a treaty accepting the king as their protector. If the king consented to their allegiance, they would be in a strong position to protect their land from the encroachments of Connecticut and incidentally to strengthen the Gortonists' claim to Shawomet. Massachusetts refused to acknowledge the validity of that treaty, claiming that the Narragansetts had been under their jurisdiction since the alliance against the Pequots in 1637. But since Massachusetts had recently abetted the Mohegan chief, Uncas, in the execution of Miantonomi, the Narragansetts believed any alliance they had with that colony was abrogated.

Gorton proved as successful with the Earl of Warwick as Williams. On May 15, 1646, he received a confirmation of the Shawomet purchase, an order to Massachusetts to desist from asserting its authority there, and an acknowledgment of the royal jurisdiction over the Narragansetts' land. Gorton promptly renamed Shawomet *Warwick;* the Narragansetts' land on the western side of the bay, south of Shawomet, became known as "the King's Province." Later, it was known as King's County, and today it is Washington County.

But these actions simply stirred Massachusetts to further action. It sent an agent to England to get both Williams's patent and Gorton's revoked. Fortunately, Gorton had the foresight to suspect such action and stayed on in London to combat it, while Holden returned to Rhode Island. Gorton successfully fended off the Massachusetts efforts to undermine his claim, and, when he got back in 1648, his friends were re-established in Warwick. The confirmation of Gorton's purchase in effect included his plantation as one of the four "towns" in the newly united colony. Even before his return, representatives from Warwick, Providence, Portsmouth, and Newport had met several times to implement a set of laws to serve as the basis for a centralized government. The most important of these legislative sessions took place in Portsmouth in May 1647. Every freeman in Newport and Portsmouth, except those still loyal to Coddington, was invited. Providence sent ten delegates, headed by Williams. Holden attended with the freemen from Warwick. The Pawtuxet proprietors, of course, refused to participate, preferring to think of themselves as part of Massachusetts.

The laws of "The Province of Providence Plantations in Narragansett," as they were called, created a ruling body of ten men, headed by a president and four assistants, all to be elected by the freemen. They also established an annual general assembly consisting of every freeman in the United colony— later, the assembly had to be changed to a representative body. In order to preserve as much local self-government as possible, all laws had to originate with the town meetings and went into force only after each town had agreed to them and the general assembly approved them. In addition, the assembly in Portsmouth in 1647 declared "The form of Government established in Providence Plantations is Democratical, that is to say, a government held by the free and voluntary consent of all, or the general part of the free inhabitants." [33] But voters or freemen

33. Arnold, *History of Rhode Island and Providence*, 1:205.

continued to be only those admitted to that privilege in town meetings.

Other laws passed in 1647 established freedom of conscience, prohibited imprisonment for debt, and allowed those opposed to the swearing of oaths to give their "solemn profession or testimony" in legal matters without swearing in the name of God. The assembly also laid a tax of one hundred pounds sterling upon the towns to repay Roger Williams for his expenses incurred in obtaining the charter. Williams had had to sell some of his own land in 1643 to pay for his trip to England. Not worshipping "God land" or Mammon, Williams never became a rich man. In fact, he died in poverty.

John Coggeshall of Newport was elected the first president of the colony and his four assistants or Council consisted of Roger Williams, William Coddington (who refused to serve), Randall Holden, and John Sandford (of Portsmouth). The settlers in Pawtuxet were asked to merge with Providence, Portsmouth, or Newport, but they refused to choose. The effort of Rhode Island to force Pawtuxet to merge with one of its towns was designed to demonstrate that the new colony did not acknowledge the jurisdiction of Massachusetts within its bounds. It was another eleven years before the Pawtuxet proprietors finally recanted their allegiance to Massachusetts and accepted membership in Providence Plantations.

Coddington's faction held out almost as long. In May 1648, Coddington moved to Boston and tried to gain an alliance with its leaders to sustain his control of Newport and Portsmouth. But the United Commissioners of the four Puritan colonies insisted that Rhode Island (Aquidneck) was within the jurisdiction of Plymouth. Coddington then left for England where, to everyone's surprise, he persuaded the Council of State to uphold his claim to independent control over Aquidneck Island and the neighboring island of Conanicut (now Jamestown). He received a patent making him governor for life over these islands and subject only to the advice of a council of six to be chosen by the freemen.

Assuming that Coddington had somehow deceived the authorities in England, the people of Aquidneck commissioned John

Clarke to go to London in December 1651, to refute his claim and support Williams's patent. Providence and Warwick townships commissioned Roger Williams to join Clarke in the effort. William and Mary Dyer accompanied the two. Meanwhile, Nicholas Easton from Newport vied with Samuel Gorton of the mainland towns to lead what was left of the central government. Gorton was chosen president of the colony by the towns of Providence and Warwick, but Easton remained president for the Aquidneck towns.

The mission to England was successful. The Council of State rescinded Coddington's patent on October 2, 1652. While Clarke and Williams remained in England to fight the claims of Plymouth and Massachusetts to Aquidneck and Pawtuxet, William Dyer returned to Newport in February 1653. But affairs were still confused when Williams returned in July 1654, with a letter from Oliver Cromwell—who, having beheaded Charles I, was now Lord Protector of the new English commonwealth. Cromwell and Sir Henry Vane had given Williams letters urging the towns around the bay to forget their differences and work together, which they tried to do. Williams was elected president of the colony for the next three years.

During that period he wrote his famous letter "To the Town of Providence," in answer to the claims of some radical pietists who still denied the right of the civil authorities to lay and collect taxes from those who conscientiously refused to pay. Williams told them that a commonwealth was like a ship at sea, in which "papists, protestants, Jews and Turks" might be passengers over whose worship the captain had no power; but "if any of the seamen refuse to perform their services or passengers refuse to pay their freight; if any refuse . . . to help in person or purse toward the common charges or defense; if any refuse to obey the common laws and orders of the ships captain concerning their common peace," then the captain, or lawful authority in the state, "may judge, resist, compel, and punish such transgressors according to their deserts and merits." [34] While that statement did not draw a precise line between church and state,

34. Arnold, *History of Rhode Island and Providence,* 1:254–255.

it clearly indicated that Williams saw the necessity for limitations of individualism in the name of the common good. It is significant, however, that Rhode Island never required the Quakers to fight in time of war; it tolerated Catholics and Jews and would probably have tolerated Moslems, had any come.

In 1656 Coddington finally gave up his attempt to rule or ruin. He returned to Newport, apologized for his traitorous conduct, and was forgiven. Furthermore, he was elected to the next Court of Commissioners and served regularly in high office until his death. Two years later the Pawtuxet proprietors gave up their futile allegiance to Massachusetts and were merged into the town of Providence. Massachusetts, however, continued to claim large parts of the western side of the bay, which a group of their land speculators, under Colonel Humphrey Atherton, fraudulently forced from the Narragansetts in the years 1658–1662.

The colony remained small during these years of controversy and confusion. According to an official census taken in 1665, Newport had only 96 freemen, Portsmouth, 71, Providence, 42, and Warwick, 37. Assuming all were married, that would total 247 families; there may have been other inhabitants who had not yet acquired the right to vote. It is probably a fair estimate that there were less than 1,500 whites in the whole Narragansett Bay area. There were at least five times that many Indians. Ultimately there was bound to be some clash between the claims of white men and red.

However, in the 1650s and 1660s, the most striking new feature in the colony's life—in fact, throughout New England— was the coming of the Quakers, the last and most radical of the Puritan pietists, if we use the term *Puritan* to apply to all those who wished additional reformation in the Church of England. Founded in England in 1647 by George Fox, the new sect repudiated all church ordinances, denied the necessity for a ministry, refused to swear an oath, refused to engage in or support war, would not take off their hats to people in authority, called each other *thee* and *thou* to demonstrate brotherly love, and dressed in a plain style to demonstrate their lack of concern for the things of this world. The most striking aspect of the Quaker faith was the belief in "the inner light" or "the Spirit of God which dwells in all men." The Quakers held that those who listened quietly and reverently for the voice of God in their hearts could commune directly with His spirit and thereby strengthen that divine principle within. Careful attention to moral principles, honesty, thrift, sobriety, and hard work in business, and a pious commitment to help the poor were the essential moral values of the new faith.

Needless to say, the Society of Friends were considered eccentric in the extreme. Their refusal to take an oath of allegiance to king or Puritan, or to fight for either side during the civil war, left them open to persecution. Many of them ended in jail, but that did not quench the evangelistic spirit within them. Because of its direct, simple, egalitarian appeal, the Quaker faith attracted many people tired of the endless bickering among religious zealots that had produced such bloodshed in Europe for so many years. With the zeal of missionaries, Quakers abandoned their homes to travel everywhere carrying their new message of peace and love. They were also willing to denounce with considerable self-righteousness the religious errors of others, especially those who placed the written word of the Bible above the inner light of the Spirit. "Witnessing" for their faith, the Quakers became the most successful evangelists in the seventeenth-century British colonies. They were ready to be mobbed, jailed, whipped, or even hanged as martyrs for the Truth.

The first two Quakers to arrive in New England landed in Boston in July 1656. Both were women. Immediately arrested, they were imprisoned, interrogated, inspected for signs of witchcraft. Their Quaker tracts were burned by the hangman. After five weeks in jail, with windows boarded lest anyone hear their heretical views, they were ordered back to Barbados. Two days after their departure, eight more Quakers arrived on another ship. They too were interrogated, imprisoned, and shipped out. But before they left, Samuel Gorton sent them a now famous letter inviting them to come to Warwick to live if they wanted a place free from persecution. They did not get the opportunity, but many later Quakers did find Rhode Island a haven from persecution.

In October 1656, Massachusetts passed the first of a series of laws inflicting harsh penalties on Quakers and Quaker sympathizers. Starting with imprisonment, fines, and banishment, these laws subsequently included whipping, branding, ear-cropping, and tongue-boring. The final step, in 1658, was a law ordering death by hanging for any Quaker who invaded Massachusetts a third time after being twice put out. Massachusetts also persuaded Plymouth and Connecticut to enact severe laws against Quakers and repeatedly urged Rhode Island to do the same. Rhode Island's legislature responded to that request on October 13, 1657, saying that, while it found Quaker doctrines strange, "we have no law among us whereby to punish any" [35] for expressing their own views of religion. Nor were they about to pass one.

After the arrival of the Quaker ship *Woodhouse* in Newport in the summer of 1657, missionary evangelists of the new sect fanned out in all directions, spreading their new light. Among the first converts were William Coddington and Mary Dyer. It was not long before some of these zealous people decided to invade Massachusetts to preach their views and denounce the laws against Quakers. A widow, Harrod Garner (or Gardner) from Newport, was given ten lashes in Weymouth, Massachusetts, in May 1658 for that offense. A month later Thomas Harris and another Rhode Islander went to Boston and denounced the sermon after Sabbath service. Both were whipped and sent home. In September, Catherine Scott, who had given up the Baptist faith to become a Quaker, received the same treatment. She was told that if she came back again she might be hanged. "If God calls us [to return]," she answered, "I have no question that He whom we love will make us not count our lives dear unto ourselves of His name's sake." To which the magistrate replied, "We shall be as ready to take away your lives as you will to lay them down." [36] And they meant it.

In 1659 William Robinson and Marmaduke Stephenson were

35. Arnold, *History of Rhode Island and Providence*, 1:269.
36. Rufus M. Jones, *The Quakers in the American Colonies* (New York: W. W. Norton & Co., Inc., 1966), p. 76.

hanged on Boston Common for returning a third time to preach their Quaker views. Mary Dyer, who accompanied them from Newport, was led to the gallows, but was reprieved at the last minute. Refusing to be intimidated, she returned to Boston a fourth time in the spring of 1660, and this time she was hanged. The fourth and last Quaker to be hanged in Boston was William Leddra of Barbados. But that year, 1661, the Quakers in England succeeded in persuading King Charles II to order Massachusetts to hang no more Quakers. Nevertheless, cruel and repeated whipping of Quaker preachers continued for another decade in all the neighboring colonies of Rhode Island. Not until 1672 were Quakers allowed to preach in Boston without arrest. Two centuries later Massachusetts tried to make up for its earlier intolerance by erecting statues to both Anne Hutchinson and Mary Dyer in front of the State House facing Boston Common.

The restoration of Charles II to the throne of England in 1660 marked the end of the Puritan movement. While it brought some comfort to the Quakers, it meant more trouble for Rhode Island. Charles II annulled all the actions taken by Parliament after the Puritans had deposed his father. Roger Williams's patent and Gorton's confirmation of Shawomet seemed of doubtful validity. The settlers of Connecticut, having no charter, dispatched John Winthrop, Jr., to get one and instructed him to see that the eastern border of Connecticut was defined as the western shoreline of Narragansett Bay. Massachusetts also claimed that area and in 1661 and 1662 arrested and imprisoned Rhode Island settlers in what are now the towns of Westerly, Narragansett, and Kingston. Plymouth not only claimed all the land on the eastern shore of Narragansett Bay, but claimed the island of Aquidneck, as well.

To protect itself, the legislature authorized John Clarke, who had remained in England since 1651, to fend off the claims of the other colonies and obtain a new charter from the king clarifying Rhode Island's boundaries once and for all. For reasons not entirely clear—except that Charles II probably enjoyed annoying the Puritans—Clarke was amazingly successful. Although John Winthrop, Jr., managed in 1662 to get a charter for

Connecticut that did mark the eastern boundary of that colony as the shore of Narragansett Bay, Clarke negotiated a modification of that charter with Winthrop in 1663 that asserted that the Pawcatuck River marked the eastern boundary of Connecticut.

In his petition to the king for a new charter for Rhode Island in the spring of 1663, Clarke stated the principles upon which Williams had founded the colony. His eloquent words still stir the feelings of Rhode Islanders. The people of Narragansett Bay, Clarke wrote, "have it much in their hearts, if they may be permitted, to hold forth a lively experiment, that a flourishing and civil state may stand, yea and best be maintained, and that among English spirits, with a full liberty in religious commitments." [37] Charles II, though a firm believer in an established church and religious conformity, was pleased to grant Rhode Island the opportunity to continue its lively experiment. On July 8, 1663, the new charter (including these words) created "the colony of Rhode Island and Providence Plantations." The charter asserted that "noe person within the said colonye at any tyme hereafter shall bee any wise molested, punished, disquieted or called in question for any difference in opinions in matters of religion which doe not actually disturb the civil peace of our sayd colonye; but that all . . . freeley and fullye have and enjoy his and their own judgments and consciences in matters of religious concernments." [38] The king also included a statement of boundaries that, though they required a century and a half to work out, were essentially those existing today.

The charter's rules of governance were so liberal that, despite the American Revolution, it remained the fundamental law of the state until 1843. It confirmed the power of the freemen to elect their own rulers and make their own laws "as to them shall seem meet for the good and welfare of the said Company," so long as these laws were not repugnant to those of England, "considering the nature and constitution of the place and

37. Bicknell, *Clarke*, p. 183.
38. Arnold, *History of Rhode Island and Providence*, 1:292.

people there.'' [39] The united settlements of the bay became a little republic, with a governor and ten ''Assistants'' elected annually and a House of Deputies or legislature with representatives from each of the towns, or any new towns to be incorporated later. The general assembly—the assistants and deputies meeting jointly—was to convene twice a year to make laws. The colony was given the right to control its own military affairs, which enabled it later to contest efforts of royal governors in other colonies who claimed they had the right to requisition Rhode Island men to fight in the king's army against the French and Indians.

So enamored did the Rhode Islanders become of their new charter that they created a ritual ceremony, a civil religion, for it, not unlike later Fourth of July celebrations. Every year when the newly elected governor was given the charter for safekeeping during his tenure, all the freemen of the colony assembled at the inauguration; the box in which the charter had been sent from England was opened, and the charter was solemnly taken out and held up for all to see. Then it was read publicly, word for word, to the assembled voters. Like the Ark of the Covenant, the charter in its box became the sacred symbol of the colony's special mission in the New World. These headstrong individualists with widely different views of how to worship God had at last found a sense of community in the worship of political freedom. Later, the states in the Union were to create the same sacred aura around their federal Constitution as the symbol of their union ''under God.''

Nevertheless, despite the possession of a royal charter, Rhode Island was still far from secure and well settled. Its boundaries remained in constant dispute, and its own settlers had become land speculators as avid as those from Massachusetts and Connecticut. The result could only arouse increasing hostility among the Indians. But land-lust was greater than common sense or even common justice. The well-to-do in Newport and Providence pooled their funds for a number of large purchases

39. Arnold, *History of Rhode Island and Providence,* 1:293.

from the Indians after 1650, the most notable of these being the Pettaquamscutt Purchase of 1657, including most of what is now the towns of Narragansett and South Kingstown as well as part of North Kingstown; and the Misquamicut Purchase of 1660, which included what is now Westerly and parts of Hopkinton and Charlestown. The Pettaquamscutt Purchase was directly challenged by the claims of the Atherton Syndicate in Boston, which managed, fraudulently, between 1658 and 1662, to force the Narragansetts to cede them a large part of the western shore of the bay. Both the Misquamicut and the Pettaquamscutt Purchases were in direct conflict with the claim of Connecticut that its eastern border extended to the bay's shore. Connecticut established townships in that area and used its authority to lay civil and religious taxes on all who settled there. Massachusetts established townships of its own there. Land titles were hopelessly confused, and continual imprisonments, fines, and even riots occurred among various claimants.

Finally, in 1664, a royal commission was sent to New England that, among other things, tried to adjudicate some of these conflicting claims. The commission decided in favor of Rhode Island's claim to all the land on the western shore as far as the Pawcatuck River—which is the present border—but its decision was not acknowledged by Connecticut or by the Atherton Syndicate. Legal appeals and petitions to the king continued until 1746. Prior to 1675, however, the area was predominantly Indian land. The white settlers were few and far between. Rhode Island, even in its most settled parts, was still a raw frontier. In the 1660s the legislature was still granting bounties for the killing of wolves, wildcats, and foxes on Aquidneck and around Providence. In 1659 harsh penalties were enacted against cattle thieves. Not until 1662 did Indian wampum cease to be legal tender. In 1664 the Narragansett sachem, Pessacus, asked that a law be passed preventing the sale of alcohol to his people, and fur trading was still lively at Smith's Castle, a trading post near Wickford.

The first great turning point in Rhode Island's early history was not really the charter of 1663, but King Philip's War, in 1675 and 1676. The war, however, was not of Rhode Island's

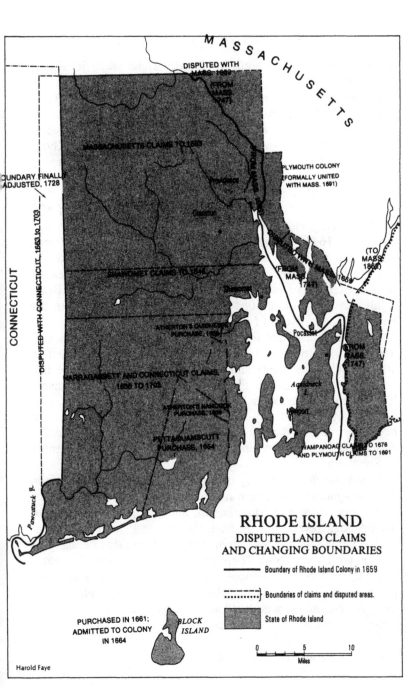

MASSACHUSETTS

DISPUTED WITH
MASS. 1659

(FROM
MASS.
1747)

MASSACHUSETTS CLAIMS TO 1658

PLYMOUTH COLONY
(FORMALLY UNITED
WITH MASS. 1691)

BOUNDARY FINALLY
ADJUSTED, 1728

Pawtucket

Cranston

(TO
MASS.
1862)

DISPUTED WITH MASS. 1659

(FROM
MASS.
1747)

SHAWOMET CLAIMS TO 1646

Shawomet

Pocasset

ATHERTON'S GUDGEON'S
PURCHASE, 1659

(FROM
MASS.
1747)

NARRAGANSETT AND CONNECTICUT CLAIMS,
1658 TO 1703

Aquidneck
I.

ATHERTON'S HANCOCK
PURCHASE, 1659

Newport

PETTAQUAMSCUTT
PURCHASE, 1654

WAMPANOAG CLAIMS TO 1676
AND PLYMOUTH CLAIMS TO 1691

Pawcatuck R.

RHODE ISLAND
DISPUTED LAND CLAIMS
AND CHANGING BOUNDARIES

——— Boundary of Rhode Island Colony in 1659

·········· Boundaries of claims and disputed areas.

▓▓▓ State of Rhode Island

PURCHASED IN 1661;
ADMITTED TO COLONY
IN 1664

BLOCK
ISLAND

0   5   10
Miles

Harold Faye

Adapted from maps prepared by the Rhode Island State Planning Board, 1936 making, nor did the people of Rhode Island wage it. Rhode Islanders saw the war as an aggressive effort by the Puritan colonies seeking to secure their claims to the land of the Wampanoags and Narragansetts and thus to assert political authority over as much of Rhode Island and Providence Plantations as they could. On the eve of the war, several prominent Rhode Islanders, led by deputy-governor John Easton, tried to negotiate a peaceful settlement with the Indians, assuring them that the king and Rhode Island would respect their rights. But matters had gone too far. The Wampanoags' courageous Chief Metacomet (King Philip, son of Ousamequin) put the issue succinctly in 1674: noting that whenever trouble arose between whites and Indians it was settled in the white man's court and that the Indians were forced to pay in land for all damages assessed, Metacomet said, "Thus tract after tract is gone. But a small part of the dominions of my ancestors remains. I am determined not to live till I have no country." [40]

Which side fired the first shot is still not clear. It seems evident that Metacomet had for some years been trying to effect an alliance of all the chiefs and tribes around the bay, but he had not yet won their assent. Even some of his own local sachems, like Queen Awashonks of Sakonnet (now Little Compton), preferred to stay out of any conflict. The Narragansetts hoped for neutrality, and so did the Nianticks on the western shore. The first bloodshed occurred in June 1675, in the town of Swansea in Plymouth.

Massachusetts, as an ally of Plymouth, exerted pressure upon the Narragansetts to remain neutral. They sent word that Chief Canonchet, the son of Miantonomi, must not give any refuge to Wampanoag people fleeing from the war in Plymouth. Canonchet struggled with the problem, but concluded that he had better side with Metacomet. There was no way to satisfy Massachusetts. Its leaders would sooner or later find an excuse to assert force to obtain the remaining land of the Narragansetts. However, the Nianticks, who lived south of the Narragansetts, under Chief Ninigret decided to remain neutral.

40. Arnold, *History of Rhode Island and Providence*, 1:395.

The Rhode Island authorities thought they too could remain outside the conflict; but they were less than neutral. They allowed the Puritan colonies to march their troops through their land, and several dozen Rhode Islanders (without official authorization) joined these invading forces against the Indians. For all its former efforts at peaceful relations, Rhode Island was involved in the land acquisitions, and it suffered heavily in the conflict. All of its settlements on the mainland were destroyed.

The first major fight of the war took place in southwestern Rhode Island, where the Narragansetts had their winter quarters. Known as the Great Swamp Fight of December 19, 1675, it was essentially a slaughter of the Narragansetts and the Wampanoag refugees among them. The Indians were betrayed by one of their own people who led 1,100 soldiers from Massachusetts, Connecticut, and Plymouth through a secret path to the one unfortified section of the Indian encampment. As the battle began and the colonists pressed into the camp, someone set fire to the first Indian wigwams, which sheltered women, children, and the aged. A heavy wind whipped the fire through the camp, burning hundreds of noncombatants to death. The Indians were routed, and the colonists killed as many as they could. But a fierce snowstorm forced them to give up pursuit. They withdrew, sending their wounded to Aquidneck Island.

Canonchet and many of his warriors escaped from the massacre at the Great Swamp and, joining with Metacomet, the combined forces of the Narragansetts and Wampanoags continued a dreadful frontier warfare throughout New England, up to the very outskirts of Boston over the next six months. Canonchet had his revenge on the English on March 26, 1676, when he surrounded a company of Plymouth soldiers sent to capture him near Central Falls, Rhode Island. He wiped out the entire force of fifty-five. The next day these warriors advanced on the town of Providence, six miles to the south. Roger Williams, though more than seventy years old, was chosen captain of the twenty-seven men who remained in a blockaded house after the rest of the population had fled to Aquidneck. Knowing they could not prevent the Indians from burning the town, Williams tried to parlay with them, asking them to depart in peace. The chief of the party surrounding Williams's men said, "Brother Williams, you are a good man; you have been kind to us many years; not a hair of your head shall be touched." [41] But it was too late to talk peace. Providence went up in flames, though Williams and his men held out in the blockaded house. In April 1676, Canonchet was captured and executed by Connecticut soldiers.

Another slaughter of Indian men, women, and children occurred near Warwick in July 1676, and thereafter the Indians were on the defensive, failing to gain the help they sought from the Mohawks. Finally Metacomet was killed by a Wampanoag turncoat on August 12, 1676, near his home at Mount Hope. Soon after, the Mount Hope area was sold to Plymouth men, who founded the town of Bristol there. The remaining warriors were relentlessly hunted down and slain. Metacomet's wife and nine-year-old son were sold into slavery along with most of the captives held by the people of Plymouth, Massachusetts, and Connecticut.

While Rhode Island had passed a law in 1674 prohibiting the enslavement of Indians, the settlers were not willing to abide by that after the war. They compromised by selling those who surrendered to them into temporary servitude in Rhode Island. Those captives five years of age or younger were to be bondservants till they turned thirty; those over thirty were to be bondservants for seven years. Roger Williams was put in charge of the committee that managed the process of selling the captives into bondage and dividing the proceeds among the inhabitants of Providence whose homes had been burned. Williams had long since lost hope that the Indians and whites could live together in mutual tolerance. The Indians, he believed, had lost their original dignity and self-respect after years of close association with the colonists and the gradual destruction of their original way of life.

The few Indians around the bay who had remained friendly or neutral during the war were placed under the daughter of Chief Ninigret (he having died in 1676) until Ninigret II came of age.

---

41. George W. Greene, *Short History of Rhode Island* (Providence: J. A. Reid and R. A. Reid, pub., 1877), p. 75.

Tribal affiliations lost their significance as survivors of Narragansetts, Wampanoags, Sakonnets, and Nianticks were all merged together. They were allowed to keep a small part of the Indian domain near Charlestown, Rhode Island, but lived on it virtually as a reservation. Under Ninigret II and his successors, they eked out a bare existence, farming, fishing, hunting, and working for the whites. Gradually they were forced to dispose of more and more of their land. Finally, in 1880, the two hundred remaining of the various tribes were officially detribalized by an act of the legislature. Except for the private plots they lived on, the remaining Indian land was sold.

The tragic story of Indian-white relations in Rhode Island—from friendly welcome to merciless annihilation—covered little more than half a century. The same scenario, with minor variations, was repeated many times thereafter as the white man moved westward. But little that happened in the Far West had not already taken place on the coastal frontier, two centuries before the days of Buffalo Bill, George Custer, and the six-shooter.

Not until the spring of 1677 did the Rhode Island refugees on Aquidneck straggle back to the burned homes in the various towns around the bay. They faced a long, slow process of rebuilding. The first generation of leaders passed away. William Blackstone died in 1675; Nicholas Easton, the same year. John Clarke died in 1676; Samuel Gorton in 1677; William Coddington in 1678. William Harris of Pawtuxet, who continued to press his land claims, was captured by Barbary pirates in 1679 on his way to appeal to the crown; ransomed in 1681, he died before he could reach home. Roger Williams lingered until 1683. The exact day of his death is not known, though he was buried with honors by the town. His grave is unmarked, his home site hidden beneath the rubble of later foundations. But his bones, removed from the original grave site, repose under a ten-foot statue on Prospect Terrace overlooking the city. His spring has become the center of a National Memorial Park. His memory is still green.

With the passing of these early pietists, perfectionists, mystics, seekers, and land-grabbers, the colony rapidly entered a new era. While everyone respected the right of each individual to believe and worship as he or she chose (or not at all), the privatization of religion led to a new emphasis on economic self-interest as the motivating force in the colony. The heavy reliance in most Rhode Island sects upon a mystical relationship with God's spirit and the widespread dislike for a learned, paid, professional clergy produced a general distinterest in education—education in that day being largely centered around religious training and directed by a learned clergy. Since neither the Quakers nor the Baptists, the two predominant groups in the colony after 1676, were interested in scholarly debates about doctrine or dogma, few books or sermons were published by Rhode Islanders. No one thought it necessary to found a college, and few sent their sons to Harvard or Yale. The absence of a professional clergy and an established church was also largely responsible for the absence of a public school system. The emphasis upon a spirit-filled, rather than head-stored, clergy left in the colony's intellectual and cultural life a vacuum that was not filled until the Anglicans and Congregationalists established churches. Once Rhode Islanders had rebuilt their towns, they turned their wits and energy toward economic survival and political rivalry with wealthier colonies.

Rhode Island continued to be a haven for religious dissent, however. The Seventh Day Baptists movement began in Newport in the 1660s, led by Stephen Mumford, William Hiscox, and Samuel Hubbard. They split off from John Clarke's church in 1671 and spread from there to Westerly and Hopkinton across the bay. With the revocation of the Edict of Nantes in 1685, thousands of French Protestants (Huguenots) emigrated to America, and forty-five of these families settled in what is now East Greenwich in 1686. The area is still known as "Frenchtown," though the Huguenots did not remain long. They unfortunately chose to settle on land in dispute between Massachusetts and Rhode Island, making their purchases from the Atherton Syndicate. For that they suffered such harassment as interlopers that they finally moved away. Gabriel Bernon, one of the few to remain in Rhode Island, joined the Anglican

Church and was influential in persuading the British Society for the Propagation of the Gospel in Foreign Parts to found the first Anglican Church in Newport in 1701. Later Anglican churches were founded in Wickford in 1707 and in Providence in 1722.

The most striking new religious group to come to the colony in the seventeenth century was the Jews. Some sources say they came as early as the 1650s; others argue that it was not until two decades later. In any case, we know that by 1677, as many as fifteen Jewish families were living in Newport, where they practiced their worship in private homes and purchased a plot for a burial ground in 1677. Led by Mordecai Campanal, Moses Pacheco, Simon Mendez, and Abraham Burgos, this small group practiced the Sephardic rites of their faith and came to America from Spain and Portugal via Latin America and the West Indies. It also appears that some of them practiced freemasonry in Campanal's home. According to the British Navigation laws, persons classified as aliens, as these Jewish immigrants were, were not permitted to engage in trade. When several of them became merchants in the 1680s, they were prosecuted by the Surveyor General, William Dyer. These Jewish merchants welcomed the trial as a test case of their status and were pleased when the jury acquitted them of any illegal practice. They were even more pleased when the general assembly formally resolved on June 24, 1684, that they were to enjoy all the protection of the law as resident strangers. None of them at that time applied for naturalization as British subjects.

This first group of Jewish settlers dwindled after 1690, but their community was revived after 1730 by a new influx from the Dutch West Indian Island of Curacao, led by the Isaacs family, the Moses family, the Judahs, the Benjamins, the Solomons, and others. They engaged mostly in small local businesses—tailoring, making brass and soap, dealing in dry goods. After 1740, more Spanish and Portuguese Jews arrived, including Isaac Touro, James Lucena, Aaron and Abraham Lopez, Abraham and Jacob Rivera, Isaac and Moses Seixas. In addition, Isaac Hart came from England; Isaac Pollock, from Poland; and Benjamin Myers, from Austria, adding an Ashkenazic tone to the predominantly Sephardic community. Touro, who led the services on the Sabbath, as a *hazzan*, or reader, was instrumental in establishing the first synagogue in Rhode Island and one of the first in America. It was built in 1763 and still holds regular services, but no rabbi was ever installed here during the colonial era.

But while increasing proliferation of varieties of religious experience continued without difficulty, the political situation of Rhode Island, like the rest of New England, became complicated after 1686, when Governor Edmund Andros was sent to Boston by James II with orders to abrogate the charters of all the colonies from New Jersey to Maine and reorganize them as one unified royal dominion. The loss of local self-government reduced Rhode Island to little more than a county in the King's Province of New England. But Andros was harder on the Puritans than on the Rhode Island pietists. He sided with the Rhode Island land claims on the western side of the bay and forced religious toleration on the intolerant colonies, suspending their right to collect religious taxes for the Congregational churches.

Like Connecticut, Rhode Island hid its charter from Andros, but could not prevent his breaking the colony's seal, which bore an anchor with the motto *Hope* above it. From Andros's political tyranny—he had no qualms about laying taxes without representation—New England was rescued by "the Glorious Revolution" in England in 1688. When the news arrived that the English had forced James II to abdicate, Andros was arrested in Boston, and all the New England colonies returned to their old political systems. Andros's chief justice, Joseph Dudley, was in Rhode Island when the news of the revolution came, so the citizens of Providence arrested him and took him to prison in Roxbury, Massachusetts, thus playing a part in the first American battle against English tyranny. The colony then took out its hidden charter and resumed its system of self-government. When Andros escaped from prison in Boston and fled to Newport, he was discovered and kept in prison there till the Massachusetts authorities came to get him. In March 1690, the General Assembly ordered a new seal made to replace the one Andros had broken. *Hope* returned.

A new era opened in New England's history under the reign of William and Mary, with the passage of the Toleration Act and the English Bill of Rights. England was at last catching up with its most radical colony. But as religious animosity died, trade rivalry grew.

2

Rhode Island Becomes an Imperial Entrepôt

ETWEEN 1690 and 1765, Rhode Island came into its own. Slowly it overcame its internal strife, its sense of inferiority, its political confusion. The resolution of its internal disputes over land titles encouraged the expansion of its settlements and population. As it secured its borders against the expansionist ambitions of Massachusetts and Connecticut, it came out from under their shadow. The towns learned to work harmoniously with each other; the legislature learned the virtues of cooperation with London. Most important, the colony's merchants evolved a commercial system that circumvented the lack of internal resources through an imaginative carrying trade on the high seas. Transporting a wide variety of goods from one part of the empire to another, Rhode Island became a major imperial entrepôt. Newport's harbor provided the key to energetic economic expansion, and merchant grandees at Newport and Providence became early symbols of the American success myth—not the kind of success a pietist like Roger Williams would extoll, but the kind embodied in the rags-to-riches dream of American free enterprise.

Fortunately—almost off-handedly—the vagaries of English politics had protected Rhode Island's freedom in the seventeenth century, despite heavy odds. But after 1690, the colony could

50

no longer live in splendid isolation; Britain began to force all its colonies into a broad perspective of colonial relationships. In that new view, Rhode Island's willful intransigence toward external authority became a stumbling block to over-all imperial integration. It took the colony some time to adjust to its new role within the empire, but after two decades of resistance, its leaders learned that swimming with the tide could be as exhilarating as swimming against it. In fact, as they gained experience in the more risky aspects of trade and shipping, they developed enormous pride and zest in their commercial skill. After 1710, they showed the same boldness and bravura in their search for markets on the Atlantic as they had formerly displayed in their quests for spiritual perfection. It was a remarkable transformation.

Politically, the transformation of Rhode Island from introverted self-containment to extroverted commerce and from subsistence farming to an international carrying trade had to begin with a revision by Rhode Islanders of the construction they put upon their charter, the symbol of their autonomy. From 1690 to 1710, the colonists interpreted their relationship with the crown in terms of their right to self-government and came close to losing the charter entirely. At that time, they had little to offer the empire and little common ground with the other American colonies. Imperial warfare and growing commercial prosperity finally put an end to such arrogance. Rhode Island found it had more to lose than to gain from provoking the Crown by a defensive protection of its "charter rights."

The years 1690 to 1765 were filled with wars in which Rhode Island could not stand alone. It came to see that the success of British arms against rival imperial powers in the world were vital to its own welfare. In King William's War (1689–1697) and Queen Anne's War (1702–1713), Rhode Island was reluctant to do its part. But in King George's War (1745–1748) and the French and Indian War (1754–1763), it offered wholehearted support. Even though Block Island was invaded three times in King William's War, Rhode Island was slow to pull its oar. Its inhabitants were poor, and tax resistance was strong; the demands of war were expensive. Rhode Islanders therefore declined to supply their quotas of men and supplies to help in other parts of the colonies. They not only pleaded poverty, but insisted that their men were needed to protect their long coastline and open harbor, that their charter placed their militia solely under the command of their own governor and legislature, hence they could not obey requests against the will of their people. However, it was difficult to support these self-interested claims against the express orders of the king giving his royal governors in New York or Massachusetts command over all military forces. Still, Rhode Island tried.

In May 1690, Governor Leisler of New York requested aid from Rhode Island in the king's name to stave off the French and Indians descending from Canada. Rhode Island refused to comply. In August 1690, Sir William Phips, commander-in-chief of New England's forces, demanded that Rhode Island's militia be put under his command, as the king empowered him to do. Again the colony refused. In March 1693, the king ordered all the colonies to send troops to aid the governor of New York, but when the New York governor requisitioned forty-eight soldiers as Rhode Island's share in August 1694, the colony refused. In 1695 the colony declined to send its quota to defend Albany from the French. Finally, the Board of Trade and Plantations in London cited Rhode Island to the crown for disobedience, and in 1697 the king started proceedings to revoke the colony's charter. The colony sent funds and documents to its agent in London to defend its charter rights against the king.

While that matter was still pending, Richard Coote, Earl of Bellomont, was made governor of Massachusetts and given power over the militia of all the New England colonies, as well as those in New Jersey. Rhode Island again refused to let its men serve under him without the consent of the General Assembly. Bellomont came to the colony in 1699 to inquire into allegations that the colony was also failing to obey the navigation acts, ignoring the admiralty regulations, and giving aid and comfort to pirates. In Newport, a group of disaffected inhabitants, known locally as "the royalists," gave Bellomont an earful of evidence against the colony. He wrote a report to the king charging that Rhode Islanders, of all the colonists under his authority, were "the most irregular and illegal in their administration that ever any government was," and demanded that they be "reduced to the subjection of the British Empire." [1] But divine providence seemed to intervene: King William and Lord Bellomont both died before action could be taken to abrogate Rhode Island's charter.

In 1701 Joseph Dudley succeeded Bellomont as governor of Massachusetts and received the same military prerogatives. He came to Rhode Island in 1702 and demanded that the militia acknowledge him as its commander. Captain Isaac Martindale, chief officer of the militia, refused, saying he took orders only from the General Assembly and the governor of his colony. Dudley then reported to Queen Anne that Bellomont was right about Rhode Island's fractiousness. The matter came again to the Board of Trade, which advised the queen to abrogate the charter and make Dudley the royal governor of Rhode Island. Fortunately, she did not heed that advice.

In 1703 Governor Cornbury of New York requested Rhode Island troops to help him defend his frontier, but again Rhode Island made excuses. Finally, in 1704 the queen sent a letter of censure to the colony, and it began to mend its ways. In the summer of 1704, Governor Cranston persuaded the general assembly to send a militia contingent to aid Dudley in preparing an expedition against the French. They went, however, because the general assembly ordered them to and not at Dudley's command. Another contingent was ordered up in February 1705, to show that Rhode Island could do its duty—but on its own terms. In 1706, and again in 1710 and 1711, Rhode Island sent such men and ships as it thought it could spare for invasions of Canada.

In addition to being censured for its obstinate refusal to help the crown's war efforts, Rhode Island was accused by Bellomont, Dudley, and other royal officials of illegally commissioning privateers, of forming an illegal admiralty court, and of tolerating piracy. The three crimes were closely related. Privateers were indeed commissioned, and the colony's governors

1. Lippincott, *Indians*, p. 113.

claimed they had the right to do so under the charter. Privateers did sometimes cross the thin line between war on enemy shipping and war on those not technically at war with England. The capture of prizes of war by privateers had to be reported to admiralty courts, to prove their legality, and in 1694 Rhode Island established its own court for that purpose. But the colony firmly denied any wrongdoing.

Privateering was partly a matter of self-defense, the creation of a colonial navy when there were no British naval ships to protect them from the enemy. One of the first privateers commissioned, Captain Thomas Paine of Jamestown, was instrumental in driving off French ships that had landed on Block Island and terrorized its people in 1690. Paine had been, according to some, a noted pirate in his earlier years. Some said that the well-known pirates Thomas Tew and Captain Want were Rhode Islanders, and everyone knew that Captain Kidd visited the colony on several occasions, dined with several prominent merchants, and might have buried treasure on one of the Narragansett Bay islands.

Privateering was also a way to turn war into profit, for the captain and crew got to keep most of the loot they captured, with ten percent reserved for the crown. Pirates may have been winked at because they brought specie into the colony and spent it freely. Privateers sometimes did not hear that the war was over and kept cruising around capturing enemy ships during peacetime. Whether a prize was captured before or after a peace treaty was signed was always open to question in those days of slow communication. But these excuses were not convincing.

By 1710, under the supple and adroit leadership of Governor Samuel Cranston, who was re-elected annually from 1697 till his death in 1727, Rhode Island had yielded on all these points. There was no way to prevent the king from establishing his own admiralty judges after 1700. The Board of Trade specifically forbade the governor to commission privateers. And as Rhode Island's own commerce grew, the profits in piracy became less important. Another important reason for establishing admiralty courts under the crown—which could commission privateers—was to make sure that all ships in and out of colonial ports paid their duties and obeyed the navigation acts. Bellomont and Dudley accused Rhode Island's merchants of habitual smuggling to evade royal duties, but while that practice became common in later years, after the Molasses Act of 1733, it is doubtful that there was much of it prior to 1710.

A large part of the willingness of the colony to acquiesce in imperial regulations was not so much the threats against its charter as the growing recognition that Rhode Island's future lay in trade. Clearly, the British army and navy protected that shipping. Furthermore, even in peacetime, it was not unprofitable to comply with the navigation acts, which gave distinct advantages to merchants within the empire.

But trade required products for export, and that meant that the colony had to develop its resources and give the fullest encouragement to the labor of its farmers, woodsmen, artisans, and fishermen. But before its resources could be developed, the colony had somehow to settle its border disputes and its internal land controversies. Only then would the hinterland fill up with people who would raise more livestock, cut more timber, plant more orchards, grow more exportable food products. Part of the problem lay in the need to centralize the colony's governance and make the towns see the advantages of yielding part of their local autonomy to the legislature. They did so just as the colony yielded some of its autonomy to the crown when distrust dissipated amid advantages gained.

The general assembly won some local support in 1696 by conceding that it should become a bicameral body, thereby giving the town deputies a chance to check the council or upper house. At the same time, it agreed that all money or tax bills should originate in the lower house. To avoid suspicions and jealousy, the general assembly agreed to transact its business in five different capitals, one in each county, thus allowing the local inhabitants to watch closely over its actions. During the course of the eighteenth century, the tiny colony was to build capital buildings in Newport, South Kingstown, East Greenwich, Providence, and—after 1746—Bristol and rotated its legislative sessions among them. Furthermore, while the general assembly levied taxes proportionately upon each town, it was lenient with towns unable to meet these levies on time. Finally, the right of electing officers of the militia, at least in the lower ranks, was left with the local units. With these concessions to localism, the central government coupled the ability to protect the towns against encroachments by influential syndicates of land speculators and by the neighboring colonies.

Through a series of intricate compromises and a bit of arm-twisting, Governor Cranston made remarkable headway against these complex land problems between 1700 and 1727. As early as 1703, he got Connecticut to agree to what is now the western border of the state, and while that colony later reneged on that agreement, it was confirmed in 1728. That settled the long conflict over the border between Stonington and Westerly. Having confirmed Rhode Island's control over that region, Cranston then clarified the conflicting land titles under the Misquamicut Purchase. Next he settled, between 1707 and 1709, the thorny questions raised by the dispute between the Pettaquamscutt Purchasers and the Atherton Syndicate, or Narragansett Proprietors. He confined Ninigret II and his tribe within a much smaller reservation in Charlestown and sold the remaining "unoccupied" Indian land in 1709.

Between 1710 and 1714, Cranston settled the long-standing dispute about the exact extent of the Pawtuxet land—essentially in favor of Providence and Warwick and against the old claims of William Harris and the Arnolds. By clarifying these various land claims and forcing the owners—or, more accurately, the land speculators—to sell off much of their holdings, Cranston opened up vast new areas in western Rhode Island for new settlement. While the northern part of this area was too hilly and rocky to be good farmland, it was good for orchards, timber, and grazing. The southwest quadrant of the colony (King's County, or Narrangansett) was extremely fertile and soon was yielding large quantities of produce and livestock for export, including the famous Narrangansett pacer.

The next most important land settlements occurred after Cranston's death. They added more land, population, and wealth, because they brought a populous, well-cultivated, already settled area within the bounds of the colony—towns that had hitherto been under the jurisdiction of Massachusetts and the old Plymouth Colony. This was the area on the eastern side of the bay. It included the present towns of Little Compton, Tiverton, Bristol, Warren, and Barrington. It also included a large triangle of land in the northeastern corner, east of the Blackstone River, then known as "the Attleboro Gore," but the town of Attleborough was not included. The charter of 1663 had stated that Rhode Island was to include an area three miles wide along the eastern shore of the bay and then directly north from Pawtucket Falls to the Massachusetts border. But Plymouth and Massachusetts had paid no attention to that, and Rhode Island lacked the power to do anything about it until the third decade of the eighteenth century. Then, with the help of royal commissioners, these boundaries were established in 1727. Massachusetts bitterly contested that decision, but in 1746 it was confirmed by the king and these towns, with their five thousand inhabitants, finally came under the aegis of Rhode Island. Though all the borders were not settled precisely in 1746, Rhode Island thereafter generally assumed the jurisdiction it has today. (Its last territorial change, in 1862, was the acquisition of eastern Pawtucket and East Providence in exchange for Fall River.)

One measure of the importance of these land settlements was the increase in population. In 1690 the colony had about 3,500 inhabitants; by 1700, it had 7,000. It more than doubled to 18,000 in 1730, and more than doubled again by 1755 to 42,000. By 1765 it had close to 50,000 people. If the number of slaves was a measure of wealth, they too increased enormously, from 426 in 1708 to 1,648 in 1730 and almost 5,000 in 1765. Even the Narragansett Indians failed to disappear as predicted. They grew more slowly, however, from under 1,000 in 1708 to 1,500 by 1765. The number of incorporated towns grew from six in 1665 to twenty-one by 1765. The two largest cities, Providence and Newport, almost tripled in size, although Providence remained only half as large as its rival. In 1708 Newport had 2,200 people and Providence 1,500; in 1765 Newport had about 8,000 and Providence 4,000. Unfortunately, we lack figures for growth in wealth, but we know that the colony's merchant fleet grew from 24 vessels in 1708 to 80 in 1731, to 120 in 1740, and to more than 500 in 1763. That was no mean feat for a colony so small and lacking in any staple crop or resource of great value. Its major resources proved to be the ingenuity and drive of its people.

A more important measure of the importance of land settlements was the trend toward a market economy. As the population increased, and new roads, bridges, and ferries were built to enable farmers to get their marketable products to the seaports, not only Newport and Providence but a group of other lively trade and retail centers arose around the bay. Bristol and Warren had grown to importance on the eastern shore under Massachusetts and continued to thrive. On the western shore, the towns of Warwick, Wickford, and Westerly also became important market centers. But this burgeoning mercantile economy had a serious flaw: it lacked a convenient medium of exchange. It lacked fluid capital and specie, or coinage. One solution that gave a decided advantage to Rhode Island over its rivals in Boston, New London, and Hartford, was paper money.

According to many historians, paper money became the bane of Rhode Island's existence in the eighteenth century, leading its neighbors once again to label it a land of irresponsible rogues and rascals. But whatever havoc that system may have wrought in the so-called critical period of the 1780s (and even that is questionable), recent studies demonstrate that paper money was an enormous boon to the merchants and the commerce of the colony between 1710 and 1750. And, being a boon to the economy, even the farmers (who at first saw little to be gained and much to be feared in this contrivance of the merchants) eventually came to support it. Rhode Island's use of paper money did not, however, please the merchants of the other colonies nor the Board of Trade in England.

The first issue of paper money in 1710 stemmed from wartime needs. Having consented finally to do its share toward supplying troops, ships, and supplies for Queen Anne's War, the colony found it increasingly difficult to collect taxes from its hard-pressed people. It simply did not have any surplus wealth for the costly expenditures needed for the invasions of Canada in 1708 and 1710–1711. Issuing paper "bills of credit" to be redeemed by taxes was seen first as a temporary wartime expedient. However, it proved so painless a way to stimulate production and trade and get taxes paid that it seemed foolish not to utilize it. At first, it met considerable local resistance, especially from pious folk who studiously eschewed going into debt. Perhaps that is why these paper bills had, in their emblem, the anchor of hope encircled by the colony's motto, *"In Te, Domine, Speramus* (In Thee, Lord, is our Trust)."

Most of the paper money (or bills of public credit) issued in Rhode Island after 1714 was based upon land, not taxes, as collateral. The colony merely used its credit to guarantee the paper money that landowners received as a loan or mortgage upon their property. The value of the paper was in theory to be sustained by the value of the land—the assessed value of the land was twice the face value of the paper issued in mortgage. The person who received the paper could use it as though it were specie (silver or gold), but he had to pay yearly interest on it (about three percent) to the state and within five years (extendable to ten), he was supposed to pay off the principal. The colony was to retire annually (that is, to burn) that amount of paper money paid off as principal.

By providing a readily available medium of exchange, paper money produced a boom in the economy from 1710 until King George's War. It was so useful that, instead of retiring it, the colony continued to issue more and more of it. The first land bank issue of £40,000 occurred in 1715; later issues in 1721, 1728, 1731, and 1738 raised the total amount of paper to £384,000. Failure to retire these bills regularly and to administer carefully the payment of interest and principal, as well as the fact that almost no mortgages were ever foreclosed, meant that the money gradually depreciated in value. By 1750 it was worth only about fifty percent of its face value. Thereafter, merchants began to oppose it. But by then the economy was self-supporting.

Nevertheless, in the years 1710 to 1750, the scheme was a success. It stimulated internal production, trade, and sales. It increased the amount of shipping tremendously. In 1708 Rhode

Island's thirty ships (mostly sloops) were engaged primarily in the coastwise trade; by 1741, it had 120 ships, many of which were in trans-Atlantic trade to Africa, the West Indies, and European ports. Not only did shipping increase, but so did ship building, harbor trade, internal retail sales, and all of the subsidiary production and manufacture needed to sustain commerce—barrel-making, wagon-building, blacksmithing, rope-making, and especially refining sugar and distilling molasses into rum. In addition, the state was able to lower taxes by distributing the interest from the payments on paper-money mortgages to the towns as a means of paying for improving roads, bridges, and ferries.

Rhode Island's paper money was never acceptable to English merchants—there was no way for them to exchange paper for land in Rhode Island; paper was not very negotiable, even at face value. However, it was accepted in most of the New England colonies, where it was most needed. It was reluctantly accepted by Boston merchants in payment for British manufactures that they imported for specie and sold to Rhode Island merchants for paper. The Rhode Island merchants made a discount gain from such exchanges, as the money depreciated, and gradually co-opted the market for the sale of English goods in the areas close to Narragansett Bay, which included southeastern Massachusetts, eastern Connecticut, and the rural areas around Worcester. Despite the 50 percent depreciation and the growing complaints after 1745 from the Board of Trade in England, the paper-money system launched Rhode Island to its self-sustaining take-off point in commerce.

By the time opposition finally curtailed the land bank in 1754, the merchants and retailers had established both credit and commerce sufficiently stable to obtain other means of exchange, notably, "bills of exchange," with a wide network of other merchants. They also had enough capital invested in ships, wharves, warehouses, stores, wagons, and subsidiary manufacturers to operate competitively with Massachusetts and Connecticut merchants. Furthermore, by 1750 they had won a major share of the lucrative "Triangular Trade" (produce, molasses, and slaves to the West Indies and Africa), which enabled them to obtain considerable specie. In short, discreditable as paper money seemed to the pious and conservative, it established Rhode Island's commercial credit. Her merchants gained a reputation for reliability, shrewdness, and energy. They also gained a less enviable reputation for Yankee sharpness.

Paper money alone did not transform Rhode Island. The general assembly used its power to stimulate commerce in other ways. It offered bounties to increase the production of needed supplies, such as barrel staves and naval stores, and bounties for the importation of fish, whale oil, and hemp. It offered subsidies and tariffs to increase the manufacture of iron and rope or cordage. To increase the value of raw materials for export, Rhode Islanders engaged not only in distilling molasses, but they built tanneries, brick-kilns, sawmills, and candle works. Shipbuilding thrived in several towns. Cheese, salt pork, and cider were prime local exports. The legislature passed laws taxing merchants from other colonies who did business in Rhode Island and made them pay duties on what they brought in.

In addition to importing British manufactures, the colony traded heavily in wines, indigo, cotton, cocoa (it had several chocolate mills), rice, and wheat. Rhode Islanders realized that, if they intended to grow up with the country, they had to agree that the business of the colony was basically commerce; all else was subservient to the goal of keeping cargoes flowing in and out. By 1750 even farmers were investing hard-earned savings in seagoing ventures the way people today invest in the stockmarket, hoping that their ship would come in loaded with profitable wares. Rhode Island put its heart and soul into trade in these years, for, as the Bible said, "Where your treasure is, there will your heart be also." [2]

Even so, expanding trade and prosperity did not come easily. Rhode Islanders were never able to sit back and relax. They had always to be on the lookout for the main chance, to cut corners, take risks, play fast and loose with every conceivable loophole in the navigation acts and other imperial trade regulations. The

2. Matthew 6:21.

word most commonly used for that kind of cut-throat competition was *enterprise*, and Rhode Island had an abundant supply of that commodity. It was a trait that at last united them in spirit to the rest of New England and America. By entering into the mainstream of imperial trade after 1710, Rhode Islanders became considerably less exceptional.

The experience in seamanship, in trade, and in privateering produced not only a large number of skillful ship captains and crews, but also a willingness to engage in the kinds of high-risk ventures that cautious businessmen in other colonies steered clear of. After 1750 some Rhode Island merchants attained a reputation (admired at home and deplored elsewhere) of being somewhat shady in their beginnings and hard-driving thereafter. Typical of the more rugged entrepreneurs of the colony in the latter half of the century was Simeon Potter, of Bristol— a seaport rivalling Providence, if not Newport. Potter is famous for remarking to his young nephew in the 1750s, "I would plow the ocean into pea-porridge to make money." [3] At the age of twenty-four, Potter was commissioned to privateer against French vessels in King George's War. That took him to the West Indies where, on his own initiative, he ordered his crew to attack and loot the small settlement of Oyapec in French Guinea. Behaving like pirates, Potter and his crew carried off every item of value in the town, including the silver plate from the local Catholic Church. A few years later, when asked by a royal official, who admired his seamanship, if he would like to join the navy and obtain command of a bigger ship, Potter answered, "When I wish for a better ship, I will not ask His Majesty for one; I will build it myself." [4]

In the years from 1750 to 1770, Potter became one of the leaders in the slave trade, a notoriously risky business requiring strong nerves and ruthless attention to profit. He instructed the captains of his slave ships to "water down your rum as much as possible and sell as much by the short measure as you can." [5]

3. Mark A. DeWolfe Howe, *Bristol, Rhode Island* (Cambridge, Mass.: Harvard University Press, 1930), p. 31.
4. Howe, *Bristol*, p. 46.
5. Howe, *Bristol*, p. 45.

Potter grew rich and respectable trading rum for slaves; he represented his town in the general assembly for many years. He also served as a vestryman in St. Michael's Episcopal Church, and in 1776 was named major-general of the state militia. One of his proudest exploits was his participation in the burning of the British naval cutter *Gaspée* in 1772. The higher law of economic survival made for a spirit of independence both in the best and worst senses of the term.

Rhode Island's three primary sources of wealth were the sugar trade, the slave trade, and the fisheries—especially whaling. Most Rhode Island merchants engaged in all three, though some specialized more heavily in one than another. After paper money had got the colony's trade on a competitive basis, the principal means of financing it became bills of exchange, supplemented where possible by the use of Spanish dollars, Dutch florins, and French livres. A good "bill of exchange" was acceptable in England and preferred by merchants everywhere over paper money. Bills of exchange worked like private checks or money orders. They were credit slips given by the purchaser of goods in one part of the realm and payable in terms of money or goods due to him by merchants in other parts of the realm. For example, if a Rhode Islander traded a couple of Narragansett pacers or a herd of sheep to a plantation owner in the West Indies who was short of specie but who regularly shipped sugar or molasses to England, the planter would write a bill of exchange payable by the dealer who bought his products in England; the Rhode Island merchant could then use this bill of 'change to obtain goods in England or wherever else the planter's credit was known to be good. Since a good bill of exchange depended upon the honesty, reliability, and affluence of the man who gave it, that method of doing business operated only among men of solid reputation and worth. The essence of Rhode Island trade was to get enough of these bills from reputable purchasers of Rhode Island exports to obtain all the manufactured imports Rhode Islanders wanted from England.

Rhode Islanders paid the merchants in Newport, Bristol, or Providence for these imports in kind—in horses, sheep, shingles, barrel staves, boards, barrels of cider, mutton, fish, leather hides, or whatever they had available; cheese and livestock were the principal items. The seaport merchant put these products on his ships and set off for some southern port or to the West Indies, where he could exchange them for tobacco, sugar, or a good bill of exchange on London. He then went to Africa, where he traded rum for slaves and bills of exchange for manufactured goods that British factors brought to that coast from England. This system of exchange gained a new stimulus with the increasing importance of the slave trade to the colonies after 1720. Up to 1730, Rhode Islanders themselves imported perhaps twenty to thirty slaves a year for work in Rhode Island. After that, perhaps twice as many were imported every year. But there was no great need for slave labor in New England, and most of the carrying trade went to the West Indies and the tobacco-growing colonies.

Slaves were essentially a convenient, though highly speculative, carrying trade closely related to the import of molasses and the distillation of that product into rum. By 1750 Rhode Island had thirty-three distilleries busily turning molasses into rum—twenty-two of them in Newport. Rum was the colony's major manufacture. The southern and West Indian colonies profited most from planting all their arable land in sugar or tobacco and utilizing the livestock, produce, meat, fish, and lumber products of New England for subsistence. By 1760 Rhode Island had 184 ocean-going vessels in the triangular trade and another 300 in the two-way lumber, livestock, and produce trade down the coast and to West Indian planters.

The slave trade was profitable, in large part because it was such a high-risk venture. Nicholas Brown and his brothers John and Moses of Providence sent a ship to Africa in 1765; on the return trip, 109 out of 167 slaves on board were lost from sickness. Occasionally, slaves successfully rebelled and took over a ship; even if a rebellion was not successful, it could cost many lives, both black and white. Still, the traffic was so lucrative that over the long haul such losses could easily be absorbed if one had the stomach for it. And Rhode Islanders had strong stomachs. Captain William English of Newport wrote to his employers, Jacob and Aaron Lopez, from the Gold Coast of Africa in 1773 that he could trade "two hundred gallons [of rum] for men and 180 for women'' and in some cases ''195 for men and in proportion for women.'' [6] The rum cost 18 to 25 cents a gallon to make, while the slaves brought $250 to $400 in Havana, Charleston, or Newport.

The highest density of slave population in Rhode Island was not Newport—although by 1760 15 percent of Newport's population was black. More slaves were used in the southwestern part of the state—''South County''—where large sheep and dairy farms utilized slaves on a plantation system. In some parts of this area, the slave population reached 17 percent by 1760. No other colony in New England had such a high proportion of slaves as Rhode Island. Yet, probably even in South County, few plantations had more than twenty slaves, and fifty was the largest number held.

The third source of New England wealth came from fishing and whaling. Rhode Island never captured a major part of this trade, but it purchased considerable whale oil and spermaceti— head matter that sailors thought was whale sperm—from Nantucket, Martha's Vineyard, and other whaling centers. Then they converted the spermaceti into candles of high quality or barreled the oil for transport. By 1760, with seventeen spermaceti factories, Rhode Island was the center for the candle trade in the thirteen colonies. Candles were also one of the few Rhode Island products that could be traded directly to English merchants in London. The two chief spermaceti manufacturing groups were the Jewish families of Lopez and Rivera in Newport and the Baptist family of Browns in Providence.

In the 1740s, Rhode Island began to manufacture pig iron, (though imperial law prevented the colonists from making it into nails, sheets, or tools). The iron deposits along the Pawtuxet, near Scituate, were the best in the colony, but there were others in Pawtucket and Cranston. The Greene family started an ironworks on the Pawtuxet in the town of Coventry in 1741, and the Browns started one in Cranston in 1765. Iron was never a major source of trade or wealth because it was of poor quality; but the attempt to smelt it indicated the effort of the colony's

6. Lippincott, *Indians*, p. 126.

entrepreneurs to convert every conceivable local resource into marketable products.

For most voyages, merchants began by gathering exportable products from farmers and dairymen over a wide area in the bay's hinterland—as far as Worcester in Massachusetts and across both the eastern and western borders of the colony. They sent agents around the countryside to buy or contract for supplies; they built slaughterhouses and coopershops near their docks and warehouses. They hired stevedores to load their ships, trained clerks to conduct their paperwork, hired farmers' sons to become their seamen. Their captains had to be as good at striking a bargain as plotting a course, for unless factors— trading agents—went along as supercargo, the captain was responsible for selling and buying along the route. Gradually, almost everyone in the colony was drawn directly or indirectly into these trading ventures, but at the top of them all were the merchant princes whose credit, planning, and experience guided each venture. Rhode Islanders staked their lives and fortunes on the sea. By 1764 the colony had twenty-two hundred able-bodied seamen, who constituted probably 25 percent of the work force; and while commerce brought about a greater disparity in wealth and social status than formerly prevailed, the road to success lay open for those with imagination, skill, and daring.

One aspect of commercial daring involved the circumvention of Parliament's efforts to regulate colonial trade to the advantage of the mother country. The prime means of circumvention was smuggling. Smuggling meant chiefly bringing sugar or molasses from French or Spanish colonies into Rhode Island without paying the duties required by the Molasses Act of 1733 and its more restrictive revisions in 1764 and 1766. Designed to regulate trade rather than produce revenue, the Molasses Act was an attempt to force the colonists to trade only with the British West Indies. But the British planters did not produce enough sugar and molasses to satisfy the commercial needs of the New England colonists, especially for making rum. The Molasses Act seemed unfair. It gave the West Indian planters a monopoly, while depriving New Englanders of a principle source of raw material needed to support their export trade. The result was to encourage smuggling despite the risks. Risks in fact increased profits.

Sometimes ships' captains undertook smuggling on their own initiative, but usually the merchant owners urged and abetted them in it, even giving explicit instructions on how it was to be accomplished. The most common instruction was to advise captains to skirt the customs officers in Newport by entering the bay at night or around an island out of sight of these officials. The cargo was then quickly unloaded at hidden coves on small wharves where local harbor vessels waited to transfer it to the company warehouses as though it were local trade. At first, British enforcement of the act was inconsistent and lax, but after 1764, when naval vessels were sent to police Narragansett Bay, trouble was inevitable.

Another common subterfuge was to forge "invoices" or "bills of lading" alleging that the molasses or sugar in Rhode Island cargoes had been purchased at one of the English plantations when it had not. During wartime, Rhode Island merchants sometimes were so eager for sugar that they traded with the enemy, especially when the British Navy prevented French, Dutch, and Spanish merchants from carrying sugar and molasses to the colonies. This meant "running the blockade"—and gathered huge profits. A third means of illegal trade was misuse of the flag of truce. During King George's War, and especially during the French and Indian War, the British captured many French soldiers who later had to be returned in exchange for English captives. A ship carrying a flag of truce was allowed to bring prisoners into a blockaded French port in the West Indies. Once in port, it was easy to take aboard a contraband cargo of sugar and return with it to the home port. The process was prolonged by returning French prisoners one or two at a time, although imperial regulations expressly said that any colony sending a truce ship was to carry on it all available prisoners.

It was claimed that, during the French and Indian War, Governor Stephen Hopkins (later to be a signer of the Declaration of Independence) charged £500 to any merchant who wished him to authorize a flag-of-truce voyage; he pocketed the money as honest graft. Some ships carrying a flag of truce did not even bother to bring a prisoner with them. "These practices," said Governor Bernard of Massachusetts to the Board of Trade in 1763, "will never be put an end to till Rhode Island is reduced to the subjection of the British Empire; of which at present it is no more a part than the Bahama Islands were when they were inhabited by Buccaneers." [7]

Merchants interested in trading opportunities paid close attention to technological advances, rumors of war, foreign finances, debates in Parliament. Keeping in touch with world affairs, they became men of the world—or, as the pietists said, "worldly." In this era, Newport began its long history of trying to keep up with the Joneses across the water in London. It was a common syndrome throughout the colonies; they were never more English than in the half century before they declared independence. With economic wealth came feelings of power and the desire to live well. Power lay in association with the imperial system, especially with royal officials. Rich men, visited by Londoners, Bostonians, Charlestonians, did not like to be thought of as provincial bumpkins, but as men of importance and standing. That brought a change in Rhode Island's style of living. It also brought about more concern for a well-ordered society in which property was safe, and business could be run efficiently.

Thus, with economic power came civic responsibility. The merchants wanted not only an efficient political and financial order, but they wanted the right judges in office, the right officials managing trade, the proper administration of laws. In addition, they wanted the places in which they lived to function efficiently—to have well-paved roads, regular stagecoach communication with Boston (which began in 1736), solid wharves, sturdy bridges, effective policing to apprehend thieves. Attention began to be drawn to drainage, sewage, street lighting, fire protection, efforts to prevent epidemics from interrupting business. Nor did men of property care to be accosted by drunkards,

7. James B. Hedges, *The Browns of Providence Plantations*, 2 vols. (Cambridge, Mass.: Harvard University Press, 1952), 1:49.

beggars, and cripples asking for alms as they passed by. So they combined enlightened self-interest and Christian benevolence and began to support institutions to give special care to the poor and needy. From there it was only a step to concern for beautifying their cities, especially the thriving entrepôt at Newport. Public buildings were erected in the latest English styles to reflect credit upon those who paid the taxes for them. Elegant new churches were built, ostensibly to honor God. Parks and shady walks made Sunday strolls or carriage rides fashionable—and of course enabled the wealthy to demonstrate their status by their equipage and dress. Public beneficence and conspicuous private consumption went hand in hand. The rich lost their pious Puritanism and decided to live well. They also expected their families to be a credit to them. Their wives were expected to entertain lavishly, which necessitated large, well-appointed homes, many servants, fine plates and silverware and furnishings.

That, in turn, provided opportunity for talented architects, portrait painters, furniture makers (like the Goddards and Townsends), silversmiths, and interior decorators to prosper. The wealth of the rich thus trickled down to the skilled craftsmen, the shopkeepers, the tailors, seamstresses, bookbinders, dancing masters, the wig and cane-makers. Black slaves also had to dress in a manner befitting their masters' station, and their uniforms became increasingly costly, until some wore wigs and buckled shoes. Early in the century, the colony had placed a tax of £3 on every slave imported into the colony, but by 1720 that had been dropped. The money from that import duty had been well spent, however, on paving Newport's streets.

An easier, more convenient way of raising local revenue was the use of public lotteries. Under earlier religious laws, lotteries had been prohibited; but after 1744, only a few religious zealots found them sinful. The promise of quick and easy riches in these gambles matched the enterprising spirit of trade for those unable to invest in large commercial ventures. The lingering objections of the pious were overcome by authorizing the lotteries for worthy religious as well as commercial causes, such as repairing or building a church. In 1744 the people of Providence financed a new bridge over the Providence River (to connect the old settlements on the eastern bank with the newer growth on the west) by means of a lottery. In 1761 Providence used a lottery to pave its streets. In 1764 Newport paved more of its streets by a lottery. The Anglicans of Newport used a lottery to obtain money for a spire on their new church in 1767. That same year, the legislature authorized the Baptists to hold a lottery to build a parsonage capable of housing the Reverend James Manning, president of the new Baptist college, and his pupils. Until 1842, when lotteries were outlawed by the new state constitution, after scandalous frauds, they played an important part in paying for local urban improvements.

Urbanism and improved housing led also to cultural improvements. In 1727 James Franklin, nephew of Benjamin, brought the first printing press to Newport and used it to publish the first codified edition of the colony's laws. His attempt to found a newspaper, the *Rhode Island Gazette,* in 1732 failed after a few months, because everyone got the news by ship or stagecoach from Boston.

An early boost to the cultural life of Newport came with the arrival in 1729 of George Berkeley, Dean of Londonderry Cathedral and later Bishop of Cloyne. An Anglican minister with a taste for literature and philosophy, Berkeley had received a charter from the king to found a university in the New World. He had chosen Bermuda as the site; but while waiting for Parliament to allocate funds to build it, he had come to Rhode Island to see whether a farm could be started to provide food for the college, Bermuda not being conducive to farming, though central to the empire. Berkeley had a reputation as a scholar and brought with him a group of gentlemen interested in his project. His decision to settle in Newport rather than Boston was a feather in the colony's cap. He also brought with him a noted portrait painter, John Smibert, who not only inspired the local painter, Robert Feke of Newport, but who painted many of the notables of the colony. Neither Smibert nor Feke, however, matched the skill of the third famous Rhode Island painter, Gilbert Stuart, who was born in North Kingstown in 1775 but never practiced his art in his native state.

Berkeley built a modest but elegant home, which he called Whitehall, that still stands, in Middletown, just outside Newport. He preached often at Trinity Church and helped to stir new interest in the Church of England. He did not confine his circle to Anglicans, however; his sparkling Irish wit and genial personality led to the formation of an intellectual group who enjoyed the prestige of entertaining him and the challenge of matching his wit. Astonished by the varieties of religious experience that he saw in the colony, Berkeley wrote back to a friend:

> The inhabitants are of a mixed kind, consisting of many sects. Here are four sorts of Anabaptists, besides Presbyterians, Quakers, Independents, and many of no profession at all. Notwithstanding so many differences, here are fewer quarrels about religion than elsewhere. The people living peaceably with their neighbors of whatever persuasions. They all agree on one point, that the Church of England is second best.[8]

He gave money to Harvard and Yale and seventy-five books to a public library started at Trinity Church. More important, he founded a society "for the promotion of knowledge and virtue by a free conversation." [9] The society met at various choice homes, had sumptuous banquets, and, over good wine, discussed the latest political and intellectual news from Europe.

While in Newport, Berkeley wrote *Alciphron, or the Minute Philosopher,* a series of dialogues defending the Christian faith against the rising tide of Enlightenment, rationalism, and deism, of which there was little in Rhode Island except among the freemasons. His most famous work for Americans was written prior to his leaving England. While Rhode Islanders were striving to imitate life in London, Berkeley had predicted that the new seat of learning and progress would be in America:

> In happy climes the Seat of Innocence,
> Where Nature guides and virtue rules,
> Where men shall not impose for Truth and Sense
> The Pedantry of Courts and Schools.

8. Lippincott, *Indians,* p. 153.
9. Carl Bridenbaugh, *Cities in the Wilderness* (New York: Ronald Press Co., 1938), p. 459.

Entitled *America, or the Muse's Refuge, a Prophecy on the Prospect of the Arts and Sciences in America,* the poem was a eulogy of America's rising glory: "There shall be sung another golden Age/ The rise of Empire and of Arts." Few believed it possible, but one verse in particular was to be remembered later:

> Westward the course of Empire takes it Way,
> The four first Acts already past,
> A fifth shall close the Drama and the Day;
> Times noblest Offspring is the last.[10]

In revolutionary years, the millennial implications of that verse were to be frequently quoted as a prescient forecast. But Berkeley had to return to England after three years, because money was not forthcoming from Parliament for his university in Bermuda.

Fifteen years later, a wealthy Quaker merchant, Abraham Redwood, who had belonged to Berkeley's literary entourage in Newport, sensed the need to move beyond the simple pietistic reliance upon the inner light for guidance. With £500 sterling, in 1747, he endowed a library, which the legislature incorporated as the Redwood Library Association. Peter Harrison, the best architect in the colony, was hired to design a suitable edifice. It still stands, along with Harrison's handsome Brick Market and his elegant Touro Synagogue, as evidence of Newport's challenge to Boston in urban splendor. Richard Munday and other local architects were commissioned to create similar public and private structures in the Georgian or classical mode, many of them adaptations in wood of Christopher Wren's stone buildings in London. Today they constitute a rich visual heritage of that colonial era.

Not until 1758 was Newport ready to support a weekly newspaper, the *Newport Mercury,* which (except during the British occupation of Newport during the Revolution) remained continually in print until the end of the nineteenth century. The first newspaper in Providence, which rose more slowly in wealth and prestige, was founded four years later by William Goddard,

---

10. Sydney V. James, *Colonial Rhode Island* (New York: Charles Scribner's Sons, 1975), p. 192.

aided by his mother and sister. During the Stamp Act crisis, the *Providence Gazette and Country Journal* published a special edition with the headline **Vox Populi, Vox Dei.** But it was founded originally as the mouthpiece of the political faction headed by Stephen Hopkins.

The first Anglican minister to preach in Rhode Island was John Lockyer, who, between 1694 and 1702, managed to raise funds for a small church building in Newport. He was succeeded by James Honeyman, who rode the crest of the wave of social aspirations among those who sought prestige by closer association with the king's church. Honeyman was sent by the missionary arm of the church, and through its efforts, Anglican churches founded in Wickford, Bristol, and Providence became centers for those who felt too urbane for the simple Baptist and Quaker meetings. Not only did Anglicanism gain a strong foothold in the colony in these years, but so did the Congregationalism of Massachusetts.

Newport had a missionary preacher from Harvard, Nathaniel Clap, sent from Massachusetts in 1696, though he did not form a church until 1720. A second Congregational church was formed in the town a few years later. In the pre-Revolutionary years, these churches were served by two of the most distinguished ministers in New England: Samuel Hopkins, the most brilliant pupil of Jonathan Edwards; and Ezra Stiles, later president of Yale. Ironically, these two men, both very different in personality and theological emphasis, became opponents of slavery and did not hestitate to so inform the people of Newport. Providence acquired its first Congregational church (by missionary action) in 1722 and its second (by schism) in 1746. The first one turned Unitarian in the early nineteenth century; the second remains as Beneficent or Roundtop Church.

Even the two Baptist churches in Newport obtained college-educated pastors early in the eighteenth century: James Callendar, a Harvard graduate, and John Comer, who attended both Yale and Harvard. Obviously, more and more people felt that piety need not be at odds with learning and that people of good social standing should be represented before God by ministers of respectable attainments and degrees. Some of the Quakers in

Newport lost their interest in egalitarianism and the plain style and strove to cut a fine figure among the well-to-do. They were dubbed "the Quaker grandees." Rural Quakers found too showy a large Quaker meetinghouse built in Newport with a cupola in 1700. In the rural areas, the pietistic preference for an unlearned, unpaid, spirit-filled ministry remained strong, indicating that the growing spectrum of social diversity in the colony was reflected in proliferating sects and churches.

By 1739 there were thirty-three church buildings and one synagogue, representing six denominations in Rhode Island. Most other colonies at the time were still trying to sustain conformity to one established church supported by religious taxes. There were twelve Baptist churches, divided among the Five-Principle Calvinists, the Six-Principle Arminians, and the Seventh-Day Baptists; ten Quaker meetinghouses; six Congregational churches (four more were added in 1747, when the new towns on the eastern side of the bay were transferred to Rhode Island); five Anglican churches. Later, a Moravian church was built in Newport. There were probably a few Roman Catholics scattered here and there, but they had no priest to minister to them. Had one appeared, he would have run into, in the colony's legal code, an anomalous interpolation that has been an embarrassment to Rhode Islanders and a puzzle to historians.

Somehow, though the legislature never enacted it, there appeared in the codification of the colony's laws in 1719 a clause stating that religious liberty was guaranteed to "all Men professing Christianity . . . (Roman Catholics only excepted)." [11] This codification was approved by the general assembly, but whether there was ever any discussion of that single exception to Roger Williams's concept of religious freedom is not recorded. Historians assume that, as part of the gravitation of the colony into the imperial orbit, and in an effort to bring the colony's laws more in conformity with those of England, those persons delegated to codify the laws simply inserted this clause on their own initiative. Perhaps the Jacobite (Catholic) Rebellion in Eng-

---

11. Patrick T. Conley, "Rhode Island Constitutional Development, 1636–1841" (Ph.D. diss., University of Notre Dame, 1970), pp. 22–23.

land in 1715–1716 had something to do with it. In any case, no Catholic ever appeared to challenge it, and in 1783 it was deleted from the laws.

Similar embarrassment arises from the cases of two eminent and respectable Jewish merchants in Newport who sought naturalization in 1761 in order to obtain full and equal rights as British subjects. After hearing their position, the state's Superior Court turned them down on the grounds that Rhode Island was a Christian colony. However, Parliament had allowed Jews to be naturalized in the empire in 1740 and there seems no reason why Rhode Island could not have granted that to Aaron Lopez and Isaac Elizer. Lopez moved temporarily to Swansea, Massachusetts, in 1763 and obtained naturalization there. When he returned to Newport, he was considered properly naturalized. At that very moment, oddly enough, the Jews were building and dedicating their new synagogue with the full approval of the community.

The first Jewish sermon printed in America was preached in 1773 by Rabbi Haym Carregal in Newport while he was a visitor. When Carregal attended a service in Ezra Stiles's Congregational Church that year, Stiles went out of his way to mention the particular friendship between Jews and Christians:

> The Seed of Jacob are a chosen and favorite people of the most
> High and the subjects of the peculiar Care of Heaven, and of most
> marvelous dispensations. . . . God hath not forgotten his Covenant
> with Abraham and his posterity, but intends them great Happiness
> and will fulfill his promise in making them a very glorious Nation
> and a Blessing to the World. . . . It should be the Desire of
> Christians and of all Nations to partake hereafter with Israel in their
> future glorious state, that we may share and rejoice in the Gladness
> of God's people and Glory in his Inheritance.[12]

Whatever their political difficulties, Jews experienced no social or economic discrimination in Newport, and Jewish merchants and businessmen entered wholeheartedly into the commercial and cultural life of the city. Aaron Lopez, among others, con-

---

12. Morris A. Gutstein, *The Story of the Jews of Newport* (New York: Bloch Publishing Co., 1936), p. 130.

tributed to the founding of the Redwood Library and participated in the city's two Masonic lodges.

Yet in the very midst of all the increasing worldliness and intellectual life of the colony, after 1740, there suddenly burst a
great religious revival, which caught everyone by surprise. Historians speak of this development as America's First Great
Awakening. It broke out in England, as well as in all the colonies, between 1730 and 1750. Probably it represented a cultural
shifting of gears as the old corporate, communal ethic of the
past gave way to the new, individualistic, competitive ethic of
America. Americans did not know quite how to fit their old
thought patterns and behavior into a totally different era in their
history. The revival was not over doctrine so much as over what
was called "conversion." Individuals everywhere, but especially under the preaching of certain gifted revivalists (Jonathan
Edwards and Gilbert Tennent in the colonies, George Whitefield
and John Wesley in England) experienced a new understanding
of their personal relationship to God. It led in many colonies to
striking divisions within the leading denominations and in some
respects can be seen as a rejection of the older, established
churches with the more formal ritual and collective structures.
In Rhode Island, where there was no establishment, the revival
led to schisms in some of the churches, but its net effect was to
break down denominational differences and to place new emphasis upon Christian unity as experienced in the process of personal conversions. It seemed almost as though the continued
diversity of religious denominations produced a reaction that
sought to find something they all had in common, a religious
search for *e pluribus unum* preceding the colonies' political
search for the same kind of union.

The Reverend George Whitefield, a Calvinistic preacher ordained in the Anglican Church but a close friend of Wesley and
part of the Methodist movement within the Church of England, seems to have inspired the most radical outbursts of religious excitement as he toured the colonies in 1740 and 1741,
preaching salvation in churches, public squares, and private
homes. He reached Rhode Island in September 1740 and stayed
only three days. His preaching at Newport and Bristol did not

seem to have the same emotional impact as it was to have in Boston. After preaching at Newport and Bristol, Whitefield noted in his journal that Rhode Islanders were badly divided in their religious sectarianism. He also noted that in Newport most of the people were engrossed in commerce and materialism: "All, I fear, place the kingdom of God too much in meat and drink and have an ill name abroad for running of goods [smuggling]." Whitefield startled some churchgoers in Newport by asking "What will become of you who cheat the king of taxes [or duties]?" [13] This, he said, made the merchants in the audience look at one another like men conscious of their own and each other's guilt. If these and other sermons by subsequent itinerant imitators of Whitefield turned pious souls to concern for their salvation, on the whole, the Awakening did little to halt the general commercial tone of the colony. Rhode Islanders had had their fill of spiritual zeal in the seventeenth century; their hearts were now set upon improving their earthly lot.

Insofar as the Awakening did have an impact, it was upon the poor, especially among black slaves and Indians. God's freely offered, miraculous grace gave them new hope. It also opened the doors of the white man's churches and spoke of Christian equality under God. Church records of the time indicate greatly increased black and Indian membership after the Awakening, but as these new members were admitted, many pastors wrote the words *black* or *Indian* after their names, indicating that equality before God did not mean social equality.

The Reverend Joseph Park (Harvard, 1724), who had been sent as a Congregational missionary to the town of Westerly, Rhode Island, reported that more than sixty Indians joined his missionary church there in the 1740s. One of these Indian converts, Samuel Niles, became a preacher to his Indian brethren, and in 1750 formed the Narragansett Indian Church in Charlestown, on Congregationalist and Calvinist principles. Some of its members adopted Baptist tenets, and Niles decided to allow "mixed communion" rather than split the church. Niles himself

---

13. George Whitefield, *A Continuation of the Rev. Mr. Whitefield's Journal* (London: W. Strahan for R. Hett, 1741), p. 22.

submitted to baptism by immersion, and his church was generally considered a Baptist church for some years thereafter. It exists today as a nondenominational church. From this church arose a second noted Indian preacher, James Simon, who became an itinerant evangelist.

The revival produced new links between the Baptists of Rhode Island and those of the Middle Colonies. Morgan Edwards suggested to the Baptists of Philadelphia that Rhode Island would be a good place to start a Baptist college, since there were so many of them there. James Manning, a Baptist recently graduated from Princeton College, came to Rhode Island in 1763 to organize such a college. He received considerable support, not only from the Baptists, but from other denominational leaders, as well. In 1764 the general assembly chartered Rhode Island College, later re-named Brown University, as the result of a liberal gift for its support by a member of the Brown family in Providence. Though its president and the majority of its corporation were by charter to be Baptists, the college's governing board also included Anglicans, Congregationalists, and Quakers.

The colony provided no money for the college, however, and it had difficulty getting started. It graduated its first class of seven in 1769 in Warren, Rhode Island. In 1770 the college moved to Providence, despite efforts of Newport merchants to have it move to their city. In 1775 the Baptists built a magnificent Baptist church in Providence, in which the commencements of the college have been held ever since, though it has long since lost its Baptist connection. A year later, on Prospect Hill overlooking the city, the corporation built a large edifice modeled after Nassau Hall at Princeton. Through this institution, which brought new cultural activity to Providence, were to pass many of the leading figures of the new state, though significantly few of them chose the ministry as a career.

The Awakening led indirectly to a new concern for Christian benevolence and an effort to abolish slavery. The Quakers, who seem to have undergone a religious revival in the 1760s, were among the first to take action against slavery, first urging their members to stop dealing in the slave trade and then putting steady pressure upon them to free any slaves they owned. The Quaker itinerant preacher, John Woolman, passed through Rhode Island in 1760 and is credited with starting the Quakers on this reform. Those Quakers who refused to give up their slaves—one of whom was Stephen Hopkins—were eventually "disowned" or expelled from Quaker meetings. By 1782 a committee established by the Quakers in the state reported, "We know not but all the members of this [Rhode Island] meeting are clear of that iniquitous practice of holding or dealing with mankind as slaves." [14]

Eight years earlier, Moses Brown, brother of the notorious Baptist merchant and slave trader John Brown, was converted to the Quaker faith. He freed his own slaves and joined with Stephen Hopkins and Henry Ward to petition the general assembly to end the slave trade and start manumitting all slaves in the colony. The Congregationalists, led by Samuel Hopkins, started their effort to end slavery in 1770; Hopkins published one of the first antislavery tracts in the colonies in 1774. But the movement met with strong opposition from the wealthy merchants who were still making large profits from the trade, and no action was taken against slavery by the legislature.

Rhode Island produced one new religious prophet in the Awakening, a true counterpart of Anne Hutchinson. Her name was Jemima Wilkinson, and she was a Quaker who was caught up in the revival at a late stage when George Whitefield returned to the colony in 1770. She was eighteen at that time, and when she began attending religious meetings outside the Quaker faith, she was disowned by the Society of Friends. In 1776 she became very ill and had a vision of heaven. Upon recovery, she was convinced that she had actually died and was then sent back to earth by God to convey a special message. An attractive, forceful, and eloquent speaker, she traveled throughout southern New England on horseback from 1776 to 1790, making many converts to her new sect, which she called the Universal Friends. Her doctrines were similar to those of the Quakers,

---

14. Mack Thompson, *Moses Brown: Reluctant Reformer* (Chapel Hill: University of North Carolina Press), p. 96.

dwelling on the inherent divinity of all people. But some of her followers believed that she was the female incarnation of God. Like her contemporary, Ann Lee, founder of the Shaker movement, Jemima Wilkinson encouraged celibacy. She also advocated pacificism (which was not popular after 1776) and predicted the imminent second coming of Christ. In 1790 she moved to western New York, where she founded a small community near Lake Seneca. She died there in 1819, without ever returning to Rhode Island. Her sect died with her.

One further outcome of the Great Awakening should be noted. In 1760 the Reverend Ezra Stiles of Newport wrote a tract entitled *Christian Union*. Ostensibly a plea for greater ecumenical union among the various Protestant denominations in the colonies, the sermon inaugurated a patriotic effort to ward off the effort of Archbishop Secker, primate of the Church of England, to send an Anglican bishop to lead that church in America. Fearing that an American bishop would try to assert the supremacy of the king's church at the expense of all others, Stiles and other ministers throughout the colonies began an ardent pamphlet campaign denouncing Secker's proposal. Most historians doubt that Parliament was prepared to back Secker's plan, anyway. Still, the important point is that Stiles, speaking from "the isle of errors," emerged as a hero of the growing nationalist movement to save the principle of religious liberty in America.

The Awakening seems to have come to an end as a general movement with the beginning of the French and Indian War in 1754, though its effect continued in many ways. Most Rhode Islanders entered wholeheartedly into the French and Indian War for a variety of reasons. War promised profit from the higher costs of trade for those willing to take risks; war offered opportunities for privateering, another source of high profits; and war required military supplies, which Rhode Islanders hoped to profit from. Furthermore, Rhode Islanders were now as determined to rid America of the French as the British government was. Ever since 1690, the coast had been raided by the French, and in various wars the French had captured many Rhode Island merchant ships.

While Rhode Island soldiers participated in the battles at Lake George, Fort Ticonderoga, Crown Point, and Fort Frontenac, they did so as only small contingents of large armies led by British regulars. Despite the hopes of easy profits, the chief effect of the war was to curtail commerce, to increase taxes, and to increase the colony's debt. The net result was a renewal of the quarrel over paper money and other means of paying off the debt. Parliament had made strict regulations after 1751 upon any further land-bank schemes. But the old land-bank money had not yet been wholly retired. The cost of supplies and men for the military campaigns necessitated issuing paper money that conformed to Parliament's strict regulations to peg it to silver values and retire it rapidly by taxation. This brought higher taxes, which in turn led to political friction within the state.

Even before the war ended, two political factions had arisen, engaging in bitter fights to gain control of the legislature. One was led by Sammuel Ward and the other by Stephen Hopkins. Ward's faction centered in the southern part of the colony, attracted mostly Anglicans and Quakers, and was sympathetic to the needs of the Newport merchants. Hopkins's faction centered in the northern part of the colony, attracted Baptists and Congregationalists, and was sympathetic to the rising merchants of Providence. Yet the lines were not clear-cut; both factions had supporters north and south, within and without the various denominations. Historians can find no distinct class identity in either party. The basic issues between them were how to assess taxes to pay off the colony's war debts, how to redeem the paper currency, and how to provide a stable, reliable medium of exchange. Yet neither party had a clear-cut program to offer, certainly no painless one. High taxes would hurt the farmer; depreciating paper hurt the merchants. While the two parties waged fierce contests, resorting to corrupt vote-buying to obtain control of the legislature, neither when in office pursued a consistent course.

Essentially, the Ward and Hopkins factions were interested in alleviating the burden of taxes and of paper-money redemption upon their own particular supporters by placing most of it upon their opponents. Whichever faction won, in the seesaw battles over almost two decades, assessed that year's taxes more heavily upon those towns that had voted for the opposite party. Similarly, each distributed party patronage to its own supporters; some 250 offices could change with each election—justices of the peace, clerkships, sheriffs, militia officers, judgeships. These practices did nothing to solve the financial crisis after 1750. It lingered on, simply because no one wanted to bite the bullet and pay up. Instead, both parties simply nibbled away at it, bit by bit. Eventually, the paper money was redeemed, private debts were stabilized in value, and hard money returned—more through the efforts of Hopkins's party than Ward's. But that was largely the result of the return of prosperity after the war.

The divisiveness of the Ward-Hopkins era was partly the result of a growing conflict of interest between Rhode Island's commercial needs and those of the empire. The Board of Trade wanted a stable, hard-money system favorable to English creditors. Rhode Island wanted a free hand in financial affairs as in trade. The war that united the colonies and England in a mutual desire to oust the French from America temporarily blurred this disparity of interest. After the war, Rhode Island began to see more clearly that money, trade, and taxes would lead to further conflict within Britain's mercantile system. The Ward and Hopkins factions began to develop an overarching consensus on imperial affairs that they lacked on internal affairs. Colonists who could not agree on how to tax themselves could readily agree that Parliament had no right to tax them.

After 1765 Rhode Island's view of its charter altered radically. Originally, the charter had been a grant by the king to a group of planatations giving them the right of local self-government within the British Constitution. But the experience of self-help—in politics, trade, and war—led Rhode Island, like the other colonies, into a different interpretation of its relationship to the mother country. The charter came to be interpreted after 1765 as a grant of quasi-independence uniting the plantations to the king only by voluntary allegiance so long as his interest and theirs coincided. When claims of English rights and royal power differed from claims of "charter rights," Rhode Islanders insisted that charter rights had equal not subordinate authority. Again, as in 1690, Rhode Island found itself at loggerheads with its king.

3

Vanguard of the Revolution and Holdout against Federal Union

STUBBORN, pugnacious, and cocksure, Rhode Island rushed pell-mell toward revolution after 1764. Its people were more united, its leaders more outspoken in favor of independence far sooner than those of any other colony. In open disobedience, it was the spearhead of the Revolution. It was the first colony to resort to armed resistance, to call for a Continental Congress, to renounce allegiance to the king, to create an American naval force. Rhode Islanders never had any doubt as to what the struggle was about: it was about economic survival and political freedom. Being small, existing on the risky margin of its carrying trade in rum and molasses, and bound to suffer first and foremost under the new imperial policies inaugurated after France was eliminated from North America, Rhode Island eagerly sought to arouse the other colonies to vigilance for liberty.

Yet, once the Revolution was won, Rhode Island wanted to go it alone. Exhausted by the high taxes of the war effort, impoverished by loss of trade, and thoroughly dislocated by the long British occupation of Newport, the obstreperous state wanted nothing to do with any new centralized control from

New York or Philadelphia. United in war, but separate in peace, was its motto. Laissez-faire free enterprise and local self-government constituted the state's understanding of the pursuit of happiness. *In deo speramus* was not the same as *e pluribus unum;* it meant every man for himself.

From Rhode Island's point of view, the blame for the Revolution rested squarely on Parliament's reckless disturbance of a perfectly good economic system. Parliament knew well enough that the colonies needed more sugar and molasses than the British West Indies produced. Five-sixths of the rum manufactured in Rhode Island came from illegal imports. Under the Molasses Act of 1733, the crown very sensibly winked its eye at such trade with the French, Spanish, and Dutch sugar islands. At least it had been so lax and lenient with those who infringed the law that the colonies felt free to follow their own self-interest in the matter. After all, it was the prosperity from molasses and rum that enabled the New England colonies to purchase the manufactured goods of British merchants. Everyone had profited from the salutary neglect and inefficient enforcement. Yet, in 1764, in flagrant disregard of these economic facts of life, Parliament passed a new Sugar Act that led to strict enforcement of duties on trade with foreign sugar islands.

Not only did Parliament send ships of the navy to patrol Narragansett Bay to enforce the duties, but it created special new admiralty courts in which to try offenders. To add further injustice, these royal judges established their court in Halifax, Nova Scotia, and were empowered to try cases without benefit of a jury. How could merchants, sea captains, and crews defend themselves so far away from understanding neighbors and without the protection of English and charter rights?

With the passage of the Stamp Act in 1765, the Declaratory Act in 1766, and the Tea Act in 1773, it became evident that Parliament was not only tightening its power over the regulation of external trade, but—more tyrannically—it was raising money for revenue by direct, internal taxation without representation of the colonists in Parliament. In effect, the new imperial regulations lowered the taxes of British subjects in England by increasing the taxes of British subjects in the colonies. And when the colonists protested and petitioned, their pleas were ignored. Where, then, could they turn, to protect their property and liberties? What alternative had they but revolution against such tyranny?

As colonial resistance mounted, Rhode Island, like the rest of the colonies, moved from defense of its charter rights and constitutional British freedoms to the laws of inalienable natural rights. Voluntary loyalty to the king grew weaker as he lent his support to the new imperial system. Eventually, appeals to a higher law than the British constitution appeared, justifying the abolition of monarchy and the establishment of an independent American republic. Rhode Island felt well qualified to speak for this heretical new political faith in which the rights of the individual were the supreme law of the land.

The political factions of Samuel Ward and Stephen Hopkins, which fought bitterly after 1760 for control of the colony's government because they disagreed over means of assessing local taxes and regulating internal currency, never for a moment hesitated to make common cause against the external powers seeking to infringe the colony's autonomy.

Rhode Island, not having any interior territory to develop, was not particularly excited by the King's Proclamation of 1763 forbidding settlement west of the Appalachian Ridge. The seriousness of the new effort to enforce duties on trade with non-English nations first hit home when His Majesty's Ship *Squirrel* arrived in Narragansett Bay in December 1763 and began making life difficult for smugglers. An incident arising out of coastal patrolling in July 1764 has been called by some local historians the first shot of the war for independence. A naval vessel, the *St. John*, assisting the *Squirrel*, was fired upon in Newport. The *St. John* had recently arrested a smuggler; some of its crew were then mobbed in Newport while trying to recapture a deserter; other members of the crew were involved in a court action on charges of stealing while on shore leave. When the *St. John* prepared to sail off in the midst of these controversies, two members of the governor's council gave orders to the gunners in the harbor fort to halt the ship. Eight shots were fired, one damaging the mainsail. The people of Newport justified their action on the grounds that the *St. John*'s captain was leaving the scene of his crimes; he claimed he was being harassed in the performance of his duties. Despite protests on both sides, no official action was taken in the matter. Four similar incidents in succeeding years testified to the mounting tension.

Stephen Hopkins was governor of the colony in 1764, when word came that Parliament was considering passage of a new Sugar Act. Trying to forestall it, Hopkins wrote a "Remonstrance" to the Board of Trade, pointing out the damage such a law would do to Rhode Island's commerce. Later, the general assembly ordered the document printed, with the title *The Rights of Colonies Examined*. It was one of the first assertions of colonial rights against Parliamentary control. Hopkins's pamphlet in 1764 was a lucid exposition of the colony's claim that strict regulation of the Sugar Act would not only severely damage colonial trade, but injure British merchants, as well. Admitting that there had been some clandestine trade and smuggling over non-British sugar, Hopkins blamed that on the shortsighted desire of the British sugar planters to obtain an unwarranted monopoly. But he went even further when he questioned whether Parliament could levy a tax on British subjects who were not represented in Parliament. "Can it possibly be shown," he asked rhetorically, "that the people in Britain have a sovereign authority over their fellow subjects in America?" The answer, he said, was negative. "All laws and all taxations which bind the whole [empire] must be made by the whole." [1] Thus early in the quarrel with the mother country, Rhode Island raised the cry "No taxation without representation." Although a group of Tories—locally called "the Newport Junto"—led by Martin Howard, Jr., and Dr. Thomas Moffat, answered Hopkins in defense of king and Parliament, the people were strongly on Hopkins's side.

A year later, with the passage of the Stamp Act, the two leading royalists, Howard and Moffat, together with the man who

1. Sydney V. James, *Colonial Rhode Island* (New York: Charles Scribner's Sons, 1975), p. 323.

accepted the job as distributor of the stamps, were hanged in ef-
figy in Newport, while mobs destroyed the interior of the homes
of Howard and Moffat. The Stamp Act went much further than
the Sugar Act in asserting Parliament's right to levy internal
taxes for revenue upon the colonies. The act required the colonists to pay for stamps to be affixed to all kinds of paper
required for legal or commercial transactions, including the
paper for publishing newspapers, playing cards, shipping clear-
ances, and legal transactions. Hopkins not only denied the legality of that, but also questioned whether Parliament had the right
to prohibit the colonies from manufacturing iron goods or textiles. But essentially he argued that Parliament was cutting off its
nose to spite its face. To damage American trade was to damage
British trade: "Will she find an advantage in disabling the colonies to continue their trade with her? Or can she possibly grow
rich by their being made poor?" [2]

While the populace vented its frustration upon those charged
with enforcing Parliament's laws, the general assembly took
more far-reaching action. In September 1765, urged on by resolutions from the various town meetings throughout the colony, it
passed a set of resolves (adopted in part from those written by
Patrick Henry for the Virginia House of Burgesses) against the
Stamp Act. These resolves argued that Parliament was abridging
basic charter rights as well as the rights of Englishmen. They
went beyond those adopted in Virginia by stating that the colonies "are not bound to yield obedience to any law or ordinance
designed to impose any internal taxation whatsoever upon them,
other than the laws or ordinances of the General Assembly" [3]
of Rhode Island. The resolves concluded by declaring the Stamp
Act null and void within the colony.

Next, the general assembly elected Henry Ward and Metcalf
Bowler to represent the colony's interest at the Stamp Act
Congress in New York. Although these delegates voted for all
the resolves put forward at the Congress in October 1765, they

2. James, *Colonial Rhode Island*, p. 324.
3. James, *Colonial Rhode Island*, p. 331.

were not able to push through the broad claims of colonial autonomy held in Rhode Island.

When stamps were sent over, a royal distributor appointed, and the law put into effect on November 1, 1765, Rhode Islanders simply ignored it. But they took elaborate precautions to make sure that no one could blame them. The mob had forced the stamp distributor to resign, and no one dared take his place. The governor said that even if someone did want the job, he was not authorized to appoint him. The stamped paper was never unloaded from the vessel that brought it from England. The governor issued statements to anyone who wished them, saying that the stamps simply were not available, and he wrote to England to explain that were was nothing he could do about it. All official business took place as usual, without the stamps.

When Parliament repealed the Stamp Act in 1766, there were great celebrations under the Newport Liberty Tree. The Declaratory Act received little attention, but the colony was again aroused to action when the Townshend Acts in 1767 imposed duties on tea, glass, lead, paints, and paper. The general assembly petitioned George III for repeal. The Providence orator and pamphleteer Silas Downer spoke from a platform built for the purpose in that town's Liberty Tree, claiming that all British taxation amounted to infractions on the natural rights of man. For a year or more, Rhode Island's merchants, seeing a chance to turn a dollar, declined to go along when their rivals in Boston, New York, and Philadelphia signed nonimportation agreements to put pressure on British merchants. That seemed grossly inconsistent and disloyal to the other colonies. They reacted by refusing to trade with Rhode Island. Rhode Island merchants pleaded that poverty drove them to it, but finally went along. The refusal of the merchants to co-operate wholeheartedly with the nonintercourse agreements did not mean that they were willing to truckle to Parliamentary regulation and taxation. It simply meant that they did not like anyone's telling them when, where, and with whom they couldn't trade.

The Townshend duties were repealed in 1770, except for the tax on tea, and while some merchants in some colonies wanted to continue the boycott on British goods, Rhode Island merchants were ready to consider the repeal a victory. Meanwhile, there was constant friction between the local people and royal officials. In 1765 the naval vessel *Maidstone* came into Newport harbor and sent a party into the city to impress men to fill its crew. The governor demanded the release of the men impressed, and when the captain of the *Maidstone* refused, a mob took one of the ship's boats tied up at the dock, manhandled the officer in charge, and after hauling the boat into town, burned it. In 1769, after the revenue sloop *Liberty* seized two ships carrying goods from Connecticut without the proper papers, the captain of one of them, pulling away from the *Liberty* in a rowboat, was fired upon by the *Liberty*'s crew. Shortly thereafter, while the captain and crew of the *Liberty* were on shore, a group of Newport roughs boarded the ship, cut down her mast, punched holes in her hull, and let her drift to a harbor island, where she ran aground. Then another group set the ship on fire. In April 1771, a new customs collector, Charles Dudley, boarded a ship in Newport to inspect its cargo; but he foolishly did so late at night and was badly beaten by unknown assailants. For none of these incidents was anyone ever apprehended or punished.

The outstanding case of violent resistance was the burning of His Majesty's Ship *Gaspee* and the shooting of its captain on June 9, 1772, a day that Rhode Islanders still celebrate. Captain William Dudingston had made himself highly unpopular, by inspecting not only ocean-going vessels for contraband, but also small boats ferrying goods from one side of Narragansett Bay to the other. (He suspected them of taking smuggled goods off ships that had paid no duty and moving them into warehouses.) Furthermore, when his men got tired of eating hardtack, they would row to the shore and kill a sheep or two for mutton, without bothering to pay the farmer who owned them. On June 9, Dudingston was pursuing the sloop *Hannah* up the bay to search her for smuggled goods. By a shrewd maneuver, the captain of the *Hannah* lured the *Gaspee* too close to shore, and she ran aground on Namquit Point (now Gaspee Point) a few miles southwest of Providence. Knowing that the tide would not come up to free the ship until early the next morning, John Brown, the leading merchant in Providence, gathered some of his trustworthy friends and employees together to plan an attack. Brown provided eight longboats with muffled oars. Four leading citizens, including Brown himself and Captain Abraham Whipple (later to be named the first commodore of the Rhode Island Navy but at that time captain of one of Brown's slave ships), volunteered to lead the attack.

As they neared the *Gaspee,* at about 2:00 A.M., the ship's sentry hailed them but was given no answer. Then Lieutenant Dudingston appeared in his shirtsleeves, fresh from his bunk. Peering into the blackness, he demanded to know who was approaching his ship. Whipple shouted, "I am the sheriff of the County of Kent, God damn you; I have got a warrant to apprehend you, God damn you; so surrender, God damn you." At that, one of the men in Whipple's boat said to his friend Ephraim Bowen, "Eph, reach me your gun; I can kill that fellow." [4] Bowen lent him his gun; a shot rang out and Dudingston fell wounded on the deck. The Providence men quickly boarded the boat, overcame the sleepy crew, and rowed them ashore. Brown had shown the foresight to bring along a doctor who treated Dudingston's wound. Bloodstains on the floor in the house to which Dudingston was taken were pointed out for a century thereafter as "the first blood of the Revolution." The patriots then set fire to the *Gaspee* and burned it to the water's edge.

Dudingston recovered and filed a protest. Rewards were offered for apprehension of the perpetrators. The British government held an official inquiry. But no one ever claimed the reward, and no one was ever prosecuted. One recent historian has labeled the *Gaspee* episode cowardly and ignoble; others still consider it heroic. Seen in the full scale of persistent colonial resistance, however, it appears just another incident by men willing to go to any length to protect their political and commercial interests.

None of these incidents caused the British to waver the slight-

4. Arnold, *History of Rhode Island and Providence,* 2:319.

est in their intention to enforce the laws of Parliament. When the Privy Council began its inquiry into the *Gaspee* affair, the Virginia House of Burgesses, fearing that some of the perpetrators would be taken to England and hanged (it was a hanging crime to burn one of His Majesty's ships), suggested the formation of Committees of Correspondence among the colonies. Most colonies already had patriot groups known as Sons of Liberty, and these groups became the backbone of colonial resistance and co-ordination thereafter. When the Tea Act was passed in 1773, Providence did not get a shipload it could throw in the bay, but two years later it did burn some tea in the Providence marketplace. The British reacted to the dumping of the tea in Boston Harbor by passing the Coercive Acts, closing the port of Boston, abrogating the Massachusetts charter, and sending troops to occupy the city. Rhode Islanders immediately sent relief supplies to Boston, which suffered from lack of food.

The continued oppression of Boston led the Rhode Island General Assembly to call for a Continental Congress in 1774, with delegates from all the colonies, to remonstrate with King George. It was the first colony to issue such a suggestion and to elect delegates (Stephen Hopkins and Samuel Ward). The call for the congress suggested that it should meet annually "to consider the proper means for the preservation of the rights and liberties of the colonies." [5] Realizing that, sooner or later, its own charter rights might be abrogated, Rhode Island wanted the united colonies to stand behind each other's acts of resistance. When the Continental Congress met and called for an embargo on all British goods, Rhode Island's merchants were wholeheartedly behind it, and its Sons of Liberty firmly endorsed it. Mobs assaulted those considered Tories, sometimes treating them to tar and feathers.

Thereafter, ten British patrol boats were stationed in Newport Harbor, and the threat of their guns held back the Sons of Liberty somewhat there. Leadership and power began at that point to pass to the more sheltered mainland city of Providence, eighteen miles up the bay.

5. James, *Colonial Rhode Island*, p. 344.

News of the battles of Lexington and Concord reached Rhode Island the night of April 19, 1775. The Rhode Island militia was called out and prepared to leave at once to join the fight; but upon learning that the redcoats had retreated into Boston, the troops did not march north. The general assembly met, however, and voted to raise an army of fifteen hundred to defend the colony. When Governor Joseph Wanton, Sr., refused to sign the commissions for such a revolutionary force, he was deposed from office, and the charter was delivered over to the new governor, Nicholas Cooke. Wanton took the view that armed rebellion was no way to protect the colony's charter rights; but by 1775, the fat was too far into the fire for his cautious position. Any plan for reconciliation with Britain was considered disloyalty to America's and Rhode Island's freedom. Henceforth, the best way to protect the charter rights was to fight for them.

At this turn of events, the captain of the British patrol fleet, James Wallace, began to block all shipping in or out of Narragansett Bay. For a time, it appeared that he might bombard Newport for its disloyalty. His landing parties demanded supplies at the threat of bombardment. During the summer of 1775, thousands of people fled from Aquidneck Island to the mainland. Fearing that the presence of these royal ships might lead Loyalists into counterrevolt, the general assembly administered an oath of loyalty to about a hundred who seemed lukewarm patriots. All but eleven were willing to take the oath or demonstrate their loyalty. Five wealthy Tories fled the colony, and their estates were confiscated by legislative action. The Quakers remained true to their doctrine of pacificism and tried to remain neutral, but their hearts were essentially with the patriot cause.

One thousand Rhode Island troops went to Massachusetts late in May 1775, to join the patriot army in the siege of Boston. The first Rhode Islander killed in the Revolution, Augustus Mumford, died from a cannon shot during that siege on August 29, 1775. What Rhode Islanders refer to as "the first American naval shot fired in the Revolution" occurred on June 15, 1775. One of the armed sloops that the general assembly had equipped for defense under Captain Abraham Whipple chased and captured an armada tender of the British naval frigate *Rose* after several shots were fired on each side. The colony now outfitted what has been called the first navy of the American colonies. It commissioned two ships, the *Washington* and the *Katy* (later renamed the *Providence*), and placed them under Whipple's command. Whipple was given the rank of commodore.

In December 1775, 150 Rhode Island men joined Benedict Arnold's force bound for the unsuccessful campaign to capture Quebec—the Canadians having declined to throw in their lot with the colonies to the south.

Political affairs in Rhode Island reached their logical conclusion on May 4, 1776, when the general assembly voted to abrogate its allegiance to the king. Though the act was carefully drawn and did not specifically declare independence, it has been taken by Rhode Islanders as amounting to the same thing. Hence May 4 has been, since 1884, officially celebrated as "Rhode Island Independence Day." Nathanael Greene was then made commander-in-chief of the state's armed forces. On July 4, Rhode Island's two representatives to the Continental Congress signed the Declaration of Independence with no qualms. The Rhode Island General Assembly endorsed that act on July 20, pledging to "support the said General Congress with our lives and fortunes." [6] Two days earlier, the legislature had altered its charter to the extent of replacing the word *colony* with the word *state*, but it made no other alteration. The colony had enjoyed such freedom under the charter of 1663 that independence merely seemed a continuation of past liberty, not a turning point requiring a new state constitution.

The jubilation over independence was of short duration. The horrors of war came home to Rhode Island with a vengeance in December 1776, when the British occupied Newport. The new state was unable to protect itself from the large fleet that brought this invasion of its soil. Its chief city and magnificent harbor fell without a shot. During its three years of occupation, Newport became a hollow shell. All shipping stopped; half the population of Aquidneck Island fled, and the British were glad to get rid of

6. Bartlett, editor, *Records of the Colony of Rhode Island and Providence Plantations*, 7:581.

the extra mouths to feed. There was a grave shortage of food and wood for those who remained, and the British occupation forces took the best of everything for themselves. The old Colony House—scene of many defiant actions against British despotism—became a stable for British horses. Those who showed open sympathy for the patriot cause on Aquidneck now received the same treatment from Loyalists that the Sons of Liberty had previously meted out to them.

It was a disastrous turn of affairs. The British roamed over the island at will, killing livestock for their troops, organizing Loyalists into volunteer military units, and building fortifications across the fields in case of a counterattack. There was little the rest of the sovereign state of Rhode Island and Providence Plantations could do but make occasional forays to the island, exchange pot shots with passing British ships, and hope that the king's army and navy would not march inland or use its cannons to bombard the towns up and down the harbor. General Washington, after ridding Boston of British occupation forces in March 1776, had departed for the Middle Colonies, hoping in vain to save New York from the British. Freeing Newport remained low in his military priorities for more than a year and a half.

Meanwhile, with thousands of island refugees crowded into Providence—reversing the situation of King Philip's War—the city was saved from starvation the first winter only by timely supplies sent from Connecticut, their old enemy—but now their closest ally. In 1778 the British sent men-of-war up the bay as far as Bristol and Warren, bombarding and landing troops in the former, but they never tried to maintain permanent control over more than the island. However, British soldiers and seamen continually harassed the farmers along the mainland shores, where occasional raids and skirmishes took place. Providence was never attacked, though it fortified itself.

The arrival of the British naval force in December 1776 caught the commander-in-chief of the Continental Navy in Providence with part of his fleet. This embarrassing situation had its beginning in November 1775. At that time, Stephen Hopkins persuaded the Continental Congress to outfit thirteen armed vessels and to commission them as the navy of the united colonies. Hopkins saw to it that Providence received the contract to outfit two of these ships. He also got his brother, Esek Hopkins, commissioned as commander-in-chief. Abraham Whipple then became a continental captain of one of these frigates. Esek Hopkins, like Whipple, had received his maritime training on a slaveship owned by John Brown. Though ordered to cruise to the Carolinas early in 1776 to protect the coast, Hopkins decided, on his own, to attack Fort Nassau in the Bahamas to get powder for Washington's army. Succeeding in that, he then returned to Providence. The British patrol ships had left Newport in March 1776, and the harbor was momentarily free. As Whipple neared Point Judith, Rhode Island, on April 6, his three ships engaged a British gunboat, the *Glasgow*. Unfortunately, the *Glasgow* outfought the three American vessels and escaped. The badly damaged American ships limped into Providence. They were still there in December, when the British fleet entered the bay eighteen miles south at Newport.

In March 1777, Hopkins was suspended from his naval command and in January 1778, he was dismissed. His failure was not entirely his fault. After repairing his ships in Providence, he tried in vain to find volunteers to man them. With its usual eagerness for the profits of privateering, Rhode Island had commissioned sixty-five privateers between May and December of 1776. Inasmuch as sailors on privateers stood to make a lot more money, with a lot less discipline than navy men, they were not eager to volunteer for the navy. Hence, when Hopkins was ordered by Congress to cruise off Newfoundland in October 1776, he could not obey. Finally, the legislature prohibited any more enlistment on privateers or merchant ships until Hopkins got his full complement; but the law came too late to save Hopkins's command.

Two daring episodes of personal courage were all that lightened the colony's dejection in those early years of the war. In July 1777, Major William Barton, stationed with American troops in Tiverton, learned that General Richard Prescott, commander of the British forces on Aquidneck, frequently left Newport to spend the night at the home of a wealthy Loyalist named

Overing in Middletown. Prescott, considering himself safe on Aquidneck, took only a few guards with him on these visits. Barton concocted a plan to land secretly on the island and kidnap the general. Using five whaleboats, Barton and his men rowed secretly from Tiverton, on the east side of the bay, to Warwick, on the west side, carefully avoiding capture by the British ships patrolling the waters. Then, in the middle of the night of July 7, they rowed from Warwick to Middletown on Aquidneck, where they landed unperceived near Overing's home. Overcoming the sentry at the door, they roused General Prescott from bed, rushed him into a whaleboat, and warning him not to utter a word, rowed him quietly back to the mainland. "I did not think it possible," [7] said the astonished general. Prescott was kept in Providence, in a manner befitting his station, until he was exchanged for the captured American general, Charles Lee. The Rhode Island legislature gave Barton a bounty for his night's work, and later the Continental Congress promoted him and awarded him a sword of honor.

Major Silas Talbot was the other local hero. He got permission to fit out a small sloop in October 1778, to try to capture the British brig, *Pigot,* which blockaded the side of Narragansett Bay to the east of Aquidneck. A native of Bristol, Talbot was stationed at Providence at the time. The British brig had twenty guns to his two. In order to reach it, he had to pass two other British patrol ships up the bay. This he did, so silently and efficiently, by night, that he captured the *Pigot* with no loss of life. The British captain was so humiliated that he wept openly.

Between Barton's feat and Talbot's occurred "the Battle of Rhode Island," the only major land contest in the state. While a technical victory for the patriots, it was part of an aborted campaign to relieve Newport, which, had it succeeded, might have greatly affected the war. In the spring of 1778, Washington agreed to make the relief of Newport a top priority. He gave General John Sullivan of Massachusetts the authority to assemble eight thousand soldiers for the attack. The French, having joined the Americans as allies, agreed to send a fleet under

7. Richman, *Rhode Island, A Study in Separatism,* p. 225.

Comte Jean Baptiste d'Estaing to attack the British fleet from the southwest, while Sullivan invaded the island from the north via Tiverton. D'Estaing's fleet of sixteen naval vessels arrived off Newport on July 29. He also had twenty-eight hundred marines in transport ships. Sullivan was not yet prepared to assault when d'Estaing arrived. Lafayette did not reach Tiverton from New York until August 4, with two thousand continental troops. Sullivan finally landed on Aquidneck on August 10.

But while d'Estaing was able to enter the harbor and drive off the British ships inside, a new British fleet of thirteen ships-of-the-line and seven frigates suddenly appeared in the Atlantic off Point Judith. D'Estaing, afraid of being bottled up in the harbor, pulled out to meet the British. A violent storm came up just as the fighting started, causing great havoc to both fleets. The British returned to New York City for repairs, while d'Estaing, ignoring his commitment to help Sullivan, withdrew to Boston for repairs. Sullivan, after his troops had pressed the British back to the final barricades around Newport, did not feel that he had sufficient strength to capture the city by assault. As they retreated, the British left the city and counterattacked. A short, sharp contest took place on August 29 in Portsmouth, Rhode Island, not far from Anne Hutchinson's old settlement at Pocasset. Sullivan's troops withstood the attack; Rhode Island's black troops—black companies in the First Rhode Island Battalion, often called the Black Regiment—inflicted heavy losses on the Hessians; but an orderly retreat can hardly be called a triumph of American arms. The first effort at American and French cooperation proved a failure. No other effort to relieve Newport was made. The British stayed until October 1779, when they withdrew of their own accord because the major scenes of action were taking place to the south.

In July 1780, Admiral Charles-Henri Louis d'Arcac de Ternay arrived in Newport with more French troops under Jean Baptiste Donatien de Vimeur, comte de Rochambeau. They stayed over the winter, complaining that American ladies, though beautiful, served too much tea and too little wine. In March 1781, General Washington came to Newport to consult with Rochambeau. Soon afterward, the French left, and thereafter Rhode Island saw no more troops or fighting. Its soldiers, however, were engaged in almost every major battle of the Revolution. Their shoeless, bleeding feet at Valley Forge brought tears to the eyes of General Greene. In the Battle of Yorktown, the turning point in the Revolution, Captain Stephen Olney and his regiment played a distinguished part.

The outstanding military contribution of the state lay in the career of General Greene, though he fought his battles in the South. Prior to the war, he had run an iron foundry in Warwick. At the start of the Revolution, he led Rhode Island's militia to aid Washington at the siege of Boston. He served with Washington in the Middle Colony campaign, fighting at Trenton, Brandywine, Germantown, and Monmouth. His fame as a general came from his brilliant campaign in the Carolinas as the head of the Army of the South after 1778. Many notable southern officers served under him, including Light-horse Harry Lee and Daniel Morgan. Though not exactly victories, his engagements with the British inflicted such heavy losses to them and so few to his own army that he in effect wore them down. As head of the quartermaster corps, he also played a key role in sustaining the army. Philip Freneau, poet of the Revolution, wrote a tribute to Greene's battle at Eutaw Springs, South Carolina, in 1781:

> At Eutaw Spring the valiant died,
>   Their limbs with dust are covered o'er;
> Weep on, ye springs, your tearful tide;
>   How many heroes are no more! . . .
> Led by the conquering genius, Greene,
>   The Britons they compelled to fly;
> None distant viewed the fatal plain,
>   None grieved in such a cause to die.[8]

After the war, Greene accepted as a gift from the state of Georgia a large cotton plantation. But he died from sunstroke at the age of forty-four in 1786. Georgia erected a statue to him in Savannah, and Rhode Islanders erected one at the base of their

---

8. Norman Foerster, editor, *American Poetry and Prose,* 3rd ed., 2 vols. (Boston: Houghton, Mifflin Co., 1947), 1:264.

state capitol. Greene's widow, born Catherine Littlefield, on Block Island, attained fame after 1793 as the patron of Eli Whitney and his cotton gin.

The war ended with Rhode Islanders heavily in debt, their trade in ruins, and Providence the new commercial capital. The state returned to its earlier paper-money system, this time to help the farmers more than the merchants. That, in turn, made the colony reluctant to join the Union after 1787, and there have been many scurrilous things said by historians about both these actions. Rhode Island, it is said in many books, contributed more than any other state toward making the 1780s "the Critical Period" in the new nation. Recent scholarship has refuted these canards. Paper money actually saved the state from the kind of despair among impoverished farmer-veterans that produced Shays's Rebellion in Massachusetts in 1786; it equalized the burden of the war debt upon rich and poor, and it paid off the state's war debts in less than two years. Refusal to join the federal Union was in part motivated by fears of jeopardizing this monetary program and in part because Rhode Island did not think it had fought a revolution against British trade restrictions and import duties simply to hand that same power over to a federated Congress in which Rhode Island would have a very small voice. It also had some criticisms of the new constitution for its lack of a bill of rights and its failure to abolish slavery.

As originally agreed to, the Articles of Confederation allowed each state to retain its sovereignty, freedom, and independence. Each state had a veto over any expansion of Congressional authority. Voluntary co-operation was the essence of the original Union, and that is the way Rhode Island wanted to keep it. The state gave generously of its manpower, its funds, and its supplies when it could. But when Congress asked the states to amend the Articles of Confederation in 1781 so as to allow federal collection of a 5 percent duty on all imports into American ports, Rhode Island resolutely opposed the motion. The leading spokesman for the state was David Howell, a graduate of Princeton who had come to Providence in 1766 to take the chair of natural philosophy at Rhode Island College. Howell was also a lawyer, and when the college suspended its affairs in 1779, he turned to politics. Elected in 1782 to represent the state in the Continental Congress, he ably defended its interests for three crucial years.

Howell argued that Congress had no right, and should not have the right, to lay and collect taxes or duties within the bounds of sovereign states. If voluntary contributions were not sufficient to support the country's needs, he suggested that the western lands of the nation be sold for revenue. Rhode Island, having no claim to any western land, was being somewhat cute in this suggestion. More important was the fact that the state was already laying its own duties on foreign imports and that revenue was part of a broad fiscal program to extricate the state from war debts. If the federal government took away the import revenue, the state would have to resort to heavier property taxes, which would hurt reviving commerce and make it harder for the state to pay its creditors. Rhode Island came in for harsh criticism over the next four years for its refusal to grant this additional power to Congress, thereby weakening Congress's fiscal credit and its administrative authority. But Rhode Island put its own sovereign needs first.

Thomas Paine became so annoyed at Rhode Island's dog-in-the-manger attitude that he rode to Providence on horseback from Philadelphia and spent part of the winter of 1782–1783 attempting in vain to convince the public that common sense dictated giving the impost power to Congress. He wrote a series of six letters to this effect in the *Providence Gazette*, and while they convinced some wealthy merchants, they did not influence the general public. Finally, in 1786, Rhode Island did empower its delegates to vote to give the impost power to Congress, but by then other states had turned against it and it was a dead issue.

The state's use of paper money to pay its debts was a more complicated but equally tense problem, producing similar bad feeling among other states. Rhode Island, not being so easily controlled by the rich as the rest of the New England states, declined after the war to adopt a hard-money, high-tax solution to wipe out its war debts. Such a program obviously would fall hardest upon the poor and indebted, on the small property holders and the farmers. Believing that the well-being of the many was more important than the fiscal repayment of the rich, the legislature used the old land-bank system to enable the poor to mortgage their land to pay off their debts as well as their current expenses. In effect, the paper-money scheme equalized the tax burdens by asking the rich to bear a slightly higher (though proportional) burden than the poor. The rich, being the creditors, bore a greater loss, because the poor paid off the face value of their debts in depreciated paper money—and so did the state. The rich at least got some of their money back, while the poor avoided ruin. Eventually, the poor had to pay off their mortgages (and also to pay heavy taxes for a few years to keep the paper viable), but as a result the state was able to retire its war debts with remarkable rapidity.

The originators of this ingenious fiscal program were Jonathan J. Hazard, Daniel Owen, and John Collins. They became so popular that their "Country party" controlled Rhode Island politics from 1785 to 1790. To carry their plan into effect, they had to refuse to accept any responsibility for servicing the Continental war debt in the state—that is, the loan certificates or promissory notes that Congress had given to individuals and towns in lieu of cash for supplies and services during the war. That meant that the value of these Continental certificates declined in value, for Congress itself, without the impost power, could not pay its debts. Since most of the Continental debt was owed to wealthy individuals or to incorporated towns (especially to Newport, Portsmouth, Middletown, and Bristol, which suffered heavy war damages) the wealthy, the people in these towns, and the merchants opposed the Country party.

When Alexander Hamilton persuaded the federal Congress to accept payment of the Continental debt and the state debts at face value, the wealthy and the people from Newport, Portsmouth, Middletown, and Bristol became firm supporters of ratification of the new government. The Country party, however, expected to pay off the state debt through its own fiscal policy and saw no advantage to the general public in joining a federal Union that had the right to lay import duties, send tax collectors, and otherwise infringe upon the rights of sovereign states.

Hence Rhode Island chose to remain outside the Union and go it alone. In the years 1787 to 1789, the legislature refused on thirteen different occasions to support resolutions leading to ratification.

Rhode Island was once again a pariah. The neighboring states particularly abhorred its policies and resurrected all the old criticisms about its being the home of rogues and rascals, heretics and ne'er-do-wells. Only now it was fiscal heresy and political heresy, not religious errors, that generated verbal assaults. Typical of these attacks was a poem printed in a Connecticut newspaper in 1787:

> [To Rhode Island]
> Hail, realm of rogues, renowned for fraud and guile,
> All hail, the knaveries of yon little isle. . . .
> Look through the state, the unhallowed ground appears
> A nest of dragons and a cave for bears. . . .
> The wiser race, the snare of law to shun,
> Like Lot from Sodom, from Rhode Island run.[9]

The last two lines referred to the law forcing creditors in the state to accept payment of all debts in paper money at face value; those who refused could be fined and disfranchised. Many creditors, it is said, left the state rather than accept these alternatives. However, in the famous case of *Trevett* v. *Weeden,* in 1786, the Rhode Island justices refused to take cognizance of the law and thus there was no way to enforce it. The Country party repealed the fine and disfranchisement but retained the law requring creditors, both private and public, to accept paper money when offered. Those who fled, "like Lot from Sodom," did not escape the law, because it allowed debtors to deposit the amount owed in a local court; if the creditor did not pick it up within a certain time, the court recorded the debt as cancelled. The law also required those who had debts against the state to accept payment in paper money or face repudiation of the debt.

George Washington called the state policies at that time "scandalous." James Madison condemned it for political

9. Frank G. Bates, *Rhode Island and the Formation of the Union* (New York: Macmillan Co., 1898), p. 143.

"wickedness and folly." Nevertheless, the paper money system worked well. It eliminated the state's debts by 1790; it enabled the farmers to pay off their mortgages, pay their taxes, get rid of their personal debts. Hence the great mass of voters steadily supported the Country party and showed no interest in joining the Union.

Various forms of pressure finally forced a change in outlook and led to the collapse of the Country party in 1790. Town meetings at Newport, Middletown, Portsmouth, and Bristol, led by those eager to get the reimbursements that Congress promised for Continental debts, joined the Providence town meeting (where wealthy merchants and those dependent on them controlled the vote) in passing resolutions favoring ratification of the new Constitution. Providence actually said it would secede from the state and join the Union if that were not done, and Newport leaders threatened the same. Some in Congress talked of dividing the state between its neighbors. Congress threatened to treat Rhode Island as a foreign nation and require it to pay duties upon all goods it shipped into the United States. Some Congressional leaders suggested prohibiting all commercial traffic between Rhode Island and the Union.

Finally, in May 1790, an adjourned ratifying convention scraped up two votes to approve ratification by thirty-four votes to thirty-two. But they did so only by agreeing that eighteen amendments should be added to the Constitution to make it palatable to Rhode Islanders' conception of individual freedom. The new state was so small that it was entitled to only one congressman, but it got its full quota of two senators. This congressional delegation was instructed by the legislature to work for twenty-one alterations in the Constitution. The first ten amendments, the Bill of Rights, made good on many of these stipulations, and with the adoption of the First Amendment, Roger Williams's principles of religious liberty and separation of church and state became part of the new nation's fundamental law.

The Country party fell out of power, and in the 1790s the new leaders voted to repay that part of the state debt lost to creditors because of depreciated paper money. President Washington, who had pointedly avoided visiting Rhode Island on his first triumphal tour as president in 1789, now made a special trip there in August 1790. The most memorable result of his visit was a striking letter he wrote in response to a memorial from the handful of Jews still worshipping in Touro Synagogue.

The letter is a landmark in the story of the nation's commitment to religious freedom: "The citizens of the United States of America," Washington said, "have a right to applaud themselves for having given to mankind examples of an enlarged and liberal policy. . . . All possess alike liberty of conscience and immunities of citizenship." Some argue that the letter was written for Washington by Thomas Jefferson, who was in Washington's entourage during this visit; but it is more likely that Washington's secretary simply rephrased the words of Moses Seixas, warden of the synagogue, who had written the memorial to Washington. Seixas had praised the "blessings of civil and religious liberty" that Jews enjoyed in America and expressed gratitude to "the Almighty Dispenser of all Events" who now beheld "a Government which gives to bigotry no sanction, to persecution no assistance but generously affording to all liberty of conscience and immunities of citizenship deeming everyone of whatever nation or tongue or language, equal parts of the great Government machine." [10]

The spirit of liberty generated by the Revolution worked also in Rhode Island, as elsewhere in New England, to bring to fruition the antislavery impetus begun in the Great Awakening. Of course, whites in Rhode Island shared the general social prejudice against blacks, and it did not occur to most of them, at first, that anything in their struggle for "the rights of Englishmen" applied to the slaves in their midst. But as the rhetoric of the Revolution moved to the higher place of "inalienable natural rights" and the claim that "all men are created equal," it became increasingly difficult to justify the institution of chattel slavery.

The year 1755 may have been the peak year for the total number of black slaves in the colony, though the statistics are

10. Gutstein, *The Jews of Newport,* p. 212, p. 210.

very unreliable and probably too low. As the Quakers set the example and moved steadily toward compelling emancipation of slaves among all their members, the proportion of slaves to free blacks decreased. Census statistics in 1755 indicate 4,697 slaves (or 11.5 percent of the population). Of these, 1,234 were in Newport, constituting 15 percent of that city. By 1774, census reports show only 3,761 slaves in the state, constituting 6.3 percent of the population. After 1770, the religious effort of the Quakers was joined by the efforts of the Congregationalists and Baptists. The first step toward making the issue political was the effort to abolish the slave trade. But so many powerful men in the state were interested in sustaining this profitable trade that the best the antislavery advocates could accomplish before the Revolution was a law prohibiting further importation of slaves into the colony. That law, passed in 1774, got through because it considerately permitted any Rhode Island slave trader who could not dispose of a cargo of slaves at a profit to keep them up to a year in the colony until the market improved.

The decision of the general assembly in 1778 to purchase slaves for £65 to £120 each from their masters and set them free if they agreed to serve in the "Black Regiment" led to the emancipation of 125 to 150 male slaves. The state expected to be reimbursed by Congress for what it paid the owners, but Congress never did so.

Moses Brown, who had freed his ten slaves in 1773, Samuel Hopkins, who never owned a slave, and James Manning, who freed his only slave in 1770, joined forces after 1778 to agitate for a law abolishing slavery in the state. In 1784 these reformers attained limited success with the passage of a gradual emancipation act. The act originally called for outlawing the slave trade as well, but John Brown and John DeWolfe, among others, were able to have that part of the bill deleted. By the terms of the law, all children born of slave mothers after March 1, 1784, were to be considered freeborn citizens. However, they were to remain in the hands of their mothers' owners, who were to be compensated for the loss of their "property" by binding them out to service and taking their wages until they reached the age of twenty-one. Of course, slaves born before March 1, 1784, remained slaves for life. In 1790 there were 985 slaves in the state and 4,370 free blacks. In 1820 there were still 47 slaves in Newport and 4 in Providence. A newspaper article in 1859 noted the death of the last slave in Rhode Island.

The antislavery reformers continued their efforts to end the slave trade, but found it difficult to abridge the concept of free enterprise. In November 1787, after great effort by the abolitionists, the general assembly passed a law fining any Rhode Island vessel's owner if it was caught engaging in the slave trade. But slave traders in Providence, Newport, and Bristol either outfitted their ships from nearby Connecticut ports or bribed the customs officials. In 1788 Connecticut passed a similar law, but no way was ever found to prevent the bribing of customs officials who were supposed to keep track of destinations and cargoes. In 1796 Moses Brown brought suit against his brother John, who was caught redhanded in the slave trade. But a sympathetic jury refused to convict such an eminent citizen and noted patriot. The DeWolfe family, the most active slave traders in Bristol, succeeded (with the backing of Thomas Jefferson) in having a port collector appointed in their town who never noticed how many ships were outfitted with chains, ankle cuffs, and iron collars for "catching blackbirds" in Africa. When South Carolina, which had banned the import of slaves in 1788, re-opened its slave trade in 1803, some fifty-nine Rhode Island vessels carried 7,958 slaves into Charleston over the next four years: 3,500 of these slaves came in ships from Newport; 3,900 from Bristol ships; and 556 from Providence-owned ships.

In 1789 Moses Brown, Hopkins, and Manning started the Providence Society for Abolishing the Slave Trade. In addition to prosecuting the illegal slave traders, this society also offered legal aid to blacks still held in slavery and sought to find employment for freedmen. It started a night school for blacks and worked with similar societies in other states to persuade Congress to act against the slave trade.

While most black Rhode Islanders were free after 1807, they remained the victims of prejudice and oppression in every sphere of life. They were segregated in the churches, kept out of the public schools, denied employment in the textile mills, and finally, in 1822, denied the right to vote. In 1780 the free blacks of Newport founded the African Union Society and in 1808 the African Benevolent Society; both organizations were designed to help educate and provide vocational training for blacks. But they lacked sufficient money to be very effective.

Newport Gardner (whose African name was Occramer Marycoo) was the leading figure in the black organizations. Though brought to Newport as a slave in 1760, he earned his freedom by teaching music. He worked closely with the white antislavery reformers for many years; but in 1823, the year after blacks were officially disfranchised by law, he gave up hope of ever getting white men to understand the meaning of equality. He and a group of friends boarded a ship in Boston to return to Africa: "I go," Marycoo said, "to set an example to the youth of my race. I go to encourage the young. They can never be elevated here. I have tried it for sixty years—it is in vain." [11] His prophecy seemed borne out when Providence became the scene of race riots in 1824 and 1831. They took place in the city's black ghetto, only a few hundred yards from the place where Roger Williams founded his haven for the oppressed. For all its zeal for liberty, Rhode Island, like the rest of the United States, fell sadly short in that area of freedom.

After 1790 Rhode Island entered a new era. While the country as a whole became obsessed with settling the West, New England tried to sustain its maritime trade, while at the same time it rapidly entered the age of industrialism.

11. Irving H. Bartlett, *From Slave to Citizen* (Providence: Published by the Urban League of Rhode Island, 1954), p. 12.

4

Industrialization and Social Conflict

*O*NCE again, in the years 1790 to 1860, the ingenuity and experimentation of Rhode Islanders enabled them to survive and prosper against heavy odds. On the map of the United States, Rhode Island shrank to a mere pinpoint within the expanding nation. Yet it grew steadily in population, in wealth, and in influence. It lived, as always, by its wits, its entrepreneurial skills, its willingness to innovate.

Despite its growing economic prosperity, however, the state displayed startling conservative tendencies in its social and political evolution. Rhode Islanders came to share, at least among the dominant middle class, the growing reputation of New England as an ingrown, stuffy, ancestor-worshipping Yankee community. It clung stubbornly to its old charter of 1663 until a local revolution took place in 1842. After 1835, it spawned an intense Know-Nothing movement—a xenophobia shared by many other parts of the country. This bigotry against "foreigners" and "aliens" was shared by the native-born among all classes. Rampant anti-Catholicism betrayed the state's heritage of toleration. Rhode Island industry needed the services of the new immigrants, but it was not prepared to treat them as equals. Somehow, the sense of community forged in the heat of Revolution had solidified the old Yankees into a block of exclusivists—white Anglo-Saxon Protestants who demanded that newcomers conform to their patterns of behavior and belief if they wished to be "American."

The nineteenth century brought great achievements in technology and industry to the state and firmly attached it at last to the rest of New England. But the benefits of modernization were slow to trickle down to the factory worker, whether foreign or native-born. Workers were mere commodities of production. While farmers and other rural folk had the social satisfaction of ancestral pride and racial affinity to the rising urban middle class and factory owners, their votes became expressions of frustration, efforts to retain a sense of control over a world passing beyond their ken. Cities, not farming communities, dominated the state. Social tensions mounted almost in direct proportion to prosperity. Rhode Island became as ethnically, socially, and economically fragmented in the nineteenth century as it had been religiously divided in the seventeenth.

Stumbling out of the debacle of war and postwar readjustments, the state's merchant leaders' first efforts were to reestablish trade relations with the West Indies. But except for those few willing to return to the triangular trade and skirt the new antislavery laws, that did not prove feasible. The British refused to let American ships enter their ports, and the Dutch, Spanish, and French imposed regulations on their islands that the old smuggling stratagems could not easily avoid. It soon became obvious that Americans were frozen out of the West Indies; neither rum, sugar, nor slaves could revive the state's trade there. Some other sources of commercial exchange had to be found.

The first of these proved to be the Baltic trade, but almost simultaneously more daring merchants tried the China trade around the Cape of Good Hope—appropriately named for Rhode Islanders. Then came the clipper ships around Cape Horn. A native Rhode Island sea captain, Robert Gray of Tiverton, was among the first to make ocean contact with the Oregon country and discovered the Columbia River; he was, however, in the employ of Boston merchants. The Napoleonic Wars and the blockades set up by the English and French fleets made both the Baltic and East Indian trades risky. And for several decades the Barbary pirates from the Mediterranean took a constant toll of American merchant ships in the Atlantic. However, by the same token, the preoccupation of the British with Napoleon gave American traders an opportunity to compete more successfully with their great rivals. From 1790 to 1810, American products such as rum, indigo, and tobacco found a ready market in Copenhagen, Göteburg, and St. Petersburg in exchange for Danish hemp, Swedish naval stores, German iron and glass, Russian duck cloth (or canvas). Occasionally, Rhode Islanders took lumber and fish to Lisbon and exchanged them for oranges, lemons, and cork to be sold in Baltic ports. Enterprise meant ingenuity in exchanging one cargo for another and gradually parlaying the original exports for cargoes that would bring a profit large enough to sustain a long and complex series of bargainings.

The trade with India, the East Indies, and China proved to be the most lucrative. Previously, the British East India Company had a monopoly on that. The first Rhode Island ships to reach the Far East came from Providence in the late 1780s. By trial and error, merchants, traders, ship captains, and factors discovered a whole new assortment of goods that could be exported and imported at astounding profits. To the ports of Madagascar, Bombay, Pondicherry, Calcutta, Java, Malaya, and Canton, the Rhode Island ships brought rum, iron, steel, sail-cloth, cotton, tobacco, sugar, cordage, and ginseng; later, seal and otter skins from the arctic replaced ginseng. They also had to carry hard cash—silver dollars or Spanish goldpieces—to deal with East Indian traders. In exchange, however, Rhode Island ships brought home tea, coffee (which also sold well in Baltic ports), and such exotic new products as silks, spices, lacquerware, chinaware, (replacing pewter dishes), flannels, muslins, cambrics, calico, and nankeens (cheap cotton goods to compete with British manufactures).

These were romantic years for Narragansett Bay. Every week brought tall ships into India Wharf at Providence or the town wharves at Newport and Bristol, with strange cargo from the Far East. Every adventurous boy dreamed of shipping out to see the world. Taverns and docks were filled with sailors carrying parrots or monkeys on their shoulders, wearing gold earrings, and spinning yarns about pirates, South Sea island girls, strange peoples with different customs and costumes, or no costumes at all. The India trade was also replete with danger from typhoons, hurricanes, and the terrors of "rounding the Cape" in a gale. Not a few Rhode Island seamen were captured by Barbary pirates, ransomed from slavery, and returned in physical ruin to tell much less romantic stories of their voyages to foreign shores. Many never returned.

While President Thomas Jefferson finally waged successful war on the Barbary pirates, his efforts to deal with the British and French seizures of American merchantmen were less helpful. Despite American efforts to remain officially neutral, neither the French nor the English believed they were so in fact. Hoping to make these countries respect America's right to freedom of the seas, the Jeffersonians placed embargoes and other restrictions on trans-Atlantic shipping from 1807 to 1812, which proved more devastating to American merchants than to the French or English public. Rhode Island's shippers, who had accepted the risks of war, blockades, and pirates, could not accept the bureaucratic restrictions put upon them by their own government. Although the state had been essentially Jeffersonian in its viewpoint, after 1808 Federalist views mounted with the decline in shipping. When the Jeffersonian party, headed by James Madison, declared war on England in 1812, the majority of Rhode Islanders (following their own interest) joined the rest of New England in opposing it.

Vehement denunciations of "Mr. Madison's War" appeared in the Rhode Island press. Resolutions passed in town meetings and in the general assembly hailed England as the defender of liberty and democracy, while denouncing Napoleon as a tyrant and barbarian. In 1812 Rhode Island, like Massachusetts and Connecticut, told the president that it would not provide troops to fight against England for policies made in Washington that stifled its economy. That same year, the general assembly voted not to allow the Rhode Island militia to be called into national service. It also complained that the government failed to increase the garrisons in the state's coastal forts. The state's first Federalist governor, William Jones—who was re-elected annually from 1811 to 1817—threatened not to obey any orders of the federal government that the state considered against its best interests: "Notwithstanding our respect for the law and our strong attachment to the union of the States, there may be evils greater than can be apprehended from a refusal to submit to unconstitutional laws." [1] The pattern of resistance to British imperial domination was being repeated in New England against the federal government.

In 1815 Rhode Island's legislature sent four delegates to the Hartford Convention, where delegates from all the New England states flirted with the idea of secession from the Union. Yet, despite its refusal to allow its militia to leave the state for national duty, Rhode Island did equip and send out five hundred men who had enlisted in the national army in 1812. In the person of Oliver Hazard Perry, a native of South Kingstown, the state produced one of the heroes of the war.

Born in 1785, Perry had enlisted in the navy at the age of fourteen and fought against the Barbary pirates from 1804 to 1806. Married in Newport in 1811, he left the navy, only to request active service when war started with England a year later. Sent to Sacketts Harbor on Lake Erie, he built and commanded a fleet of ten small vessels whose task it was to clear the British off that lake. In the famous battle of Put-in Bay on Lake Erie, on September 10, 1813, Perry's fleet engaged the more powerful British warships on the lake. One quarter of Perry's sailors and four of his captains were from Rhode Island. In the course of the battle, his flagship, *Lawrence,* was so badly battered that he had to leave it and fight on from another ship. After desperate fighting, the British ships surrendered, and Perry sent his famous message to General William H. Harrison: "We have met the enemy and they are ours." [2] The handmade flag that Perry hoisted at the start of the battle, with the motto "Don't Give up the Ship," is today preserved at the United States Naval Academy. (Perry's younger brother Matthew later attained fame for his arrogant negotiation of America's first

1. Richman, *Rhode Island, A Study in Separatism,* p. 276.
2. Richman, *Rhode Island, A Study in Separatism,* p. 277.

trade treaty with Japan in 1853–1854.) A statue of Oliver Perry stands today in Cleveland, Ohio, and another flanks the steps of the Rhode Island State House, along with that of Nathanael Greene.

While the China trade continued into the 1820s, it was an expensive, risky business, and only two or three firms were capable of maintaining it. The War of 1812 hastened the diverting of capital in the state from shipping to manufacturing. British competition in trade and new European impost duties after 1815 accelerated the shift. Successful manufacture of textiles had started this flow by 1805. With the rise of manufacturing, Rhode Islanders switched their antipathy toward federal regulation to one of support, at least insofar as federal power was utilized after 1816 to support protective tariffs for the state's infant industries.

In 1824 the state voted for John Quincy Adams over the frontier hero Andrew Jackson—an expression of its preference for industrial development over western expansion. Moving now into the orbit of New England Whiggism, the state cast its votes for "the American System" of Henry Clay and Daniel Webster—for government support of turnpikes, canals, railroads, and manufactures. Rhode Island had at last found the blessing of national union, at least so long as the business of America was business.

For a few years, as the maritime trade lingered on, there were conflicts between the local interests of the merchants and the manufacturers. As late as 1828, the important firm of Brown and Ives in Providence led a movement to petition Congress against increasing the tariff on textiles and manufactures, which they imported from England. However, after 1830, Brown and Ives completely shifted their capital to textile and metal manufactures and joined the rising industrial interests in support of high tariffs against competing British imports. They concluded that manufacturing (with the aid of high tariffs) offered a safer and more profitable investment than the China trade in which they had pioneered. By 1840 maritime interests in Rhode Island were almost extinct. The only important shipping that remained consisted of coastal trade, which brought lumber, coal, and raw cotton in for the mills and shipped textile products out. In its effort to preserve this mutually profitable link between government regulation and manufacturing, as well as in its concern to maintain a supply of docile and disciplined labor, Rhode Island, like the rest of New England, started down that path toward conservatism that was the mark of a dominant power bloc. Progress henceforth meant technological and managerial improvement within the existing industrial system. Political and economic change were welcomed only if they meant "more of the same." By the end of the century, that was to pay handsome dividends for those at the top and to the native-born middle class. But it seemed increasingly repressive to those on the bottom.

At the outset, the thought of making Rhode Island an industrial state seemed not only risky, but bizarre. Where would it get the capital? How could it possibly compete with British textiles? Where would it obtain the machinery and the skilled mechanics to build, service, and operate the necessary machinery? Moses Brown, Quaker abolitionist and member of the well-to-do Brown family in Providence, proved to be the man with the vision, the capital, and the persistence to carry out the initial experiment. Water power proved to be the hidden resource that provided inexpensive means to operate the mills. Protective tariffs offered the answer to British competition. A transport revolution through canals and railroads provided the means to distribute the production. A rapidly growing nation provided the raw material in the South and the necessary domestic market. Immigration held the answer to a continually expanding need for cheap labor. Tariffs weakened British competition. With hindsight, it all seems so logical as to be inevitable. But at the start, it seemed an almost hopelessly visionary notion.

When the glaciers that covered New England in the Ice Age receded, the melting ice cut numerous river beds along the four-hundred-foot decline from the northern and western borders of Rhode Island down into Narragansett Bay. They also left numerous ponds, lakes, and coves amid the ridges and island peaks. The Blackstone River, the Moshassuck, the Woonasquatucket, and the Pawtuxet rivers were fast-moving, almost never frozen, and never dry. Their various falls and small ponds (for water storage behind dams) proved perfectly adapted for mill wheels to generate steady and certain sources of power. All that was needed was the capital to build the mills and the mechanics to run them. Rhode Island had always been a sheep-raising community. Its men and women knew how to spin wool, cotton, linen, or flax and how to weave them into various kinds of cloth. But most of that was done simply for household or local use on spinning wheels and hand looms. The refusal of the British government to allow the colonies to engage in manufacturing and the British prohibition against the exportation of textile machinery (or even of the blueprints for that machinery) seemed to doom Americans to remain consumers or traders, rather than producers.

Moses Brown and his business partner, William Almy, made the first efforts to overcome these obstacles in 1787. They hired a Providence clothmaker, John Bailey, to go to Beverly, Massachusetts, to study some crude spinning jennies being used at a short-lived mill there. But the machinery was inadequate, and the Beverly mill soon failed. After further investigation, Brown bought a spinning and carding machine built by two Providence mechanics, Richard Anthony and Daniel Jackson, and in May 1789, started a small spinning factory in Providence. These first machines were manually operated and proved ineffective. Brown then looked into the use of waterpower. That same year, he bought a water frame and carding machine built by John Reynolds of Providence and hauled them to Pawtucket, where he installed them in the first water-driven cotton mill in America.

However, these machines also proved inadequate, and none of the mechanics in New England seemed capable of constructing a workable machine. After a few weeks of operation in the fall of 1789, Brown shut down his mill. The problems seemed insoluble. But, providentially, Brown's efforts were heard of by Samuel Slater in New York City. Slater, who had worked for seven years in the cotton-spinning factories of Derbyshire, England, wrote to Brown on December 2, 1789, and offered his services. He said he had emigrated in defiance of British law forbidding skilled mechanics to leave the country and that he could reproduce from memory the complicated blueprints for the most up-to-date British spinning machinery, the invention of Richard Arkwright. All he needed was someone with enough faith in him and enough capital to build it in America.

Brown sent money for Slater to come to Providence and gave him the funds and assistants to build the first successful Arkwright cotton-spinning machine in America. It was installed in Brown's Pawtucket watermill in December 1790. The results were spectacular. Brown's persistence had paid off. Soon "Slater's mill" (the firm was henceforth that of Brown, Almy, and Slater) was carding and spinning more thread and yarn than the hand weavers could possibly utilize on their home looms. The surplus was temporary; it lasted only until Slater developed effective marketing methods for the new manufactured product.[3] Brown and Slater at first used the "put-out" system to make cloth; that is, they put out the yarn to be woven in weavers' homes. But that proved inefficient. The weavers set their own hours and often held other jobs. The manufacturer could not fill his orders on schedule. So Slater built a large, two-story mill building and installed row upon row of looms adjoining the cotton-spinning machines. The weavers were told to come to the factory, where they worked under close supervision for wages for sixty to seventy hours a week. That proved much more efficient, but it also aroused the opposition of these skilled craftsmen. Unaccustomed to such implacable regimentation, they protested. The first workingmen's strike in American history occurred in Slater's mill in 1800, when the weavers walked out and left their looms idle in protest against Slater's hard-driving system. But protest was useless. Workers henceforth followed the relentless pace of the machines.

The next step was obvious, but it took time to implement. The British had already automated the weaving process, and Americans repeated the practice of copying British plans. Wil-

3. Charles Carroll, *Rhode Island: Three Centuries of Democracy*, 4 vols. (New York: Lewis Historical Publishing Co., 1932), 1:405.

liam Gilmore built the first power loom in Rhode Island in 1815. Power looms, however, did not replace hand-weaving overnight. Not until 1830 were most cotton factories running water looms. These machines had tremendous advantages, despite their complexity and cost. They increased production, stabilized it, made a more standardized product, and cut costs. Moreover, once installed, they could be tended by the unskilled labor of women and children, who, with little complaint, took over the work formerly requiring hundreds of skilled craftsmen—and they did so at much lower wages. Alexander Hamilton had said in his famous "Report on Manufactures" in 1792 that the man who would find such work for women and children would be a benefactor of his country. Ironically, the philanthropic Moses Brown was that man. He proudly wrote, "As the manufactury of the mill yarn is done by children from eight to fourteen years old, it is as nearly a saving of labor to the country as perhaps any that can be named." [4] At that time, with skilled labor scarce and expensive, machines tended by women and children did seem a great boon to the nation. Rhode Island initiative had found a new source of prosperity. With the perfection of the power loom after 1815, the production of cotton cloth began to rank with cotton yarn as a primary area of investment capital in New England.

In addition to cheap water power and cheap labor, the success of Rhode Island's textile industry owed much to climatic conditions that produced just the right amount of moisture in the air to keep the threads from drying out and snapping on the fast-moving machines. Equally important, however, was the attitude of the Rhode Island people toward hard, menial labor and of the state government's eagerness to encourage free enterprise. The state lesiglature, believing that industrialization served the public interest, allowed the needs of the mill owners to take precedence over those of farmers and fishermen. Farmers might sue for compensation when mill dams flooded their land, but they

4. Edmund Brock, *The Background and Recent Status of Collective Bargaining in the Cotton Industry in Rhode Island*, Catholic University of America, Studies in Sociology, vol. 8 (Washington, D.C., 1942), p. 84.

could not stop the dams from being built or continuing in operation. Fishermen could require that dams be opened at designated times to allow fish to pass through (up or downstream), but they could not obtain laws preventing manufacturers from polluting the streams. Within a short time, most rivers and many fishing areas and shell beds became polluted by industrial waste from cleaning, bleaching, and dyeing the cotton. Nor did the state give any thought in the nineteenth century to regulating working conditions or safety hazards in the mills. Nor was it concerned about the living conditions in the factory towns. In the interest of progress, it chose to overlook, not oversee.

The education of the mill operatives' children was at the mercy of the local taxpayers, and once parents thought their children old enough to go into the mills, that was the end of their education. The decline of farming (as new fertile areas in the West were settled) and of the maritime trade left the common people no other source of gainful employment. They took what they could get and resented those who came later and were willing to work for even lower wages. The old Puritan work ethic, taught by schoolteachers and ministers and firmly held by lawgivers, held that hard work and strict discipline were good for children, and few parents disagreed. A few millowners tried paternalistically to provide good housing and working conditions, but as competition increased, philanthropy in business decreased. Efficiency meant cutting costs. Long before the end of the century, millworkers were treated with less concern than the machines they tended.

The cultural emphasis upon individualism, the uncritically accepted "success myth," kept the workers from banding together. Religious prejudice complemented economic competition for work and produced the nativist resentment of Irish Catholics. The first attempts at labor unions in the 1830s were defeated by these frictions that the employers played upon. *The Voice of Industry,* an early labor newspaper, expressed the angry frustration of the native-born workers in 1846:

The manufacturers of Rhode Island seem to prefer foreign laborers, not only because there is no prospect of their exercising the right of suffrage but because . . . they are more submissive under corporation tyranny. And the factory despotism is therefore increasing here faster than in any other portion of New England.[5]

Between 1830 and 1850, the percentage of foreign-born in Providence increased from 1 percent to 16 percent; the jobs they found had formerly been held by native Americans.

From 1790 to 1803, the Brown, Almy, and Slater Company owned the only spinning manufacturies in America (the partners added subsidiary mills in 1794 and 1799). Between 1803 and 1805, competitors started four new cotton-spinning mills; and by 1815, there were a hundred cotton-spinning mills in the state, employing seven thousand workers; twenty-one of the state's thirty-one towns had found some river capable of sustaining a spinning factory. Part of this stimulus came from the Embargo of 1807 and the maritime decline; part, from obvious profits to be made from manufacturing. In addition, the cutting off of British supplies and the invention of the cotton gin boosted the new industry. By 1815, Rhode Island was consuming 29,000 bales of raw cotton a year. Raw cotton soon became the state's leading import. This new link between southern planters and northern cotton manufacturers quickly became a potent political factor, another aspect of his investment that the abolitionist Moses Brown had not foreseen.

In the years 1790 to 1815, Rhode Island dominated the yarn and textile production of the nation; but after 1815, when John Cabot Lowell developed the integrated system of cotton manufacturing (by placing the carding, spinning, weaving, bleaching, dyeing, and finishing process all under one roof), the textile manufacturers of Massachusetts began to surpass those in Rhode Island. Nevertheless, as of 1831, Rhode Island was manufacturing one-fifth of the nation's yarn and one-sixth of its cloth. It ranked second to Massachusetts in New England as a producer of cotton goods and ahead of much larger states like New York. At first its mills were small and required only small investments to build. But by 1832 the larger ones were capitalized at more

5. Brock, *Collective Bargaining in the Cotton Industry,* p. 7.

than $100,000 each. The total capital invested in cotton manu-
facturing in the state in 1832 was $5,600,000, which was more
than triple the amount invested in maritime commerce. By 1860
one out of every three persons in the state's work force was
employed in some aspect of the textile business. More than half
the mill operatives were children, and three-fifths of the adult
workers were women. By the 1830s, manufacturing, having absorbed the available native-born workers, was eager for the new
immigrants from Europe.

From manufacturing cotton products, it was only a small step
to woollen products. But woollen manufacturing always lagged
behind cotton in those years. Its beginning dates from the efforts
of Rowland Hazard in South Kingstown in 1804. Hazard was
one of those early philanthropic millowners who tried to produce utopian working conditions in his milltown. Peace Dale
was to Rhode Island what the early Lowell mills were to Massachusetts—a model town with a school, a library, a church,
and neatly arranged workers' housing, all built by the mill-
owner. But most woollen mills differed little in their conditions
from cotton mills.

The Providence Woollen Manufacturing Company, founded
in 1812, may have been the first textile mill in America to
employ steam power to drive its machines. However, it went
bankrupt in 1815. Wool manufacturing became profitable only
after a more efficiently integrated system of production was developed and when, after 1828, an adequate tariff was placed
upon the import of British woollen goods. By 1832 there were
twenty-two woollen mills in the state, capitalized at $335,000
(about 6 percent as much as the capitalization of cotton mills).
While 9,071 workers were employed in cotton manufacturing in
1832, only 380 worked in woollen mills. Woollen mills also
united "the Lords of the loom and the Lords of the lash," since
the chief product of Rhode Island's woollen companies was the
"kersey cloth" used primarily to make clothing for slaves.

The rise of textile manufacturing can be measured against the
decline of the state's maritime trade. The sum of import duties
collected on foreign shipping in the port of Providence dropped
from $400,000 in 1804 to $100,000 in 1830. By 1860 only

$36,000 was collected from foreign import duties. The same decline can be seen in re-export values out of Rhode Island to foreign ports. These dropped from $1.5 million in 1805 to only $10,000 in 1860. Rhode Island was turning away from the sea, after two centuries. Home markets replaced foreign markets. Shipbuilding almost disappeared. Seaports like Newport, Bristol, Warren, Wickford, and Westerly faded into quaint backwater towns, while inland farming communities sprouted enormous wooden and brick factory complexes along their rivers. Crowded, smoky cities in the northern half of the state became the center of enterprise, prosperity, and power, while Aquidneck, South County, and the eastern shore—except at Fall River—stagnated.

Textile manufacturing spread rapidly after 1830, largely because steam power first supplemented and then replaced water power in the mills; and steam power in the mills was matched by steam power in the railroads and the steamboats. Samuel Slater built the first large steam-driven cotton mill in 1827 in Providence. At first, steam engines merely provided power in the summer, when streams were low and the water wheels did not turn as fast as desired. But manufacturers soon discovered that steam engines were more efficient all year round. They provided a smoother, steadier, more easily regulated source of power. In winter, ice sometimes blocked the water wheels, but freezing weather did not bother the steam engines. Steam power also freed new manufacturers from obtaining water-power rights upon the swiftly moving streams. A plant could be built almost anywhere, though some water was needed for washing, bleaching, and dyeing purposes, as well as to provide water for the steam engine and an easy way to dispose of wastes. Steam power enabled textile manufacturing to move farther out into the country and down the bay, where tidal inlets could be used for dumping waste. Textile mills on the bay were also handy for importing cotton and coal and for exporting finished products.

Use of steam power avoided the need for costly building and upkeep of dams, locks, water wheels, and reservoirs. True, the need to import coal raised the cost of production, but that was more than compensated for by the greater efficiency it provided.

The quality of yarn and cloth improved with steam-driven looms and spindles. Most important, steam power reduced labor costs. However, the heavy machinery involved meant a loss of flexibility for the Rhode Island economy. Capitalization was costly and so were upkeep, repair, and modernization. Efficient and profitable when working at full speed, idle steam-driven engines and machinery became costly when broken or when surpluses piled up that could not be sold. Gradually, the state was becoming overspecialized with both the advantages and disadvantages of a single-staple product.

Steam power developed rapidly after 1830 and, together with the railroad, led to ever-increasing investment in textiles. Capitalization in that industry alone doubled from $5.6 million in 1832 to $12 million in 1860. The labor force in textiles rose from 9,071 to 15,700 in the same period. The mills themselves grew larger and more complex. The largest mill in 1832 was capitalized at $240,000, while in 1860 there were at least six firms in Providence County alone operating at that scale, with three capitalized at half a million each. The 1830s were the period of most rapid textile increase in pre-Civil War years. In that decade, the number of mills almost doubled, from 126 to 226. Profits resulting from tariff protection allowed investment in high-grade machinery, which permitted the production of special calicoes and other complex fabrics hitherto produced cheaper in England. By the 1840s, New England was effectively competing with British textile manufacturers in the home market.

Still it would be a mistake to attribute the state's prosperity simply to textiles. The manufacture of textile machinery, steam engines, and metal tools flourished. New banking and insurance facilities developed. A profitable new industry in jewelry, silverware, and precious metals arose. Jabez Gorham started his nationally famous silver company in Providence in 1813. In 1846 Thomas H. Lowe discovered a new method of "sweating" gold plate that further advanced the jewelry industry. George H. Corliss gave a tremendous boost toward making Providence the center of steam-engine production when he brought his remarkable engineering talent to the city in 1844.

Four years after founding his company, he produced the first reciprocating rotary-valve steam engine, a discovery that revolutionized the whole steam-power process. It has been called the most important single advance in steam design since James Watt invented the steam engine. Two other prominent companies involved in metal casting—the Union Butt Works and the Barstow Stove Company—also located in Providence prior to the Civil War. Both sold cast-iron products throughout the northeast.

The development of these metal and machine industries helped to diversify somewhat the state's manufacturing products and kept its economy from being totally at the mercy of fluctuations in the textile industry. By 1860 the precious-metals industry had 91 firms in the state, capitalized at $1.5 million and employing 2,043 workers. The base-metals industry had 173 firms, capitalized at $4.1 million, with 4,691 workers. The plants that made machinery for the textile industry consisted of 51 firms, capitalized at $1 million, employing 1,560 workers. Nevertheless, all the money invested in these industries together (and including what little was left of maritime trade) amounted to less than was invested in textiles in 1860. Another way of measuring the shift that had taken place in the state's economy within half a century is to note that, by 1860, less than 3 percent of the total work force was engaged in maritime trade, while more than 50 percent was engaged in manufacturing. Agricultural employment occupied only about 10 percent. With more than 80 percent of the state's capital invested in manufacturing (textiles and metals), Rhode Island in 1860 was the most highly industrialized state in the Union.

With industrial expansion came population explosion and diversity. Rhode Island's population increased two and one-half times between 1776 and 1860, much of it through foreign immigration. Between 1830 and 1860, the population increased by 77,000, reaching a total of 174,000 in 1860. While the growth was not exceptionally high in terms of the national population growth, the concentration of so many new people in so small an area gave the feeling of intense crowding. And in that narrow confine, the tensions between native and foreign-born became close to explosive.

The other important change that took place in the early nineteenth century was the rise of the city of Providence and the metropolitan area contiguous to it. By 1800 it had clearly replaced Newport as the maritime hub of the state. Its industrial growth in the next sixty years turned Rhode Island into a city-state. Three of the state's largest rivers debouched at the head of the bay, thus creating a heavy concentration of textile mills in and near Providence. Providence also became the center of the metals industry, the banking and insurance companies, and the transport entrepôt for the distribution of imports and exports. As the state's business center, Providence was the place where middlemen served as agents or factors for all imports and exports—handling the raw cotton and the fuel that entered the state, as well as distributing the multifarious kinds of textiles, jewelry, and machinery exported from it. The offices and warehouses of these middlemen naturally arose at the point where transport facilities and manufacturing firms came together, and that point was Providence. Roger Williams had chosen a better site than he could ever have guessed. And while the population of the state as a whole increased by 154 percent between 1820 and 1860, the population of Providence grew by 1,004 percent. The northern sector of the state, which in 1790 held 50 percent of the population, by 1860 held 80 percent. The density throughout the state averaged 223 per square mile; in Providence, it reached 7,560.

The city of Providence not only had a good harbor through which heavy goods (coal and raw cotton) could be cheaply shipped in, but it also became the railroad center through which manufactured goods were distributed inland to the rest of the country. The first railroad came into Providence from Boston in 1832. It was soon extended southward to Stonington, Connecticut, (in 1841) and then to New York City (in 1848). It radiated north to Worcester in 1842 (where Providence men had invested heavily in textile mills), west to Hartford and Fishkill in 1854, and eastward to Fall River and Bristol by 1855. Similarly, the turnpike-and-canal system radiated from Providence, starting with the Blackstone Canal in 1828. Between 1803 and 1842, thirty-six turnpike companies were incorporated in Rhode Island, and while railroads thereafter surpassed wagons and stage-coaches for long-distance travel, that network of roads continued to be a prime system for internal local travel. After the perfection of the steamship, Providence also became the center for passenger traffic from New England to New York. Even Bostonians traveled to Providence to catch the overnight steamers. After 1845, however, the steamship companies built larger, more efficient facilities at Fall River, and new railroad connections to that more open seaport created a more direct and faster passenger service to and from New York.

As the state's economic center, Providence attracted people of wealth, imagination, and talent. It became the cultural as well as financial and political core of the state. Although the legislature continued to rotate its sessions between five capitals until 1854, and then between Newport and Providence until 1900, clearly metropolitan Providence wielded the economic power that dictated most important decisions and set basic policies. Providence also became the most cosmopolitan city in Rhode Island, attracting a large proportion of the new immigration. While the new ethnic groups added variety to the city, they played at first little social or political part in it. The immigrants lived in the worst houses near the factories and were excluded from the mainstream of the cultural life. Yet they increased so rapidly that they could not be ignored. The first signs of anti-Catholic bigotry and class friction developed naturally enough in Providence.

However, in one crucial respect, Providence did not dominate Rhode Island. It had only four votes in the general assembly, out of a total of seventy-two, and could be easily outvoted on any questions opposed by rural legislators. It was in part for that reason that Providence also became the scene of the main events of the Dorr Rebellion in 1842. While that political movement also contained many aspects of anti-Catholic and antiforeign feelings, it has generally been described as an effort of the middle-class Yankees to extend the suffrage and alter the old charter without accepting the prevailing concept of universal manhood or altering the social balance. There were some elements of class friction involved in the conflict, and the reenfranchisement of the state's black population became a major issue. But the Yankee middle class managed to contain the more radical elements, so as to produce minimal change.

Known locally as "the Dorr War," the political crisis of 1840–1842 had ramifications far beyond Rhode Island. While it involved no loss of life and very little armed conflict, it shook the state to its foundation and led to an important case before the United States Supreme Court. The contest was an early test of the Constitution, forcing the question of the extent to which the federal government could or should interfere in a sovereign state to enforce the maintenance of a republican form of government guaranteed to each state by the Constitution. In a more profound way, the national reaction to the Dorr War may have laid the basis for the angry reaction to the secession of the southern states in 1861. In effect, it helped solidify the ideal of nationalism and union in opposition to the Revolutionary theory of popular sovereignty. The defeat of the radical aspects of the movement advanced the growing conservatism of the new nation.

The critical issue was: What constitutes true republicanism, the voice of the people or respect for duly constituted authority? Or, to put it another way, can the principles of natural rights and popular sovereignty justify circumvention (or replacement) of the prevailing, formal institutions of law and order? Thomas Dorr and his rebels argued that they were conservatives, conserving the Revolutionary principles of "no taxation without representation" and majority rule. The defenders of the old charter system argued that these Revolutionary principles were no longer operative in America. Dorr said they were operative whenever an outmoded political system, like the charter of 1663, deprived so many citizens of their natural right to participate in government as to produce minority rule. Rhode Island was only one of several states and territories that went through this kind of struggle after 1830, but it provided the test case for conservative constitutionalism against radical natural-rights theory. Ironically, it resulted in an expansion of the suffrage, at the same time that it exacerbated the growing antagonism between the enfranchised native-born and the effectively disfranchised foreign-born. While native-born citizens could vote by paying a one-dollar registry tax, naturalized foreign-born citizens could vote only by meeting the old—and prohibitively high—property qualification.

By 1840 Rhode Island had fallen badly behind the times in its political institutions. Formerly the most democratic of the colonies, it was, in 1840, the only state that still limited voting rights to persons who owned real property. Dorr and his followers also criticized the old charter government because, under it, the first-born sons of freemen were allowed to vote upon coming of age, even though they personally did not meet the property qualification. This hangover from feudal concepts of primogeniture was peculiar to Rhode Island and totally out of step with the egalitarianism of the Age of Jackson, but Rhode Island's conservatives clung to it from tradition and because it kept the dominant group further entrenched in power. In 1775, when almost everyone in the colony owned his own piece of land, 75 percent of the adult white males voted, but by 1840, with the tremendous increase in landless, urban dwellers, only one out of three white male inhabitants had the vote.

Equally important, representation in the state's legislature was severely overbalanced in favor of the small towns. Representation had been fixed by charter regulation in 1663, and in 1840 Newport was still entitled to six seats in the general assembly, while Providence was entitled to only four. Yet, by this time, Providence had a population of 23,000, while Newport had only 9,000. By charter regulations, all towns incorporated after the original four were entitled to two representatives. By 1840 some of these rural towns, which had declined to a few hundred people, sent the same number of representatives to the legislature as burgeoning industrial centers five or ten times their size. Furthermore, the charter provided no way to redistribute the seats in the legislature or to district the state without the consent of the general assembly. Since the general assembly was controlled by those who benefited from the outmoded system, the suffrage reformers argued that the state was locked into an increasing unrepresentative or antirepublican form of government. As of 1840, the minority dominated the majority. Rural town meetings were still controlled by the handful of farmers or middle-class property owners, while hundreds of mill workers who owned no property in the towns had no voice in their community affairs. In the urban centers, shopkeepers who rented the buildings in which they lived and ran their businesses and clerks who lived in boarding houses were considered among the propertyless because they owned no real estate.

One of the difficulties the suffrage reformers faced was whether to extend the vote to propertyless foreign-born inhabitants (if naturalized) or only to propertyless native-born inhabitants. The conservative reformers felt it would be dangerous to follow the Jacksonian policy of granting all males over twenty-one the right to vote; neither blacks, Indians, nor recently naturalized "foreigners" seemed truly capable of exercising such a privilege. If the foreign-born were to be given the vote, then some thought the requirements for the number of years' residence in the country prior to naturalization should be extended. It might take twenty-one years for an Irish Catholic to assimilate.

Thomas Wilson Dorr, leader of the reformers and one of the more radical of them, was the son of a prominent Providence merchant and industrialist. Educated at Harvard, he became a lawyer and served in the Rhode Island legislature as a Whig from 1834 to 1837. Young, personable, dedicated, Dorr worked to reform the system of public education and to promote the antislavery movement as well as to extend the suffrage. It seemed wrong to him that men who paid taxes and were required to serve in the state militia were often denied the vote simply because they did not meet the property qualification. Among Dorr's followers were a number of working men led by Seth Luther, a Providence millworker and carpenter who took a more radical view than many of the Dorrites. Luther had founded one of the first working-man's organizations in Rhode Island and was a Loco-Foco (or radical) Jacksonian egalitarian. Like Dorr, he worked hard for free public education and against the exploitation of women and children in the factories. He thought every adult male should vote. While that attracted support to the movement from the Irish, it frightened away many of the more conservative Yankees.

Frustrated in his efforts to get the Whigs to support his suffrage reforms, Dorr became a Democrat in 1838. He came to view the suffrage as a natural right, not a privilege. But many native-born workers and many middle-class Whigs who wanted to change the charter to give themselves the vote were not particularly eager to go so far as Dorr and Luther in this matter. It was this cleavage within his own ranks and his refusal to compromise his principles that ultimately wrecked Dorr's revolution.

The first efforts toward political reform had started before Dorr rose to prominence. In 1821 and 1822, the towns had voted down efforts to draw up a new constitution; and in 1824 and 1834, though conventions were called, they accomplished nothing. Efforts to persuade the Whigs to support constitutional reform from 1834 to 1837 failed because they feared the Democrats would gain the most from it. In 1840 the reformers created the Rhode Island Suffrage Association to gain grass-roots support for replacing the charter and reapportioning the legislature. Soon it had local organizations in every town. In 1841 the association forced the legislature to call a constitutional convention. But when the legislature allowed only qualified property-holders to elect delegates to that convention and specified that only property-holders would ratify the results, the Suffrage Association decided that the convention would accomplish little. Led by Dorr, the reformers turned to the radical concept of popular sovereignty, arguing that, where the will of the people was consistently frustrated, they had the power to take matters into their own hands against would-be despots.

The Suffrage Association therefore called its own convention. They now spoke of themselves as "the People's party," and there is no doubt that they represented a widespread feeling that the old charter was no longer adequate. All adult, white, male citizens were entitled to vote for delegates to the "People's Convention." In the fall of 1841 the people of Rhode Island were faced with a choice between "the People's Constitution," drafted in August, and "the Landholders' Constitution," drafted in November. The legislature considered the People's convention totally illegal, but could not entirely ignore the wide popular support it received. In order to weaken support of the Dorrites, the Landholders' convention drew up a somewhat more liberal constitution than they would otherwise have done.

Comparison of the two constitutions consequently reveals less difference than might be expected. While the Landholders had moved to the left, the conservative reformers had forced the Dorrites to move to the right. For example, Dorr simply could not obtain a majority in the People's Convention to favor extending the suffrage to black citizens. Moreover, while both constitutions extended the suffrage to all white male citizens over twenty-one for elections to statewide office, both maintained some property qualifications for those who were allowed to vote on questions of taxes and government expenditures, which meant that persons not meeting these qualifications could not vote in town meetings on tax questions nor elect city councilors who drew up city tax levies. The People's Constitution had a slightly less restrictive clause in that respect than the Landholder's Constitution, but the principle was the same in both. The Landholder's Constitution required twice as long a residence in the state (two years as opposed to one) before a citizen from another state could vote and three years' residence for naturalized citizens before they could vote, unless they owned sufficient real property. The People's Constitution was more consistent in establishing a tripartite separation of the executive, legislative, and judicial branches (which the charter had united in the general assembly), but neither constitution adequately reapportioned the legislature to conform to the new demographic structure of the state. The People's Constitution gave somewhat more seats in the legislature to the urban areas under its reapportionment than the Landholders' party, but nowhere near what they rightly deserved. Under the existing charter system, the urban-industrial towns had roughly one-third of the seats in the legislature, though almost two-thirds of the population lived in such areas. Under the Landholders' Constitution, these urban towns would have received 40 percent of the seats; under the People's Constitution, they were to receive 50 percent. Fair representation would have given the urban towns 67 percent. Clearly, the People's party was willing to settle for a limited improvement favoring the middle class; they believed the rural areas were places of old Yankee virtue and saw no harm in giving them a somewhat larger share of votes than, demographically, they deserved.

The refusal of either constitution to return the suffrage to black citizens aroused considerable anger among blacks and among the growing number of abolitionists. In 1840 there were 3,238 blacks in a total state population of 108,837; 50 percent of them lived in Providence. William Lloyd Garrison, the great Boston abolitionist, denounced both constitutions in *The Liberator* for that shortcoming. Some of the most powerful abolitionist speakers in the country came to the state in the winter of 1841–1842 to demand equal political rights for black citizens. Frederick Douglass, Abby Kelly, and Stephen Foster held meetings in Newport and Providence on that topic; the speakers faced angry mobs with people from both parties defending black disfranchisement. The Reverend Alexander Crummell, then a lay reader in Christ Church Providence (an Episcopal mission church for blacks) worked strenuously to re-enfranchise black Rhode Islanders. So did other black leaders in Providence—James Hazard, Alfred Niger, Ransom Packer, Edward Barnes, and George C. Willis. In the end, they were successful, but not, ironically, with the People's party.

The People's Constitution came up first for ratification, before the Landholders' convention had finished its work. In the vote, under the auspices of the Suffrage Association, held in December 1841, 13,944 adult white male citizens voted in favor of this constitution, while only 52 opposed it (most opponents of course abstained from voting for an extralegal constitution). The Dorrites claimed that 13,944 constituted a majority of the state's free white males and hence (under the principle of popular sovereignty) the majority had spoken for a new government. Not only was the old charter now replaced, said the Dorrites, but the legislature elected under it must give way to one elected under the terms of the new People's Constitution. Furthermore, to clinch the case, Dorr noted that 4,960 voters identified themselves as qualified voters under the charter system—that is, they were "freemen" or holders of real property; that constituted, he said, a majority of the qualified voters, even by existing charter and statute regulations. The old legislature, however, would not concede that it had been superseded by the new popular movement. These legislators not only remained in office, but proceeded to hold a vote for ratification of the Landholders' Constitution in March 1842, as though the People's party did not even exist.

In a last-minute switch, the Landholders' Convention agreed to allow all native-born white males to vote for or against ratification of its constitution, thereby making its own claim to popular sovereignty. But the Dorrites opposed the Landholders' Constitution, and it was rejected by a vote of 8,689 to 8,013. If Dorr expected the old government to step down and let his party take over, however, he was sadly mistaken. The legislature and its executive officers simply continued to operate under the old charter. Fearing that the Dorrites would try to put their constitution into effect by force, the old legislature got a ruling from the State Supreme Judicial Court denying the validity of the People's Constitution. Then the legislature passed a law stating that any overt acts against the charter government would subject the perpetrators to trial for treason against the sovereign state of Rhode Island. Seth Luther said the workingmen of the state would obtain their civil liberties, "Peacefully if we can, forcibly if we must." [6]

The situation became tense, and nativist aspects of the rebellion came to the surface as the supporters of the charter government began to say in speeches, broadsides, and newspaper articles that the People's party (especially its radical wing led by Dorr and Luther) represented ignorant Irish Roman Catholics, labor union radicals, and persons interested in mob rule as opposed to respectable law and order. The People's party, ignoring the ruling of the State Supreme Court and the treason law, proceeded to conduct a statewide election for candidates for office in order to put the People's Constitution into effect. Dorr ran for governor, risking life imprisonment under the law. Since anyone who tried to assume office under the People's Constitu-

---

6. Louis Hartz, "Seth Luther," *New England Quarterly* 13, no. 3 (September 1940): 107.

tion took that risk, it was not easy to obtain candidates. In April 1842, a total of 6,359 citizens (by the new suffrage standards) voted for the People's party candidates. Those elected assembled in Providence in May, inaugurated Dorr as governor, and declared themselves the legitimate government. Meanwhile, the Landholders elected Samuel Ward King as governor, in Newport. The state now had two complete sets of officers, as well as two constitutions.

Governor King ordered Governor Dorr's arrest; but before he could be caught, Dorr left for Washington, D.C., at the request of his legislature, to try to persuade President John Tyler to take "the people's side" in the quarrel. Dorr argued that the federal constitution required Tyler to guarantee a republican form of government to each state, and that the charter government was not republican. Tyler would make no commitment, except to say that, if Dorr resorted to force, the federal government would support the charter government. Since Tyler was a state's-rights Southern Democrat, his stand indicated some political inconsistency. Stopping in New York City on the way back to Rhode Island, Dorr was given a banquet by the Tammany Hall Democrats, who offered the support of New York militiamen if he needed help.

The climax of this struggle occurred after midnight on May 17, 1842. Dorr, back in Providence and fully supported by Seth Luther and the Irish, obtained two old cannon and led a group of his supporters in an armed attack on the Providence arsenal. His force of 234 faced 200 defenders of the arsenal, but when Dorr ordered the cannon to be fired, they did not go off. Some claimed the guns were sabotaged. Great confusion then prevailed, and a fog settled over the area at about 2:00 A.M., as local militia rushed to the defense of the arsenal. Dorr's supporters retreated. No one was hurt, but the resort to armed rebellion lost Dorr the support of most moderates in the state and within his party. Many of those elected to serve under him thereupon resigned.

Fearing arrest, Dorr fled to Connecticut. On June 25 several hundred of his diehard supporters, again with Luther in the fore, rallied in the village of Chepachet, near the Connecticut border. Dorr came to lead them in a march on Providence. The charter government rallied the forces of law and order, and many black citizens in Providence volunteered to serve to protect the city—a shrewd political move, as it turned out. As the charter-government forces, twenty-five hundred strong, advanced, Dorr ordered his badly armed and outnumbered forces to disband. Dorr went to New Hampshire. The charter government, now calling itself "the Law-and-Order party," declared martial law and arrested several hundred of those who had participated in the arsenal attack, the armed assembly in Chepachet, and other treasonous acts. Luther was a prime target of political vengeance and, after arrest and trial, spent a year in jail in Newport.

In November 1842, the Law and Order party, now under Governor James Fenner, called another constitutional convention. This convention's work closely resembled the defeated Landholders' Constitution, except that, as a reward for their loyalty in defense of the city, black males over twenty-one were given the same suffrage rights as white males. This constitution specifically gave native-born citizens more liberal voting rights than naturalized citizens. Duly ratified by the voters, the new constitution went into effect in 1843, and the old charter was gone forever. In effect, Dorr won his point against the inadequacies of the old charter, though he failed to sustain the popular-sovereignty ideology of 1776 and 1787.

The Constitution of 1843 gave the urban industrial areas in the northern part of the state thirty-seven of the sixty-nine seats in the general assembly; though less than their fair share, that was far more than they had formerly had. To a great extent, that gain was nullified by the fact that each of the thirty towns in the state, no matter how small, was allowed at least one senator. Thus the rural areas still retained a majority of the upper house and a veto on the urban voters. Furthermore, while the new constitution increased the electorate by 60 percent, the extension benefited Yankee Protestants more than foreign-born Catholics. By express wording, the constitution made second-class citizens of naturalized (foreign-born) Americans who lacked the old real-property qualification. They could not vote in statewide or federal elections, although every male native citizen could vote without owning real property simply by paying a one-dollar "registry tax." A propertyless Yankee was considered a better citizen than a propertyless Irish-born citizen or a citizen born in any other country. Furthermore, nonpropertyholders and non-taxpayers, whether native or foreign-born, were not allowed to vote in town meetings when taxes or expenditures were concerned, nor could they vote for members of the city council in Providence—at that time the only city governed by a mayor and council. This meant that, in Providence, the native-born property holders would continue to control the city government though vastly outnumbered by the poor, who lacked property.

At that time, there was no secret ballot, and hence the practice of intimidating voters remained possible; that was especially effective in mill villages, where the millowners were all-powerful. Judges, while appointed without terminal dates, could be removed under this constitution at any time by a majority vote of the legislature, thus keeping the judiciary subservient to the Yankee property holders and those living in rural areas. Not until 1928 did naturalized citizens get full political equality; not till 1935 did the urban areas gain power over the rural areas; not till 1966 did the principle of one man, one vote prevail in Rhode Island.

In October 1843, Dorr returned to Rhode Island, gave himself up, stood trial, and was convicted of treason against the state. He was sentenced to life imprisonment at hard labor but was released after serving one year. His theory of popular sovereignty finally reached the United States Supreme Court in 1848, in the case of *Luther* v. *Borden*. Daniel Webster argued for the State of Rhode Island that Dorr's concept was nothing but an excuse for anarchy. In deciding that the matter was a political one and not subject to adjudication in the courts, the Supreme Court in effect gave Webster the victory. The decision ended the possibility that there was any peaceful way for the people to assert their sovereignty against a government legally elected, however corrupt it might be. Nevertheless, the Rhode Island legislature revoked the charge of treason against Dorr in 1854, just prior to his death at the age of 49. Dorr has, over the years, been reinstated to popularity as a hero of democratic egalitarianism, but his was a Pyrrhic victory if ever there was one.

Efforts by working-class reformers, like Seth Luther and Thomas Man, to ameliorate the condition of the millworkers in those years met with as little success as efforts by middle-class reformers like Welcome Sayles and Elizabeth Buffum Chace to help the poor. The operatives were powerless to help themselves because of the oversupply of cheap labor that made it easy to fire troublemakers and hire strikebreakers. The middle-class reformers were hamstrung by their own limited perception of the causes of poverty, their tendency to blame the poor for their plight.

There are records of sporadic strikes in the pre-Civil War years: one in 1824 is said to have been the first industrial strike in which women played a major role. But the only successful one appears to have been in the early 1830s, when some textile owners tried to extend the work day during winter by the use of candlelight in the mills. Middle-class reformers concentrated upon moral evils like intemperance, prostitution, and child labor. Welcome Sayles investigated the latter in 1851 and presented a devastating report on the exploitation of children in the state. Some effort was then made to prohibit employers from hiring children under twelve and to see that children were released from mill work for at least three months of schooling a year. But many families could not live without the income made by children, and millowners accepted false certificates of age and schooling. The early effort of Samuel Slater to provide schooling to children on Sundays at his own expense was not copied by other employers.

Elizabeth Buffum Chace, wife of the owner of a textile mill, wrote and worked constantly to help the poor from 1840 to 1880, but admitted in 1881 that the cause was "so difficult of solution" that she was discouraged. Recognizing that parents felt obliged to put their children to work because they needed their meager wages to survive, she nevertheless noted that most of these mothers were poor housekeepers and many of the fathers intemperate. She found it difficult to sympathize with "this class of our population who learn to depend as easily on the labor of young boys and girls for bread as for rum and tobacco.'' Moreover, she could not, after discussing the matter with her husband, find the wage system to blame. ''The employer is not wholly responsible,'' she wrote, ''partly because such labor is cheaper, partly because some work in factories can best be done by children.'' [7]

The workers themselves, whether native-born farmers or former Irish peasants, had always worked hard, and to them the family had always been a working unit. They welcomed the steady jobs and regular wages; poor as their pay was, they believed they were better off than they had been on their miserable farms. They too shared the dream that with hard work they might somehow lift themselves by their own bootstraps. Even when their grievances made them sympathetic with workingmen's associations, the millworkers could not afford union dues nor risk their ''future'' by going on strike.

Rhode Island did make some start toward a more widespread system of tax-supported public education in those years, even if the working class did not generally benefit by it. In 1800 John Howland, leader of the Providence Association of Mechanics and Manufacturers, persuaded the legislature to pass a law requiring every town to establish a free school. But three years later, only Providence, Bristol, Middletown, and Smithfield had complied with that law. Moreover, even these ''free schools'' required students to provide their own books and pay fees for school expenses, such as heating. (Children were asked to bring in their quarters and dollars to the schoolteacher, who bought the coal to fill the pot-bellied stoves in the classrooms.) The records show that in 1819 there were 192 schools of that sort scattered around the state. In 1828 the legislature established a permanent $10,000 school fund to supplement local taxes. That constituted the real beginning of public education. Three years later, the number of public schools had jumped to 592.

Even with state aid, most pupils in local schools were still charged for school supplies and fuel, until Thomas W. Dorr obtained a law preventing that in 1840. With the appointment of

7. L. B. C. Wyman and A. C. Wyman, *Elizabeth Buffum Chace*, 2 vols. (Boston: W. B. Clarke Co., 1914), 2:151.

Henry Barnard as state commissioner of education after 1842, Rhode Island at last joined the general movement throughout the nation to see that public schools with uniform standards for buildings, equipment, teachers, curriculum, and schedules were available—at least to the middle class. Barnard made a thorough study of the school system in 1843 and discovered that, while there were 30,000 children of school age, only 18,000 attended with any regularity. He estimated that the state needed at least 405 schools, while the number had dropped to 312, and at least 86 of them he found totally unfit. Black children attended all-black grammar schools and until 1868 were not allowed to attend public high schools where they would have had to be integrated with white children.

Despite notable efforts by Barnard and others to improve public education, only about 45 percent of the school-age children attended school regularly prior to the Civil War. As a result, Rhode Island had a very high illiteracy rate, especially for a northern state. The illiteracy rate was naturally highest among the Irish immigrants, whose children had so little opportunity for schooling, even after parochial schools began in the 1850s. But what was most startling was that the illiteracy rate increased faster than the population. Between 1850 and 1870, the state's population increased by 50 percent, while illiteracy increased by 367 percent. Obviously, the prosperity brought by industrialism was not trickling down to improve life at the bottom of the social ladder.

Economic and social divisions were magnified by religious and political antipathies. When not under pressure from the millowners (before the secret ballot), the foreign-born gravitated toward the Democratic party, thus further alienating themselves from the native-born Whigs and Republicans. As the Democrats became increasingly proslavery, middle-class Yankee reformers found another reason to dislike the Irish. The Irish made no secret of their disdain for the antislavery cause. Black Americans being the only group socially and economically below them, the Irish viewed blacks essentially as competitors for scarce jobs. Psychologically, the blacks demonstrated to the Irish that they were not absolutely at the bottom of society.

Much of the tension in the Dorr War stemmed from the anti-

Irish and anti-Catholic feeling among Dorr's opponents. With
the founding of nativist societies such as the Order of the Star-
Spangled Banner, in 1849, anti-Catholic bigotry became an
organized movement in Rhode Island, as it did throughout the
nation. Even before that, the Irish had been viewed as dangerous to the republic. A vote for "the People's Constitution,"
said one nativist broadside in 1842, "will place your government, your civil and political institutions, your public schools
and perhaps your religious privileges under the control of the
Pope of Rome through the medium of thousands of naturalized
foreign Catholics." [8] Newspapers—like the *Providence
Journal*—that were closely allied with the textile mill owners
and the Whig party filled their pages with such propaganda. It
was not coincidental that Yankee conservatism, Whig-
Republicanism, and anti-Catholicism helped to elect to the Senate a man like Henry B. Anthony, an owner and editor of the
Journal in these years. The fusion between politicians and Yankee businessmen was to dominate Rhode Island politics until the
1930s.

Roman Catholicism came late to Rhode Island and until the
1840s, its institutional growth was slow. A Boston priest who
traveled to Providence to conduct services occasionally in 1813
found only four communicants at mass; in 1820, he had eight.
The first Catholic parish was organized in 1828 in Newport and
the first Catholic church, Saint Mary's, was not built until 1829
in Pawtucket. Regular worship in Providence began in 1832,
but the church of Saints Peter and Paul was not completed until
1837. The influx of Irish immigrants began in the 1820s, and by
1835, there were about a thousand Catholics in the state. Two
decades later, however, Catholicism had become a major denomination in the urban areas. In 1844 Bishop William Tyler of
the diocese of Hartford took up residence in Providence, and ten
years later there were nineteen churches, sixteen priests, six parochial schools, and a Catholic orphanage in Rhode Island. The
Catholic population in Providence alone was almost ten thou-

8. Cited in Larry A. Rand, "The Know-Nothing Party in Rhode Island," *Rhode
Island History* 23, no. 4 (October 1964): 107.

sand by 1854. Parochial schooling started in the basement of
Saints Peter and Paul in 1845, but the first school building was
not erected until 1851, Saint Xavier's Academy. In 1855 there
were six hundred children in parochial schools; in 1865 the figure had doubled. But that constituted only a tiny fraction of the
Catholic children in the state.

The Know-Nothing or anti-Catholic movement reached a
peak in Rhode Island in the early 1850s, when the Whigs were
badly split over slavery (cotton being essential to the textile industry). The foreign-born had reached a proportion of one out of
every five inhabitants, and the old Yankee folk were beginning
to fear that control of their culture might be slipping from their
grasp. In 1854 a mysterious "Independent party" appeared, ostensibly campaigning for temperance but obviously including in
its ranks a large number of anti-Irish nativists. The movement
was also stimulated by new efforts by Thomas W. Dorr, Philip
Allen, and the Democrats from 1850 to 1854 to expand the
suffrage of naturalized voters by amending the constitution of
1843. Governor William Hoppin, a Whig, lent support in 1854
to an idle rumor of an armed Catholic conspiracy in the state.
He supplied arms and uniforms for the formation of a military
unit known as "the Guards of Liberty," whose enrollment was
conspicuously limited to native-born white Protestants. The
Providence Journal gave editorial support to increasing nativist
sentiment and facetiously suggested, in December 1854, that
restaurants and boardinghouses stop serving "Irish stew" and in
place of that "odious dish" they "substitute one which must
recommend itself to every real Yankee, viz. Johnny cake and
molasses." [9]

In March 1855 the Know-Nothings held a secret convention
in Providence and announced a complete slate of candidates.
That same month, Rhode Island almost had an anticonvent riot
when mysterious handbills were circulated on March 22, 1855,
falsely claiming that a young woman was being held against her
will in the convent of the Sisters of Mercy in Providence. The
next day, an angry mob milled around the gates of the convent

9. Cited in Rand, "The Know-Nothing Party in Rhode Island," p. 110.

for hours, while Bishop O'Reilly and loyal Catholic stalwarts stood guard within the gates. The incident ended without violence, but the furor created by it helped elect the Know-Nothing candidates a month later. They completely dominated the legislature (as they did also in Massachusetts, Connecticut, New Hampshire, and several other states)—a prime example of "the paranoid style" in American politics. Five out of every seven votes in the Rhode Island election went to the new party. The Whig and Know-Nothing tickets were both headed by William Hoppin, who won the governorship by 11,130 to 2,729. The vote for lieutenant governor showed 9,733 votes for the Know-Nothing ticket, 1,309 for the Whigs, 2,705 for the Democrats.

Little significant legislation emerged from this party sweep. A law was passed preventing state courts from naturalizing aliens, which meant that the foreign-born had to apply to the less easily available federal courts. A law empowered the state commissioners of education to visit nunneries and nonpublic schools. However, a bill requiring twenty-one years' residence by foreign-born before they would be eligible to vote was defeated. Such legislation might discourage immigration and cut into the supply of cheap labor.

In 1856 the mounting furor over the antislavery issue and the rise of the new Republican party led the Know-Nothings to unite with them on most nominations. Hoppin was re-elected, but the three-way vote for lieutenant governor showed the Know-Nothings now with only 7,882 votes, the Democrats coming back with 7,227, the Republicans with 1,306. Rhode Island was not vigorously supportive of the Republican party dedicated to alienating the cotton planters. Still, as the Know-Nothing movement faded from the scene, most of its ardent supporters moved into the Republican camp. Whig bigots like Henry Anthony rose quickly to leadership in the new party.

Rhode Island was not a vigorous antislavery state. The movement that had started with Moses Brown and Samuel Hopkins in the 1770s had virtually ceased after 1800, and slave traders were still evading the laws as late as 1818. The debate over the Missouri Compromise in 1820 revived the issue briefly. James Burrill, Rhode Island's federal senator, spoke strongly against the compromise because he feared it would expand the area of slavery. In 1835, at the request of William M. Chace, president of the Providence Anti-Slavery Society, the American Anti-Slavery Society, led by William Lloyd Garrison, agreed to send Henry B. Stanton to Rhode Island to promote the new doctrine of immediate abolition. With the help of James G. Birney, William Goodell, the Grimke sisters, and other abolition speakers, Stanton finally was able to form the Rhode Island Anti-Slavery Society in 1836 as the state branch of Garrison's national abolition movement. An abolition convention was held in February of that year at "Round Top" (Beneficent) Congregational Church in Providence at which 185 citizens resolved to support total, immediate, uncompensated emancipation of the slaves. Soon they had enlisted 300 members and raised $2,000 for continuing activity. They gained the support of Thomas W. Dorr and a few other Whig reformers, established headquarters in the stunning new Arcade Building in Providence, and petitioned Congress to abolish slavery in the District of Columbia.

Newport, which continued to attract many southern visitors every summer, as it had done since pre-Revolutionary days, when slaveholders felt at home there, became the center of antiabolition sentiment. Benjamin Hazard and Richard K. Randolph of Newport spoke strongly in the legislature in favor of an effort to prohibit the publication of abolitionist newspapers in the state in 1835. Randolph was a native of Virginia; he had married a Newport woman and settled there. As the Newport representative, he strove to prevent the legislature from instructing its congressmen to support abolition of slavery in the District of Columbia.

When the antislavery movement split nationally in 1840, the Rhode Island group sided with Garrison, rather than Stanton and Theodore Weld. Rhode Islanders opposed the formation of a third party dedicated to abolition and gave no support to the political side of the movement. Dedicated to higher moral principles, several of these abolitionists became involved in the underground railroad, helping fugitive slaves who got to Fall River or Providence by boat to get through the state to Worcester and from there north to Canada. Several Rhode Island homes still standing served as "stations" on this escape network. However, the abolition movement remained weak, actually declining in membership after 1840.

The state did not care for the war with Mexico in 1846. The legislature resolved that it was an unnecessary and most expensive war and suggested that President James K. Polk merited impeachment for his useless and constitutional invasion of that country. But undoubtedly that action, like the legislature's opposition to the annexation of Texas and the admission of California into the Union, was motivated by Whig political partisans. As a manufacturing state, Rhode Island, like the rest of New England, was dedicated to the Whig support of high tariffs and tended to use any political club it could to beat its opponents over the head. The Democrats, split between the native-born Jeffersonian agrarians and the foreign-born urban Jacksonians, were seldom any competition for the Whigs. The state voted for the Democrat, Franklin Pierce, for president in 1852, on his promise to ignore antislavery agitation and try to bind the country together.

Typical of the conservative Whigs in the state in these years was the Reverend Francis Wayland, president of Brown University from 1827 to 1855. Wayland was one of the leading Baptist ministers in the nation in those years and quickly established an enviable reputation as an educational reformer, raising Brown to a prominent position among American colleges. However, his attempt to reform the university's medical school so antagonized its staff that they resigned, and the medical program was eliminated. Wayland thought of himself primarily as a moral scientist and published important books on this subject, as well as on political economy. He had no use for Andrew Jackson, and his opposition to the Dorr Rebellion carried much weight with the community. Locally, he supported the efforts to expand public education, to reform the prisons, and to improve the hospitals, but he deplored more radical reforms like women's rights. He devoted most of his energies toward Baptist home and foreign missions and tried desperately to prevent the Baptist denomination from splitting into proslavery and antislavery factions. For that he was lauded by the southern Baptists and damned by northern abolitionists. His efforts proved unsuccessful, however; the denomination did split into northern and southern branches in 1845, much to his regret. Though morally opposed to slavery, Wayland could find no practical solution to the problem. However, after the Whig party collapsed, he transferred his support to the Republicans and became a great admirer of Abraham Lincoln.

By contrast, Rhode Island also produced an early leader of the feminist movement in Paulina Wright Davis. After the death of her first husband, Francis Wright, she married Thomas Davis, a wealthy jewelry manufacturer of Providence. Starting as an antislavery reformer, she discovered that, even in reform organizations, women were supposed to defer always to men and never speak in public. She concluded that a campaign for women's rights was as important as the effort to free the black slaves. In 1850 she helped to organize, in Worcester, Massachusetts, the first National Women's Rights Convention. In 1853 she published and edited one of the first women's rights newspapers in the country, entitled *Una*. After the Civil War she helped found the New England Woman Suffrage Association in 1868 and served as its president until 1870. Later she supported the National Woman Suffrage Association, along with Susan B. Anthony and Elizabeth Cady Stanton. Davis was as radical in her sphere as Wayland was moderate in his; but it was then a man's world, and he was more representative of Rhode Island's cultural viewpoint than she. As Wayland wrote, in his *Elements of Moral Science* (published in 1835 and frequently reprinted and used as a college textbook), "The law of marriage . . . makes the husband the head of the domestic society . . . . Hence the duty of the wife is submission and obedience."

Rhode Island opposed the Fugitive Slave Act in 1850, voted for John C. Fremont in 1856 and for Lincoln in 1860. It was firmly committed to holding the Union together. In 1860 it elected the wealthy and prestigious Democrat and textile manufacturer William Sprague as governor, because his opponent, Seth Padelford, was considered much too radical an abolitionist. The two Rhode Island congressmen elected in 1860 ran on the

Union ticket, a remnant of the Whig moderates who took no position on slavery (the Union party had nominated John Bell of Tennessee to run against Lincoln). Rhode Island's voters tried as strongly as they could to show the South they were not going to interfere in its peculiar institution.

Even after the southern states began to secede, Rhode Island demonstrated considerable sympathy for them. The legislature authorized Governor Sprague to appoint five delegates to the Virginia Peace Convention in November 1860. They were instructed to give a sympathetic ear to whatever concessions the South might want, to remain in the Union. In addition, in order to appease the South, the state ignominiously repealed its "personal liberty law" passed to thwart slave-catching after the Fugitive Slave Act. To sustain its economic relationship to the cotton planters, the state would have accepted almost any compromise.

But when the Confederates fired on Fort Sumter, Rhode Island rose to arms. The state immediately exceeded its quota of volunteers to meet Lincoln's call to sustain the Union. Throughout the war, the state never resorted to a draft, though it did have to spend considerable sums in bounties to meet later quotas. It also supplied soldiers for most of the major engagements and, in General Ambrose E. Burnside, produced a general worth erecting an equestrian statue to afterward—although his military record was far from distinguished, and the Irish remembered him chiefly for heedlessly sacrificing Irish foot soldiers in storming impregnable Confederate positions. A black regiment served for two years in the South. Symptomatic of the state's maritime decline was the fact that it played little role in the naval aspects of the war.

From the state's point of view, the most important aspect of the war was that it provided enormous profits in the textile and other manufacturing industries, despite the shortage of cotton. The population and assessed wealth of the city of Providence doubled in the decade 1860–1870. The need for additional labor combined with a farm depression in Quebec led to the beginning of French Canadian immigration during the war years; it proved to be one of the important new ethnic groups of the state in years to come.

After the war, Rhode Island, like the rest of the nation, entered what came to be called the Gilded Age. For the state, it was the beginning of a fabulous era of wealth and middle-class comfort. It was also the beginning of a long period of intensive political conflict and corruption, as the Yankees strove desperately to sustain their control against a growing ethnic majority. While factory smoke marked the prosperity of the northern part of the state, Newport suddenly revived as a glittering summer resort for the nation's new millionaires; their palatial mansions on Aquidneck still attract hosts of tourists who come to see how "the Four Hundred" used to live it up in the days before the income tax.

5

Prosperity, Respectability, and Corruption

*T*HE half century following the Civil War was the halcyon era of Rhode Island. In those years, the system worked. Not for everybody, but for enough. Never before had Rhode Island as a whole been so prosperous, so attractive a place to live and to invest in. Never before was the middle class so contentedly affluent—never before, and never again. But for that period, Rhode Island at last tasted national respectability, power, and recognition. Its manufacturers hobnobbed with the rich and powerful who controlled the nation—not only hobnobbed, but shared power, helped make the nation's decisions and policies. At last, Rhode Island reached the pinnacle of success as success was measured in the age of the Robber Barons.

Nelson Wilmarth Aldrich, the Rhode Island senator who dominated the tariff schedules in Congress at the turn of the century, was described, with considerable truth, as "the General Manager of the United States." [1] He was a master both of politics and business when these two were intimately related. He himself had risen from poverty to riches. Yet, with power came corruption—for Aldrich, for the Republican party he led,

1. Lincoln Steffens, "Rhode Island: A State for Sale," *McClure's Magazine* 24, no. 4 (February 1905): 337.

and the state he controlled. High-handed manipulation of the electoral process kept the Yankee Protestant majority in power and allowed the employers to treat their workers—men, women, and children—as mere elements of production. Rhode Island, the most densely populated, most heavily industrialized and urbanized state in the Union, was ruled by a small minority of business oligarchs and rural voters.

Lincoln Steffens, the muckraking political analyst of the Progressive Era, concluded after a visit here in 1904 that "The political condition of Rhode Island is notorious, acknowledged and it is shameful";—"Rhode Island is a State for sale and cheap." [2] The state was no more corrupt than many others; but, because of its size, the mechanics of the system were harder to hide. More ominous, but less visible, was the dangerous extent to which the state had mortgaged its future to the textile industry—lost its industrial flexibility and its zest for adventurous experimentation. The manufacture of cotton and wool seemed so solid and profitable that it bred a conservative impulse to keep a good thing going. Without realizing it, the state was suffering from economic hypertrophy.

Many essential features of Rhode Island's success and sickness can be delineated through the careers of Nelson Aldrich, his friends and cronies. Born in Foster, Rhode Island, in 1841, Aldrich's family heritage stretched back to the 1630s. His mother was a descendant of Roger Williams. His father was a ne'er-do-well mechanic who moved from one cotton mill to another, repairing the machines. Aldrich had a common-school education and attended a Methodist academy in East Greenwich, but never went to college. In 1858 he left home to seek his fortune in the rising city of Providence. He started work as a clerk in a wholesale grocery firm. During the Civil War, he spent three dull months in the Union army near Washington, D.C. He saw no action, but afterwards it proved helpful to his career that he was a war veteran, a member of the Grand Army of the Republic.

In 1865, he returned to the grocery business, at which he

2. Steffens, "Rhode Island: A State for Sale," p. 337.

proved very competent, especially at collecting back bills from debtors. He tried to educate himself by reading and debating; he joined the Masons and advanced to a junior partnership in the grocery firm. Marriage and a growing family led him to consider other ways of advancing in his career. In 1869 he ran for office in the Providence City Council. In that venture, he was backed by "Boss" Henry B. Anthony, the former owner and editor of the *Providence Journal*.

Anthony had gone to Congress in 1856 and was the state's senior senator in 1868. He headed the Grand Old Party, as the Republicans modestly called themselves, and basked in its reputation of saving the Union against treasonous Democrats and slaveholders. Anthony's faction in the party, sometimes known as "the *Journal* Ring," had for years used the *Journal* as the party's mouthpiece. Anthony's close colleagues were George W. Danielson, the editor, Henry W. Gardner, president of the Providence Steam Engine Company, and General Ambrose Burnside. Other Republican factions in Newport, Bristol, and Warwick sometimes challenged Anthony's dominant group in Providence, but they seldom succeeded. With the Democrats branded first as rebels and then as supporters of free trade and Populism in the rural areas and of Irish Catholic working men in the cities, the Republicans had politics pretty much to themselves. They represented solid patriotism and sound business enterprise. Those who ran the party ruled the state.

Unlike Roger Williams and Thomas Dorr, Aldrich had chosen—if he ever thought a choice was necessary—to go along with the dominant group and conform to its mores. That was the road to the top. Within a few years, he rose to the presidency of the City Council and proved so adept at politics that in 1875 the party asked him to run for the state legislature. Aldrich was elected and in 1876 became speaker of the house. Two years later, he ran successfully for Congress, and when old General Burnside died in 1881, Aldrich succeeded him as the junior senator from Rhode Island. Appointed to the influential Finance Committee, he found the perfect spot for his statistical and business abilities. He was an intelligent, hardworking man, a shrewd judge of people, and completely dedicated to the business ethic of his day. His greatest asset was his ability to persuade. He believed sincerely that his job as senator was to do what the big businessmen of Rhode Island wanted him to do, because what was good for them was good for his state and for the country. But he was never just a lackey for his constituents.

By 1881 the industrial revolution had reached the stage where co-operative effort was needed to prevent wasteful conflict among different business interests in the nation. Men like John D. Rockefeller and J. P. Morgan saw that; cartelization and concentration of control, not rugged, cut-throat competition, was essential for efficient, harmonious business and financial operations. Aldrich agreed completely. Rhode Island businessmen, deeply involved in textiles and metal manufacturing, were often short-sighted, he believed, in putting their local interests ahead of national interests. Aldrich realized that, if he simply looked out for his own constituents, he would pit himself in fruitless fights against other senators eager to aid their local interests. What American businessmen needed in Congress was a mediator, an honest broker, a man who could see all sides of a broad range of interests and harmonize the related needs of each for the best interests of all. Every businessman wanted the government to help him prosper (by raising tariffs on his products and lowering tariffs on his raw materials). Aldrich became "the General Manager of the United States" by heading the Senate's Finance Committee and its Steering Committee so as to set the best course for the most—or most important—businessmen. He learned to do that well. His word was reliable, and he performed what he promised. Because he was trusted, he was able to obtain more for his local constituents than if he had simply pushed aggressively for Rhode Island at the expense of everyone else. American businessmen, he said, should be partners, not competing enemies. That way, they could most effectively make the government work for them.

The major issues of the day, as businessmen saw them, being sound money and a high tariff to protect the nation from foreign competition, Aldrich made himself master of these basic policies. He agreed with the business community that agrarian reformers who supported the Greenback movement, the Grangers, the Populists, and William Jennings Bryan's Free Silverites, were "bad for business" and must be adamantly put down and kept down. He agreed also that tariffs should be high in order to keep out "unfair" competition. But here it became necessary to mediate between conflicting interests in the business community. Textile manufacturers wanted no tariff, or a very low one on raw materials—fine Egyptian cotton and Australian wool; but that pitted them against southern agribusiness interests in cotton and against western wool growers interested in high tariffs on foreign cotton and wool. Metal manufacturers in Rhode Island wanted a high tariff on British metal manufactures, but a low tariff, or none at all, upon various kinds of iron and steel imported by them to make their products. Yet, a low tariff on British iron and steel enabled the British to undersell firms in Pittsburgh and their subsidiaries in Birmingham, Alabama. Aldrich took on the delicate task of trying to satisfy everyone, persuading each to give a little here and there for the sake of the whole.

He thereby became the grand strategist of the Republican party on the all-important question of the tariff. He mastered not only the complex needs of the textile and metals industries, but the needs of manufacturers and businessmen throughout the nation. For example, he learned how to balance the West Coast (Spreckels) Hawaiian sugar interests against the East Coast (Havemeyer) Cuban sugar interests. And in the process, he dabbled in sugar investments himself and was duly rewarded to his immense financial gain. Eventually, since every tariff bill was a matter of horse-trading or log-rolling, since Aldrich mastered all the complex details of commerce in virtually every raw and manufactured product in the nation, and since largely on his say-so Congress moved tariff schedules up or down, he became the most indispensable man in the Senate.

Next to his deals in and for the sugar refiners, his prime personal interest was in tobacco. (He carefully stayed out of textiles, but not out of other Rhode Island business and commercial interests). He owned at one time more than one million dollars in the stock of the American Tobacco Company. Later he became interested in rubber. Because his work required constant attention to details, constant adjustments to changing technological improvements at home and abroad, Aldrich had to be totally dedicated. In keeping up with this immense task, he relied heavily on business lobbyists for essential information on business needs. From 1881 to 1911, when he retired, Aldrich managed to remain "the political boss of the United States Senate." He let others manage party politics and tried to keep himself out of the limelight, to give the appearance of nonpartisanship. Meanwhile, he kept iron control over party patronage and electioneering in his home state and amassed a large fortune for himself.

In his last years in office, Aldrich worked to create the Federal Reserve System, to provide a more efficient and stable currency for the American banking system, though that did not come into being until after his death. The driving force behind Aldrich's career was not bribery, though his henchmen did plenty of that at the local level, but love of political power. The fact that his business cronies frequently offered him positions of importance in their enterpises and lent him money to invest in sugar, tobacco, rubber, banks, street railways, gas, and electricity, he accepted as his due. In 1911 he retired to a palatial estate that he built for himself in Warwick; and his family, by marrying into the Rockefeller family, became members of the new "power elite" which still dominates American politics, society, and economic affairs. His Warwick estate (now a Roman Catholic seminary) was known in his day as "the house that sugar built."

To read the authorized version of Aldrich's biography, one would never know that he took any interest in Rhode Island politics or played any significant part in local business manipulations for his own profit. But, as Lincoln Steffens showed, that was not the way American politics worked. "Boss" Aldrich was put into political power by "Boss" Anthony and the *Journal* Ring. He was kept in office by "Boss" Brayton and the local ward and town machine bosses under him. Hence the story of Boss Brayton is an integral part of Senator Aldrich's and Rhode Island's success story; but it is the seamy side that his biographer was persuaded to ignore.

Charles R. Brayton was born in Warwick of an old Yankee family. His father had been a Republican congressman from

1857 to 1859. Brayton himself served with distinction in the Civil War and was discharged with the breveted rank of brigadier general. As a reward for his war service, Senator Anthony got General Brayton the position of United States Pension Officer for the state. This job required him to keep in close touch with all the state's veterans and enabled him to cajole them in one way or another into voting for the Anthony faction of the Grand Old Party. Later, Anthony had him appointed postmaster general of Rhode Island, which allowed him to dispense all local postmasterships and postal clerkships on a strictly party basis. Brayton was personable, resourceful, and when necessary, forceful. He made a fine art out of buying elections and managing the state legislature. He utilized every quirk in the Rhode Island constitution to keep Senator Anthony and his businessman's party in power.

Brayton and Anthony not only took care of all federal and local patronage positions, but gathered money for the party from the wealthy men who ran the textile and manufacturing concerns. In return, these businessmen obtained local legislation they needed and national tariff support. If they coveted power, they were allowed to run for various local offices. The governorship of the state, for example, became a kind of honorary office for big businessmen who liked to think of themselves as capping their private careers in "public service." Out of twenty-five governors of Rhode Island between 1860 and 1929, fourteen were millowners, bankers, or manufacturers; five were small businessmen; four were corporate lawyers, one a doctor, and one a newspaper editor. The latter two were "reform" governors. From 1856 to 1887, the Republicans elected every governor, every United States senator, every congressman, and controlled every legislature, with one exception. And they did almost as well in Aldrich's day. When Anthony died in 1884, Aldrich inherited his tight, efficient political machine and wisely kept Brayton to direct it.

Known as "the Blind Boss" after he began to lose his sight in 1900, Brayton was a professional politician who had no desire to run for high office. He was satisfied simply to manage political campaigns for others and make a modest fortune for

himself locally. He sported a walrus moustache, a Union officer's hat, and was described by one reporter as "a big, coarse,
powerful, dominant, masterful man." He used to address his
party workers as "Gentlemen and Fellow Machinists." [3] But
sometimes he overreached himself and embarrassed his party
chief. In the 1870s, vote-buying in Rhode Island had become so
blatant that two committees in the United States Senate examined the state's election frauds. Senator William A. Wallace of
Pennsylvania led one committee, and Senator Matthew C.
Butler of South Carolina, the other. Wallace's committee reported wholesale bribery and intimidation of voters by employers; it also noted that the property qualification disfranchised ten to fifteen thousand naturalized citizens—a fact that
his committee considered "unconstitutional." Senator Butler's
committee found Brayton guilty of breaking the civil service
regulations by requesting Republican party contributions from
all postal employees and firing those who refused. But neither
senatorial committee could get the Republican Congresses of
their day to take any action against such a loyal Republican
state. And of course Senators Anthony and Burnside, along with
Congressman Aldrich, stoutly denied all the charges.

In 1880, however, even Anthony and Aldrich could not save
Brayton from temporary disgrace. He had taken a bank loan of
$37,000 for some personal business venture and used postage
stamps belonging to the Post Office as collateral. When Anthony found out about it and made him get the stamps back,
Brayton foolishly embezzled $37,000 in postal funds to pay
back the loan. He was discovered and forced to resign, escaping
prosecution only when Republican party leaders surreptitiously
raised the money for him to repay the government. After only a
brief "vacation" outside the state, Brayton returned in 1881 to
resume his work for the party. Three years later, Aldrich helped
him obtain two new federal jobs, one as Indian Inspector for the
state and one as Postal Inspector. Brayton seemed throughout
his life to be the indispensable man for the respectable party

3. Mary C. N. Tanner, "General Charles R. Brayton," *The Rhode Island Yearbook*
(Providence: R. I. Yearbook Foundation, 1969), p. H–173, p. H–174.

chiefs. Every election year, Brayton carefully canvassed the state and estimated how much the party needed to win the election. Balancing patronage plums with bribes, he then conferred with Aldrich, who assessed the required sums upon the party's wealthy backers. Brayton then distributed these "donations" to meet the needs of the party workers in each town.

Brayton's job was made easy by the malapportionment in the state legislature, which gave the rural towns majority control. The small electorate in rural towns made vote buying easy and efficient. The going rate for a Rhode Island vote in Brayton's day was two dollars to five dollars in ordinary elections (according to Brayton) and fifteen dollars to thirty-five dollars in hotly contested elections. Some high-principled Yankees could not be bribed to vote against their consciences, but they were willing to accept money not to vote.

Brayton ran into difficulties only when party factions quarreled over important offices or when reformers raised ideological issues that could not be dealt with pragmatically. Prohibition was one of them, woman suffrage was not. The Democratic party regularly attacked the issue of malapportionment and the property qualification, but its most effective challenge was to Republican discrimination against ethnic groups. Not until the first and second generation of "born-in-America" ethnic groups reached voting age in large numbers, however, did the Democrats pose a significant threat. Until the 1930s Rhode Island's Yankee Protestant Republicans managed by hook or by crook to stave off that challenge. But occasionally, when corruption became too blatant, reform fervor cut temporarily into party loyalty.

Underneath, the system was changing in ways that no party bosses could prevent. To run its industrial system, Rhode Island needed cheap labor. The state became a lodestone for immigrants from Europe and Canada. Although the Irish predominated (if one included their children and grandchildren), the French Canadians were rapidly catching up. Known as "the Chinese of the East" for their docile willingness to work hard for low wages and for their loyalty to their language and culture, the French Candian foreign-born in Rhode Island outnumbered the Irish foreign-born 34,000 to 30,000 by 1910. Then, after 1890, a tremendous influx of Italian immigrants raised the total number of Italians to 27,000 by 1910 (1,000 below the number of English-born immigrants). The fourth prominent but smaller ethnic group came from Portugal (sometimes via Massachusetts), the Azores, and Cape Verde Islands. By 1910 there were 6,000 foreign-born Portuguese in the state, in addition to many who had been born here since the first immigration in the 1850s. Woonsocket, Central Falls, and Pawtucket in the Blackstone valley were the major centers of French and English Canadians; the Irish, Italians, and Portuguese centered in Providence and in the Pawtuxet valley.

By 1910 only 30 percent of the population in the state was of old Yankee stock; one-third of the population was born abroad and another 36 percent had at least one parent born abroad. After 1900 the majority of inhabitants in the state were Roman Catholic. Other important ethnic groups included Polish, Armenian, Scandinavian, English, Scottish, and Anglo-Canadian. Rhode Island had become a perfect patchwork of European settlements, as originally it had been a patchwork of ultra-Puritan sects. But Rhode Island did not become a melting pot.

The first desire of the immigrant in a strange land was to congregate near relatives and others from his native land who spoke his language, understood his customs, worshipped in the same manner. These immigrants also hoped to sustain the ethnic heritage they brought and pass it on to the next generation. For that purpose, parochial schools, where nuns and priests taught in the language of the parishioners, enabled the children to sustain their mother tongue, maintain the faith, keep up the customs, holy days, and saints' festivals. In many cases, the immigrants spoke little English; they were poor, divided, unfamiliar with American customs; they therefore became pliant tools of the industrial machine and did not at first realize how they were excluded from the political rights and privileges of their adopted land. Their priorities were to earn enough to stay alive, to send money back home, to buy a steamer ticket for a wife, brother, sister, or parent.

Whether huddled in the growing cities or isolated in the rural mill villages, the immigrant working class became a group apart from the dominant political and social structure, partly by choice, partly by exclusion, partly by ignorance of the system. The Irish, who came earliest and in the greatest numbers, could speak English—and thus adapted more quickly and were the first to learn how the political system operated. In learning to use it to their advantage, they rose to dominance in the Democratic party, and later immigrants had to challenge their leadership. But so long as the state constitution excluded naturalized citizens from voting by setting a high real-property qualification for them, the immigrants had to gain such power as they could by the same kind of political manipulation and bribery that they saw practiced against them. Brayton and the Republicans consequently found the Irish and the Democrats to be wily, if less affluent, opponents.

Rhode Island politics hinged upon the constitution of 1843. The dominance of the Yankees rested on the fact that the landless poor could not vote, and the urban areas were underrepresented. By 1910 the seven large factory towns around Providence (including that city) held two-thirds of the state's population, but twenty-two small towns with populations of fewer than 5,000 controlled the state senate. Furthermore, native-born but landless citizens were entitled to vote simply by paying the one-dollar registry tax one week before each election. Republican party workers happily paid that fee for those who supported their party. Qualification for foreign-born but naturalized citizens was not by a registry tax, but by ownership of more real property than most of them could afford to buy. Bribery of the rural Yankees was covered by the euphemistic claim that they deserved a few extra dollars to cover the expense of leaving their work and coming to the polling booth. In 1888 the *Providence Journal* reported, to no one's surprise, ''There is a purchasable and corrupt element in the state which has existed for many years sufficient to decide elections and both parties attempt to gain it. The Republicans had the most money [this year] and were successful.'' [4] But the Republicans always had

4. Caroll, *Rhode Island: Three Centuries of Democracy,* 2:659.

the most money. The Democrats won only when Republicans became angry with their own party and switched or stayed home.

Brayton at first had more trouble with the Prohibitionists than with the Democrats. They tended to be pious, rural Yankees or urban church folk who normally voted Republican. These Baptists, Methodists, Presbyterians, and Congregationalists exerted sufficient pressure on the legislature in 1886 to force through a constitutional amendment prohibiting the sale of alcoholic beverages throughout the state. Brayton found a way to kill two birds with one stone: first, he had the legislature appoint him chief of the state police (a newly created post) with a large staff in order to enforce the law; second, he had twelve new judges appointed to try those he caught. Being a noted tippler himself, he reported a year later that the law was "unenforceable"— unless, of course, the taxpayers wished to spend a lot of money hiring more state policemen and local judges. Outraged at Brayton's flouting of their will, the temperance-minded Republicans switched parties in 1887 and elected "Honest John" Davis, the first Democratic governor since pre-Civil War days. Brayton resigned as police chief, but a year later won back the governorship for his party. In 1888 the prohibition law was repealed.

To salve the pious Protestants' feelings, the legislature passed a local option law the same year, empowering those strongholds of prohibition sentiment to pass local ordinances prohibiting the licensing of taverns and saloons within their town limits. Since that left the urban areas, the real dens of iniquity, free to consume, the prohibitionists were not satisfied. They formed a Prohibition party that drained off sufficient votes to give the Democrats a fighting chance to win elections. It was in these years that the "expenses" for a rural vote increased to twenty-five or thirty-five dollars. To prevent that nuisance, the Republicans, who managed to win pluralities, if not outright majorities, in the three-party races, passed a law declaring that henceforth a plurality of votes would suffice to elect the governor. Despite the strong support of the Anti-Saloon League after 1896, the prohibition efforts always remained weak in Rhode Island. In 1919, when the rest of the nation adopted the eighteenth amendment, the Democrats and antitemperance Republicans in the state legislature not only voted against ratification but instructed the state's attorney general to challenge the legality of it.

The woman suffrage movement proved less difficult to contain, though in 1919 the state legislature did ratify the nineteenth federal amendment. Like the prohibition movement, woman suffrage arose in the 1880s. Supported chiefly by upper-middle-class, educated, urban-dwelling, Protestant women, it received little support either from the Democrats or the Republicans. Both parties feared that women's votes might be less amenable to machine control. Pious Protestants and traditional Catholics both thought women's place was in the home. But the movement was ably led by Elizabeth Buffum Chace, Sarah E. Doyle, Abby D. Weaver, Sara Algeo, and Eliza C. Weeden. In 1886 the feminists finally persuaded the legislature to consent to propose an amendment to the state constitution giving women the vote. The voters turned it down 21,957 to 6,889, and that ended legislative interest. Brown University, under the liberal leadership of President E. Benjamin Andrews (whom the conservative corporation almost fired in 1897 for his espousal of free silver) and under pressure from Sarah Doyle, consented to admit women for all degrees in 1892. Perhaps the fact that Elizabeth Buffum Chace's son was treasurer of the university helped. In 1897 the corporation established a women's counterpart to the college, called Pembroke College in Brown University—abolished in 1972 to make Brown coeducational. Women also obtained representation on the committee governing state prisons, the Rhode Island Institution for the Deaf, and the State Home and School for Children—all thought to be well within women's proper sphere. In 1893 married women won control over their own property and in 1896 won custody of their children. But not until the federal government took action did they acquire the vote.

Men were more successful in extending the suffrage to each other. In 1886, after twenty years of frustrating effort, the reformers finally persuaded the legislature to allow any soldier or sailor who had served in the Civil War to vote without meeting the property qualification. That increased the electorate by about two thousand voters, most of them naturalized Irish veterans. Two years later, the legislature took a major step by passing the Bourn Amendment, which ended the real-property qualification for naturalized citizens. That, in one sweep, increased the state's electorate by almost fifteen thousand. Much of the credit for that reform belongs to Charles E. Gorman, whose supporters became known as Gormanites or "neo-Dorrites" in the 1880s. Gorman was a major thorn in Brayton's side.

Born in Boston in 1844, he moved to Providence as a child, later studied law, and in 1870 became the first Irish Catholic elected to the legislature. In 1878 he and his supporters, mostly Democrats, presented a petition to Congress claiming that the Rhode Island constitution was in conflict with the federal constitution because it denied to the citizens of the state "a republican form of government." When the Senate Judiciary Committee denied the petition, Gorman organized an Equal Rights Association to lobby for a constitutional convention to do what the legislature refused to do. But the state supreme court stated in 1883 that, by the terms of the constitution of 1843, it was impossible to call a convention. Amendments, said the court, could be made only as specified in the constitution, by the vote of two consecutive legislatures (a general election intervening), ratified by 60 percent of the voters. Nevertheless, Republican arrogance and corruption at the time temporarily alienated sufficient voters in 1888 to force the legislature to pass the Bourn Amendment.

Augustus O. Bourn, a Republican state senator and wealthy rubber manufacturer from Bristol, was no friend of the Gormanites. His amendment, while framed to increase the electorate for general state officers, actually decreased the electorate who could vote for city councils. That is, Bourn's amendment dropped the real-property qualifications for naturalized citizens in state elections and mayoral elections but continued the real-property qualification for voting for city councilors or in town meetings where tax measures were being considered. Since other cities than Providence were now being run by city councils, this amendment, when ratified in 1888, actually extended Republican control over city government in the state. Moreover, because of rural malapportionment, it did not really alter Republican control of the legislature. In fact, many of the naturalized foreign-born enfranchised in 1888—especially among Anglo-Canadians, Scandinavians, English, and Scottish (most of whom were Protestants)—voted Republican. Other ethnic groups, resenting the tight Irish control of the Democratic party, often voted with the Republicans, especially when the Republicans began to give French Candians a place on their ticket. At best, the Bourn Amendment gave the Democrats an occasional chance to elect a governor or a mayor.

In 1901, when it seemed that the Democrats were close to winning the governorship with more regularity, Brayton engineered passage of "the Brayton Act." This effectively deprived the governor of his power to make administrative, judicial, or executive appointments; that power passed to the Republican-dominated senate. Deprived of this patronage, the governorship became thereafter largely an honorary post. Dr. Lucius F. C. Garvin, an ardent Democratic reformer and a follower of Henry George, was elected governor in 1902 and 1903, but he was so frustrated by the Brayton Act, the absence of a gubernatorial veto, and the willingness of many of his own party to play along with the Republicans for a few paltry gains, that he delivered an angry public message to the general assembly in 1903 frankly accusing most of its members of obtaining their seats by bribery: "That bribery exists to a great extent in the elections of this state is a matter of common knowledge," he said. "Many assemblymen occupy the seats they do by means of purchased votes. . . . bribery takes place openly [but] is not called bribery. . . . The money paid to the voter, whether two, five, or twenty dollars, is spoken of as 'payment for his time.' " [5] It was Garvin who provided much of the information for Lincoln Steffens's muckraking article in *McClure's* in 1904.

But as Steffens pointed out, bribery was not only a Republican enterprise. A Democratic boss of a small mill town told him, "The Republicans can come in there with more money than I have, and I can still hold it [that is, keep the town Demo-

5. Steffens, "Rhode Island: A State for Sale," p. 342.

cratic.] Suppose they have enough to pay ten dollars a vote and I can give but three; I tell my fellows [voters] to go over and get the ten and then come to me and get my three; that makes thirteen, but I tell them to vote my way. And they do." [6]

When Steffens asked Brayton about his use of bribery, Brayton defended it. "The Republican Party shouldn't be blamed for the present state of affairs. The Democrats are just as bad, or would be if they had the money." Brayton was also frank in noting that many wealthy millowners contributed to his slush fund only for congressional and presidential campaigns because they controlled the voters in their own towns without Brayton's help: "They give to the Republican campaign fund in Presidential years, but usually when you go to them to get money for state elections they say, 'Oh, we'll take care of our town'; so in that way all the towns in the state are peddled around, each manufacturer caring for his own town. Some of them haven't treated the party just right. The Republicans have never passed any legislation that would bother them, like the ten-hour law and things like that." [7]

Garvin explained part of the problem when he said, "The blame for the present order of things . . . belongs to the educated manufacturers and businessmen of the State who are too busy making money to pay attention to political conditions." [8] But of course most businessmen paid very close attention to politics when it concerned them directly.

However, the main roadblock for the Democrats was the malapportionment of the legislature. In 1905 Providence contained 40 percent of the population in the state but could elect only 16.75 percent of the members of the legislature. In 1905 several country towns, each with as few as 500 people, were entitled to one senator; and Pawtucket, a city of 43,000, also had one senator. Providence, with 175,000 people, elected just one senator. Or, to put it another way, 77 percent of the population

---

6. Steffens, "Rhode Island: A State for Sale," p. 342.
7. Steffens, "Rhode Island: A State for Sale," p. 343.
8. Edward Lowry, *To the People of Rhode Island: A Disclosure of Political Conditions* (n. p., n. d.), p. 7.

in 1906 elected only eight out of thirty-eight senators; 23 percent of the population elected the rest. Through control of the state senate (one town, one senator), 7.5 percent of the state's population (40,000 out of 428,000) controlled the state government. That 7.5 percent could block passage of any legislation asked for by the other 92.5 percent. Although control of the lower house was not as greatly distorted, malapportionment almost always gave the Republicans control of that as well.

The ultimate function of politics—at least as the leading merchants, businessmen, and manufacturers understood it—was to protect and promote the economic prosperity of the community. And if one believed in the theory of individualistic free enterprise, as Rhode Islanders obviously did, who knew better than the men of trade and finance what was best for Rhode Island? Their initiative, their judgment and imagination had kept the smallest colony and the tiniest state at the forefront of America's great success story. In making themselves rich, they provided opportunities for others to improve their lot. The wealth might be unevenly distributed, but in the long run everyone's standard of living rose. The best way to help those at the bottom was to help those at the top. And who was to deny that Rhode Island was prospering mightily under the leadership of its businessmen and bankers? By every conceivable measurement of economic growth, the state was a huge success in the Gilded Age and the Progressive Era.

Sparked by the textile and metal industries, which constituted 80 percent of its investment, Rhode Island's economy doubled and tripled in the two generations following the Civil War. Its rate of production, its volume and scale leaped prodigiously. Capital investment by domestic and foreign sources grew. Old factories cut costs, increased output, developed a wider variety of products, and improved technical skills. New, more complex, highly integrated mills and factories arose, and old ones were up-dated and consolidated. The number of employees increased; profits to investors increased, and the affluence of the middle class who served the growing population as wholesalers, retailers, lawyers, doctors, ministers, clerks, and shopkeepers increased. Rhode Island's humming mills and belching factories turned out such technically skilled work that at last it was able to enter the world market in competition with British and other European manufacturers. If the United States in those years finally achieved international status as a world power, as a manufacturing nation, shouldering its way into every market around the world as well as meeting the enormous needs of its own expanding empire, then Rhode Island was not only playing its part, but was at the forefront.

By 1890 Providence was, next to Philadelphia, the largest woollen-producing city in America. Rhode Island led all the states in the production of worsteds. It was among the five top states in the manufacture of cotton goods. Its jewelry and silverware were prized throughout the world. Its production of rubber goods, steam engines, and metal tools ranked with that of the largest industrial states. It had achieved such technical skills in the production of textiles that there was no form of cotton or woollen goods that its factories could not compete with. Simply to list the manifold variety of its textile products is the best way to indicate the richness and variety of its production. While it specialized in staples, such as cotton thread, yarn, cotton cloth, and cotton webbing, it also produced copious supplies of corduroy, velveteen, plush, twills, satin, broadcloth, voile, corded shirting, jeans, sheetings, flannels, draperies, bedspreads, blankets, broadloom jacquard fabrics, fine lawns, muslins, cross-barred muslins, cambrics, velours, pile fabrics, tire cord, tire fabrics, cotton wadding, book cloth, corset cloth, mohair, and upholstery materials of all kinds. Its companies were known across the nation for the quality and durability of their goods: Brown and Ives, Manville-Jenckes, Coats and Clark, B. B. & R. Knight, Dunnell, Lippitt, Chace, Hazard, Sprague, and Sayles were the leading family names in textiles, though their companies had many brand names—like "Fruit of the Loom"—which were more widely known.

In addition to producers of cotton and wool, the state contained a variety of nationally known manufacturers of other products: the Nicholson file, the Corliss steam engine, Rumford baking powder, Gorham silver, Manton ship windlass, Household sewing machine, Cottrell Printing, the Banigan, Davol, and Dunlop rubber companies, Providence Machine Company, Grinnell, American Screw Company, Brown and Sharpe tools— not to mention Horsford's Phosphates, Kendall's "Soapine" (the first soap powder for washing), and Perry Davis's "Pain Killer," a patent medicine praised by ministers and missionaries everywhere.

There were other companies, some of them big in their day, which became over-extended and failed. And there were opportunities started and lost—notably in the manufacture of locomotives, automobiles, and auto tires. Banigan Rubber was the founding company of United States Rubber Company, but the state could not hold it. Probably the outstanding business failure in the whole history of Rhode Island (and one that rocked other states as well) was that of the Sprague family business in 1873. It illustrated how big one Rhode Island firm could get and how mighty could be its fall.

Started in 1808 by William Sprague in Cranston, the company grew to be a three-million-dollar cotton-manufacturing firm by the time of his death in 1836. His sons William, Jr., and Amasa doubled its value in the next two decades. After 1856, William Sprague III increased the family worth to fifteen million dollars; A. & W. Sprague was now the largest business concern in the state and one of the giants in the nation. The Sprague family's investments went far beyond cotton textiles and far outside the state, extending from Georgia to Texas by 1870. They included lumber forests in Maine and water rights to possible mill sites in the southern states. There were investments in the New York Steamboat Line, Providence street railways (horsedrawn), agricultural land in Kansas, a horseshoe foundry, a mowing machine company, and several banks. Sprague had begun to speculate in coal and oil in Pennsylvania when the end came. Net value of the Spragues, the most powerful and wealthy family in Rhode Island, was said to be worth at least $19 million in 1873.

By entering politics, William Sprague III created many enemies, especially when he flouted Anthony's machine and spent $125,000 to get himself elected governor in 1860. After the war, he went on to become United States senator. His flagrant use of his wealth to muscle his way into the Senate was resented by the supporters of the *Journal* Ring in Providence. He then offended certain respectable old families by marrying the beautiful and ambitious daughter of Salmon P. Chase, whittling down "Boss" Anthony's power, and engaging in a riotous (some said drunken) social life in Washington, which he then extended to Rhode Island by building a fabulous mansion in Narragansett. Sprague helped to revive Narragansett as a summer resort area, building a track for trotting horses and bringing his wealthy political and business friends there for gala social affairs. Many Washington socialites preferred Narragansett to Newport.

However, Sprague developed powerful financial enemies in the state, especially those connected with the Providence firm of Brown, Goddard, and Ives, who were his chief rivals in wealth and power. They waited patiently for the flamboyant Sprague to overreach himself. Their opportunity came in the late 1860s, when Sprague's speculations exceeded his liquid capital, and he was forced to borrow heavily at high rates of interest. When the government gave up the wartime "greenbacks" and returned to hard money, Sprague found himself unable to meet his debts. As he tried desperately to hold off his creditors by borrowing from Providence banks, the Browns and Goddards used their influence to stop his credit. Sprague lost his head and attacked his rivals on the floor of the Senate in a wild speech. Finally, in 1873, with the collapse of Jay Cooke & Son, and the beginning of the great financial panic that year, the A. & W. Sprague Manufacturing Company had to declare itself bankrupt. The economic shock to the state was enormous. Few banks were not involved in some way, and thousands of small and large investors and creditors faced ruin. In addition, with 25 percent of the state's textile industry and 12,000 of its operatives tied up in the firm, it appeared that Sprague's ruin might drag countless others with him. His creditors consequently took steps to alleviate the situation. Although Sprague was in debt to the tune of $11 million, his assets were worth $19 million. With careful manipulation, the creditors might yet get their money returned. They joined together and appointed a trustee for the Sprague Company, a Providence ironmonger named Zechariah

Chafee. Chafee was given the power to take charge of all Sprague's enterprises and agreed to continue to run them. Their profits were to be turned over to the creditors each year until all were paid off. Chafee was given four years to work out the firm's financial problems.

However, Chafee was incompetent, if not crooked. He betrayed his trust and enriched himself by defrauding both the Sprague family and the creditors who appointed him. Almost $14 million of the Sprague assets were lost before the creditors discovered what Chafee was up to. Not even Nelson Aldrich could straighten out the mess, though he tried his best. The case went to court and dragged on until 1882. But Chafee, by clever legal maneuvers and special favors, managed to save himself from indictment. The creditors finally permitted Chafee to sell off the firms' remaining assets one by one. They were bought for a fraction of their value by competing firms, and Chafee emerged a rich man.

Yet so great was the impetus for industrial production in Rhode Island that what seemed like a catastrophe in 1873 scarcely impeded the tremendous expansion of the state's economy. But it did provide a warning that even the greatest firms and financial wizards could fail if they became overextended and inattentive to business.

Along with its dynamism in industrial growth, Rhode Island developed another source of wealth and fame almost as a byproduct. After 1865, "the Ocean State" revived as a summer resort, the playground of millionaires. Although this resort era is generally associated with Newport, half a dozen other places around the bay were equally attractive to different groups of summer visitors. Watch Hill on the southwestern tip of the coast was less lavish than Newport, but very fashionable to the quietly rich; Block Island and Jamestown were popular for those who wanted to hide away; Wickford and Narragansett Pier were popular for the more sporty crowd. And in addition to these exclusive places for the very rich, a score of other coves, bluffs, and beaches drew the middle class every summer. Large hotels and rows of cottages dotted the shore both east and west; and for the lower-middle class and the poor, amusement parks became the place to spend a day at the shore if one could not afford to rent a cottage for the season. Excursion boats paraded the bay night and day; mixed bathing became acceptable; anyone with social pretensions went sailing. Rocky Point, Riverside, Crescent Park, Boyden Heights built large piers, roller coasters, dance halls, and tried to rival Coney Island. The seaside was no longer a place for simple clam-diggers, but for gigantic clambakes. Of course respectable people carried parasols when they walked on the beach; suntans were associated with the working class or the hayseed farmer. Yachts of all shapes and sizes now cruised where formerly China clippers and African slave traders plied. Rhode Island was a pioneer in the new consumer art of summer vacations, resort places, and of tourism. This new area of enterprise was a huge success.

Newport became the most palatial, extravagant, and expensive summer resort the world had seen since the days of the Roman Empire. Here the big businessman was king and Aquidneck his country seat. Here he retired from the heat of the city and the bustle of business or sent his wife and family to demonstrate his affluence. Rhode Island profited, not only by its international fame as a resort area and not only by the thousands of dollars spent by these visitors, but also by the creation of magnificent architectural structures that, even today, though empty of gaiety, still stir the imagination. Yesterday's summer homes are today's museums and historic sights.

The Harvard philosopher George Santayana, who saw the idle rich in Boston at the turn of the century, said that Americans did not love money for itself but only for what they could spend it on. What else was business success for, if not to enjoy the fruits of one's labor in lavish recreation? The turn-of-the-century sociologist Thorstein Veblen looked upon Newport and coined the terms *conspicuous leisure, conspicuous consumption,* and *conspicuous waste.* But it was not all wasted. In fact, sociologically, it was put to very good use. Spending money properly became a sign not of wealth or power, but of breeding, refinement, and respectability, commodities that many of the

nouveaux riches millionaires and their wives sadly lacked and
frantically craved. And if money could buy these qualities, they
determined to acquire them.

Newport had been a summer resort for the out-of-state rich
long before the Gay Nineties made it internationally famous.
But in quieter ways. From 1750 to 1850, it was a summer resort
for southern slaveholding aristocrats fleeing summer heat and
malaria. In 1783 George Washington sent his ailing nephew
there to regain his health. A much different group of summer
residents came down from Boston after 1840—artists and literary people, mostly: Henry James, Sr., Henry Wadsworth Long-
fellow (who immortalized "the Viking Tower" in verse);
George Bancroft, Thomas Wentworth Higginson, Julia Ward
Howe (related to Rhode Island's revolutionary governor, Samuel Ward). With these literary folk came the artists John Singer
Sargent, John LaFarge, and William Morris Hunt. For a season
or two, Robert Louis Stevenson and Bret Harte joined these cul-
tured Bostonians. (Edgar Allen Poe found romance in Rhode
Island and became temporarily engaged to the beautiful local
poet, Sarah Whitman; but this was in Providence.) Summering
with friends or at resort hotels, the Bostonians did not feel the
necessity of establishing their rank in society by building gran-
diose summer houses. As of 1852, there were only twelve summer homes in Newport, and only four of them were built by
Bostonians. Summer life before 1870 centered at the Ocean
House Hotel, the Redwood Library, the Art Association of
Newport, and the Newport Reading Room.

But as industrial wealth increased after the Civil War and
new-rich New Yorkers began to seek the prestige of recreating
where the Boston Brahmins summered, Newport underwent its
third metamorphosis. Samuel Ward McAllister is generally
credited with bringing the New York upper class to Newport.
He coined the term *the Four Hundred* in 1888 to help New
Yorkers establish the social register of families worth knowing
and inviting to one's parties. Born in Savannah, Georgia, in
1827 (but also a descendant of the Rhode Island Wards), McAllister had come to Newport as a boy with other southerners.
After making a small fortune as a lawyer in San Francisco and

marrying the daughter of a millionaire in 1853, he bought a summer home in Newport but lived in New York. By the 1870s, he had become the confidante and advisor of Mrs. William Backhouse Astor and helped her persuade the leaders of New York's Four Hundred to make Newport the summer extension of their New York social life. While their husbands continued to work in the city, (making only hurried weekend trips on the Fall River steamers), the wives of the nouveaux riches at last found a place where they could dominate every aspect of activity.

The women who created and sustained the complex ceremonial life at the top level of America's social hierarchy from 1875 to 1920 were not brainless big-spenders, but talented, shrewd, and forceful administrators. Fitting counterparts to their husbands in managerial skill, these women were given huge summer budgets (sometimes $100,000 to $300,000 for a season—which would be worth five times that sum today) to administer their palatial estates. They were the board of directors of magnificent luxury retreats operated upon very demanding standards. The amount of planning, organization, and creativity needed to maintain the pace of Newport's summer social events year after year was tremendous. Only astute women of great energy, will, and efficiency could cope with it. Though they called their summer homes "cottages," these places were, in effect, resort hotels or palaces, with fifty to seventy rooms, large stables, horses and carriages, spacious lawns and gardens, greenhouses for daily flowers. To keep such extensive establishments functioning required the careful overseeing of scores of employees—butlers, maids, groundskeepers, stablehands, caterers—perhaps as many as fifty to a hundred for ordinary daily routine and twice that for special events. These women had to be able, on short notice, to plan elaborate dinners, balls, and outings involving scores of guests. If the southern lady of the antebellum slave plantation is to be praised for her managerial skills as mistress of a huge estate and retinue, the same credit must be given to these determined, capable, businesslike women.

There was more to being a leader of society than simply

knowing what to wear, how to hold one's parasol, and which fork to use. To run these establishments without friction, to keep them functioning smoothly for an endless stream of guests, to provide new and exciting ways of passing the time, and yet always to seem a lady of leisure, grace, and wit—these skills required talent of a high order. Money alone could not do it. In its subtle way, Newport society life was a training ground for the second generation of the industrial elite. It was anything but frivolous or leisurely. At Newport, women were given the task of establishing and sustaining the prestige and power of their husbands. Mere money, which the men made in the jungle of business and finance, was not sufficient to establish "class." Nor was mere ostentation. Class was established by an increasingly rigid code of conduct and behavior that took training and patience. Women's role in this upper echelon of power was to create an aura of taste and refinement in the lavish expenditure of disposable wealth. Sometimes the effort became ludicrous, among those without skill or wit—the mere aping of European manners, the uncontrollable urge to marry into royalty. Many women made fools of their husbands and pawns of their sons and daughters in the scramble. One estimate lists five hundred American heiresses married to titled Europeans by 1909, with doweries totalling $220 million. The outstanding example was the marriage of Consuela Vanderbilt to the ninth Duke of Marlborough in 1895; the Duke is alleged to have set $10 million as the price for making her his duchess. (The marriage did not last, and she returned to Newport sadder and wiser.) In the end, "high society life" at Newport became as cutthroat as the stock exchange on Wall Street. Summer leisure was as serious as winter business. Only the cleverest survived.

In another respect, for those who dabble in psycho-history, it might be said that Newport society life was the place where wealthy women had their revenge upon their husbands. Here women were the queen bees and the men mere drones—conveniences to hang an arm upon or to manipulate for purposes of display or marriage. Not only did husbands have to foot the bill, but they had to play the women's game at Newport. A businessman's prestige hung upon his ability to dance to the tune set by his women. The women were the peacocks of the walk; their men often appeared drab and boorish beside them—out of their element. Some men, lacking in grace and charm, ill at ease in dress suits and formal functions, inept at small talk, were unable to play this game nearly so well as their wives and daughters. To escape the endless round of teas, luncheons, dinners, cotillions, musicales, and picnics, they formed men's clubs or built huge yachts and took to the high seas.

Few Rhode Islanders participated in this social set, though they built summer homes at other resort areas around the bay. Newport, like these other resorts, benefited from the spending-and-building summer visitors both in the short and the long run, for these homes are still wondrous to behold. Fortunately for the colonial architecture of Newport, the New York set built their palatial mansions around the rocky southern tip of Aquidneck, rather than in the old harbor area. Still, to keep up with the Astors, Vanderbilts, and Van Rensselaers, a great many older wooden houses and hotels had to be torn down. In their places arose immense palaces of limestone, granite, and marble, costing hundreds of thousands of dollars—sometimes millions. The most expensive were William K. Vanderbilt's Marble House (1892), Cornelius Vanderbilt's The Breakers (1892–1895), and Oliver Hazard Perry Belmont's Belcourt (1894), each costing from five to ten million if one includes the outhouses, stables, landscaping, and interior decorating. Rhode Island's wealthy manufacturers could not compete in that class.

Unfortunately, original architectural genius did not flourish in that climate. American artists were as unsure of themselves as American socialites, when it came to taste and refinement. So they took the easy way out and imitated the art and taste of the European upper class. The architecture of Newport's golden age was fabulously expensive, but exhibited a hodgepodge of transplanted styles. E. J. Berwin, the Pennsylvania coal magnate, had his architect, Horace Trumbauer, build The Elms in 1902 in imitation of the eighteenth-century Chateau d'Asnière near Paris. O. H. P. Belmont's architect, Richard Morris Hunt, based Belcourt upon a hunting lodge of Louis XIII of France. W. K. Vanderbilt's Marble House (also by Hunt) was made of

Italian marble and modeled after the Grand Trianon at Versailles. Visitors today may marvel at seeing these European chateaux on the island of the Narragansett Indians, but they added little to the development of American architecture. In fact, the most creative American architects at the turn of the century lashed out bitterly against this sterile, conformist, "Beaux-Arts school."

The mad whirl of Newport summer society lasted only a generation. Today its monuments can still be seen along Bellevue Avenue, Ochre Point Road, and Ocean Drive, but the grandeur is gone. The tiny southern tip of Aquidneck proved too small for the motorcar life-style of the Jazz Age. The rich found new summer spots, and the income tax and rising property taxes made the cost of maintaining these chateaux prohibitive, even for millionaires. The Fall River Steamship Line faded into decay. The Old Colony Railroad, which had carried the Four Hundred from the wharf at Fall River to Newport in plush parlor cars, abandoned its tracks. With the Wall Street crash of 1929, Newport's third era as a summer resort fell, too. Since then, it has become bad form to display one's wealth, and one "jets" to foreign islands for exotic surroundings. One by one, the great Newport mansions were boarded up, destroyed by vandals and fire, sold for taxes, torn down, or converted to other uses. Mrs. Stuyvesant Fish's palace is now cut up into middle-income apartments, its lawn and garden filled with sandboxes, jungle gyms, and Volkswagens. The French chateau Ochre Court, (built for Ogden Goelet in 1888), is now a Catholic college, Salve Regina, with crosses on its battlements and a statue of Jesus in front of its massive porch.

Thanks to the lavish gifts and splendid organization ability of Miss Doris Duke of the Newport Restoration Foundation and Mrs. G. H. Warren of the Preservation Society of Newport County, half a dozen of these mansions have been preserved and restored, along with some of the older colonial mansions and ordinary colonial homes in the city. The former inspire awesome gasps (and settings for Hollywood movies), but the latter seem more livable, honest, and American—though of course they too were imitations of European models. Worth remark, however, is one native craft that developed to a high form of art in catering to the rich in the Gilded Age: yacht building. Just as local colonial craftsmen like the Goddards and Townsends developed magnificent skill and originality in designing furniture for the merchant grandees of eighteenth-century Newport, so the Herreshoff family in Bristol developed a similar talent in building racing and pleasure yachts for those who could afford them in their day.

John B., Nathanael, and James Herreshoff established their shipyard in Bristol in the 1840s. Their skill at nautical engineering brought them many commissions from the rich of Newport and elsewhere to design and build yachts, but the most famous ships they ever built were those to defend the America's Cup. Although the America's Cup races did not take place off the Newport coast until after 1930, the Herreshoffs were building the world-championship yachts in the 1890s. Their first such boat was the *Vigilant,* which won the cup in 1893. Over the next twenty-seven years, Herreshoff racing yachts won eighteen of twenty individual races with British contenders and never lost a match of the best three-out-of-five to any contender. The Herreshoffs designed every cup winner from 1893 to 1937. It is a pity that these beautiful craft cannot be preserved the way Goddard furniture and Newport mansions have been; they constitute a truly original form of American artistic skill.

One other form of native craftsmanship in this era deserves mention in connection with the new interest in summer resort activities. While the Herreshoffs were master builders for the rich, Charles I. D. Looff was a folk artist catering to the summer pleasures of the middling poor. He built carousels, the most beautiful and unique ever produced in America. His wood-carving art was central to the new business of amusement parks, and before he came to Rhode Island, he built the first steam-powered carousel for Coney Island. Looff established a factory to build merry-go-rounds in Riverside, Rhode Island, in the 1890s. His entrepreneurial skill brought to that town the title "the Coney Island of New England." It took millions to own a Herreshoff yacht, but for a few pennies, anyone could ride a Looff merry-go-round. Looff's hand-carved horses, camels, and dragons were masterpieces of action and color; the music of his steam calliopes lifted the spirits of thousands as his mechanical levers lifted the whirling wooden managerie. Owners of amusement parks came from all over America to commission Looff to build carousels to their specifications. Each one was handcrafted and so well constructed that they still function daily in parks around the country. (Only recently, a marvelous specimen of Looff's work was removed from Roger Williams Park in Providence to a resort in Virginia). The most fabulous carousel of all, which Looff used as a showcase for his varied animal figures, is still in daily use at Cresent Park in Riverside.

In the same years that Newport mansions were being equipped with exquisite crystal chandeliers lighted by gas, the city of Providence was undergoing a dramatic transition to electric lighting and electric power. The man who engineered that transition and became a millionaire in the process was Marsden J. Perry. At his death, Perry was referred to as "the man who owned Rhode Island." His career, like that of "the General Manger of the United States," is a perfect example of the integral relationship between politics and industrial progress. Without the ability to control the city councils of Providence and its related metropolitan area, and without important assistance from "Boss" Brayton in the state legislature, Marsden Perry could not have become the utility baron of the state. Which meant, of course, that he had to work closely with "Boss" Aldrich, as well. Yet, in many respects, like Aldrich, Perry was considered a self-made man, a living example of the Reverend Horatio Alger's stories so popular at the end of the nineteenth century.

Born on a farm in Rehoboth, Massachusetts, just across the eastern border of Rhode Island, in 1850, Perry came to Providence at the age of twenty-one with little money and no friends. But he was of good old Yankee stock. He formed a small loan-broker's office in 1874, when the nation was in the grip of a depression, and cash was hard to get. By charging high rates of interest on short-term loans, he earned enough within seven years to start the American Ring Traveler Company, which manufactured a special piece of equipment for textile firms. When he sold the company in 1889, he obtained his first large sum for capital investment. Meanwhile, he had entered the banking business by buying some shares in a small Providence bank called the Bank of America. It was capitalized at only $287,000 when Perry became its director in 1881. But the bank's president was Zechariah Chafee, the crooked executor of the great Sprague estate, and Chafee found Perry a valuable accomplice in milking that trust. By 1905 the Bank of America had been reorganized as the Union Trust Company, with assets of $30 million, and Perry had succeeded Chafee as its president. But by 1905, Perry had made his own mark on Rhode Island finance. He did it by seeing, as Chafee did not, the important opportunity available to the man who could corner the new source of power that would replace water and steam as the basis for all the state's manufacturing.

In 1882 the electric power business was just beginning, and Perry got in on the ground floor. First, he bought up the small Fall River Electric Lighting Company and then the Narragansett Electric Company in Providence. The latter was then so small that Perry got it for $25,000 in 1884. Five years later, he bought out its only rival, the Rhode Island Electric Lighting Company. Utilities were able to fly in the face of the American shibboleth about competitive free enterprise by adopting the term *natural monopolies*. It made sense to have only one firm running electric lines in a city (or gas pipes or water mains), but somehow it never seemed possible to regulate these "public" utilities adequately. Many cities took them over for the public, but not in Rhode Island.

In 1889 Perry built a large power plant in Providence, encouraged manufacturers to switch to electric power and home owners to switch from gas lighting to electric lighting, and then used his profits from electricity to buy out the gas companies. For a time, gas remained competitive for lighting purposes and home cooking, so Perry took over both. Then he moved into water companies, and finally, as streetcars left horsepower for electric trolley lines, Perry took them over, as well. No one ever doubted his keen business judgment and shrewd managerial skill. But it is also apparent that he rode the crest of a massive technological change taking place throughout the nation.

The revolution in streetcar services also stimulated a demographic revolution, as millions of city dwellers moved to the suburbs to get away from the increasing crowds, smoke, dirt, and noise. Electric streetcars were the key to rapid, efficient, easy, cheap commuting, in the days before the automobile. Furthermore, gas, water, and electricity were the keys to more comfortable living conditions in the suburban home. Though Perry started in Providence, he soon expanded his utilities empire to the whole metropolitan region of northern Rhode Island. In 1896 he acquired the East Providence Water Company. His streetcar lines extended first to Pawtucket, the state's second-largest city, then to North Providence, Cranston, and Warwick. Perry's utility monopolies served 70 percent of the state's population and its most concentrated textile and manufacturing area.

Perry could not have accomplished all that without inside political help. Aldrich and Brayton proved more than willing to assist him. To protect the heavy investment required for these utilities in the early years, Perry needed "exclusive" and "long-term" franchises from Providence and the surrounding city councils, otherwise he could not get the banks to lend him the money for buying up the horse-car companies, laying new tracks and trolley wires, purchasing new trolley cars, expanding power plants, digging gas and water pipelines, building repair shops and trolley stations, and so on. With Brayton's help, he got the legislature in 1891 to pass a law permitting towns and cities to grant monopoly franchises for up to twenty-five years. With Aldrich's help, he obtained the millions he needed for investment.

Aldrich had connections with Philadelphia's Havemeyer Sugar Refining Trust, which was grateful to him for help with tariff rates on sugar—and expected more help. The Havemeyers agreed to lend Aldrich $5 million to go into the electric-streetcar business with Perry. The Havemeyers were closely associated with the Elkinses and Wideners, who were managing the streetcars of Philadelphia and knew a good deal when they saw one. Then, with the backing of carefully selected New York and Providence bankers, the Perry-Aldrich-Havemeyer syndicate bought up all the horse-car companies and their franchises in Providence and Pawtucket, early in 1893. On March 1, 1893, the syndicate incorporated the United Traction and Electric Company in New Jersey, where incorporation was easy and flexible, as the holding company for their Rhode Island streetcar system. Aldrich became the company president; John Searles of the sugar trust became vice-president; William G. Roelker, a Providence lawyer and Republican state senator, was secretary-treasurer. Perry was the leading figure on the board of directors, which included the bankers concerned.

The company issued eight million dollars' worth of watered stock, and the Central Trust Company of New York granted a forty-year mortgage to raise another eight million. Several million shares of this stock were given outright to Aldrich, Perry, and Roelker. Using that money, Perry supervised the electrification of the streetcar system of metropolitan Providence (his own electric companies provided the power), and by 1895 Rhode Island had an up-to-date trolley system. In 1900 there were 218 miles of trolley track in the state, carrying fifty-three million passengers a year. Brayton was retained as legal counsel for Perry's company and more than earned his legal "fees" by seeing that the necessary local and state legislation was passed to grease the wheels of progress. The most important service Brayton performed was the passage in 1896 of a law granting a "perpetual" franchise to the street railway company to replace the old twenty-to-twenty-five-year franchises. It was not popular because people feared "perpetual" grants to monopolies, but it passed at a special session of the legislature held at Aldrich's convenience in Newport; he personally testified on the importance of the measure to the public welfare. That law also included a ridiculously low tax rate on the company; it also effectively took control of the streetcar system out of the hands of the cities concerned and turned it over to Perry and his board of directors.

Perry's influence over the streetcar and other utilities was so dominant that he was easily able to manipulate the power of the political system to control his workers. When a strike broke out among the streetcar workers in 1902, the police force was used to see that the cars ran on time, with strikebreakers at the controls. When the legislature made the mistake of passing a ten-hour work law that applied to streetcar workers, Perry got Brayton to have it repealed. "Governors may come and go," said one newspaper, "but General Brayton never loses his grip on the trolley." [9] After breaking the strike, Perry sold his control over the company to the Rhode Island Company for more than a million dollars, though the Philadelphia syndicate that owned the company retained him as president. He was now sufficiently well off to purchase the splendid colonial mansion built by the merchant buccaneer John Brown in 1786, on the corner of Benefit and Power Streets.

Perry's career did not stop there. He was also influential in reorganizing the banking structure of the state. With the founding of the Rhode Island Hospital Trust in 1867, the Industrial Trust Company in 1886, and Perry's Union Trust Company in 1890, this form of banking institution became more popular with investors than national banks. Chartered by the state, they were less rigidly regulated than banks operating under federal control; hence they could pay higher interest rates to depositors and better dividends to stockholders. Perry joined the trust company bankers in liquidating the oversupply of national banks and consolidating the state's banking facilities into a few giant firms dominated by the big trust companies. The intricacies of these maneuvers were devious, but the results made millions for Perry and those like Samuel Pomeroy Colt (head of the Industrial Trust) who were in on it. As president of the Union Trust Company, the Narragansett Electric Company, and the Rhode Island [Streetcar and Gas] Company, Perry in 1906 was one of the most powerful men in Rhode Island.

One of Perry's last accomplishments was to solidify the control of the New Haven Railroad over New England's railroad and steamship system. Appointed as receiver for the bankrupt New York and New England Railroad in 1893 by "Boss" Platt of New York, Perry delivered its assets to the New Haven a year later, as Platt expected him to do. Though the New York and New England had no track in Rhode Island, its system

9. Tanner, "General Charles R. Brayton," p. H–173.

posed the only possible competition for the New Haven's monopoly of rail traffic from New York to Boston and Springfield. Thereafter, the New Haven and its managers became a basic force in the economy of every New England state. Within Rhode Island, however, Perry's complex interurban electric railways were able to offer effective carrying competition with the New Haven for short-haul freight. Consequently, in 1906 and 1907, the New Haven Railroad Company, aided by J. P. Morgan and Charles S. Mellen, bought up the Rhode Island Company at four times its real value and thereby ended that competition for its freight business. Perry, a large shareholder in the Rhode Island Company, again profited handsomely by that consolidation of power.

Perry's downfall came partly as a result of the panic of 1907 and partly as the result of mounting public antagonism toward his (and Brayton's) arrogant management of the public service monopolies. The latter temporarily weakened the political power of Brayton during a rebellion of "Progressive reformers" in the Republican party and prevented the election of Aldrich's friend Samuel P. Colt to the United States Senate in 1907. It also led to the election of a Democrat, James Higgins, as the first Irish-Catholic governor. The triumph of the Democrats and Progressive Republicans was short-lived, but the impact of the panic produced a run on the Union Trust Company that ruined Perry's financial power base. He was forced to resign in 1908, both as head of the Union Trust and of the Narragansett Electric Company. Though hardly reduced to poverty, he ceased after that to be a significant political or financial force in the state.

Even during the Progressive Era, the old Yankees found it difficult to overcome their prejudice against foreigners. Higgins was a respectable lawyer, but most of the Irish, French Canadians, and Italians were seen as racially inferior to the Anglo-Saxons—at least, by the best social scientists of the day and the informed public. One political scientist at Brown University wrote, in 1909, "In certain respects the growing numbers of the Irish have contributed their share to social instability and accentuated certain social prejudices of a grave sort. The unfortunate historical environment of the race in its native land, and the systematic representation of Great Britain as a copious source of injustice and oppression, have unquestionably helped to retard in certain elements of the Irish people that distinctive regard for government, law, and order which characterizes the highest Anglo-Saxon civilization." [10] The Irish, it was noted, were of Celtic ancestry. While the "decent" citizens of Rhode Island sometimes deplored the corruption of the Republican party, they could seldom bring themselves to vote against it.

However, in 1909, the Progressive Republicans did join with the Democrats to obtain a constitutional amendment that took a small step toward legislative reapportionment. It increased the size of the lower house from seventy-two to a hundred members and required that seats be reapportioned by population, according to prescribed districts. However, no city (meaning Providence) was to have more than twenty-five representatives, and every town was entitled to at least one in the lower house. That meant an increase of from twelve to twenty-five representatives for Providence, (though by population it deserved closer to fifty seats). The state senate continued to have one senator from each town. In drawing the lines for districts in the lower house, the Republicans carefully gerrymandered them so as to assure the election of as many Republicans as they could. In 1910 the governor's role was strengthened somewhat by giving him the veto power, though the Brayton Act was not repealed. Despite its heavy urbanization and the fact that the majority of its citizens were now Roman Catholics of recent immigration, Rhode Island remained in the hands of the rural and Yankee citizens for another quarter century. And despite the fact that the Democrats needed all the unity they could muster, they frequently quarreled among themselves—Bryanite farmers against urban workers, Irish party leaders against new ethnic groups.

There is no way to find out the precise size of each ethnic group because census statistics do not include those who, though born in the United States, were the children or grandchildren of immigrants and associated socially and politically

10. William McDonald, "Population," in *A Modern City,* edited by William Kirk (Chicago: University of Chicago Press, 1909), p. 50.

with their ethnic ancestry. It seems clear that the Irish constituted the largest of these; the French Canadians were a close second; the Italians, third, and the English (or British, including Welsh, Scottish, and Anglo-Canadians), fourth. Far below these numerically, but collectively significant, came the Russians (mostly Jews), Scandinavians, Portuguese, Germans, Polish, and Armenians. By 1920, 71 percent of the population was of foreign stock (that is, born abroad or with at least one parent born abroad); the next-closest state to that figure was Massachusetts, with 66.8 percent.

The Irish were the first ethnic group to play a significant role in Rhode Island politics. By 1890 they were high in the ranks of the Democratic party. In 1900 they held three-fourths of the ward positions in the Providence Democratic party. In 1907 the election of James Higgins gave them their first governor. With growing political power came patronage jobs and minor elective and appointive offices. But the Democratic party remained split between its Populist rural wing and its Irish urban wing. The populists, following William Jennings Bryan's lead from the early 1890s until World War I, campaigned on national issues in favor of free silver (cheap money), low tariff, railroad regulation, opposition to imperialism, and antimonopoly. The urban wing campaigned on local issues, for better working conditions, election reforms, social welfare legislation. The Bryanites, like Bryan himself, tended to be Protestant fundamentalists. The urban Democrats tended to be a combination of working-class Catholics and Protestant professionals. However, many workers, accepting the high tariff and "full-dinner-pail" policy of McKinleyism, favored Republicanism as the basis of job security. Because it was impossible in Rhode Island for the Democrats to gain control of the legislature, they could obtain important appointive offices or legislation only by co-operating with their opponents, which some of them (known as "yellow-dog Democrats") did openly, and others did secretly. This did not strengthen the party's image or integrity.

Having achieved a small share of power within the party, the Irish were not at first willing to share it with newer immigrants. Such jobs and offices as they controlled went to loyal Irishmen.

The Republicans were able to play upon the antipathy that produced between the Irish and the French Canadians. The same was true later for the Italians. (Providence did not get its first Italian mayor until 1975, and he was a Republican.) French Canadians, who frequently split their vote in the early part of the century, had a governor (Aram J. Pothier) in 1909 who served until 1915 and again in 1925–1926. They also elected Emery J. San Souci to serve as governor from 1921 to 1923. Both were Republicans. Pothier, a wealthy banker, was born in Quebec; San Souci, a department store owner in Woonsocket, was born in Saco, Maine. The Democrats were not able to get a French Canadian elected to high office on their ticket until Felix Toupin became lieutenant governor in 1923. The Italians did not gain political influence until after the Democratic party came to dominance in 1935.

Since the rise of the Know-Nothings in the 1840s, nativism and anti-Catholicism had played an important role in Rhode Island politics. The steady increase in Catholic immigration did nothing to reduce that friction. But Catholicism was the religion of the poor, and the Roman Catholic Church itself was so busy trying to minister to the spiritual, charitable, and educational needs of its congregations that it took no active part in politics. Moreover, the various ethnic groups and nationalities did not get along well and the dominance of the Irish in the hierarchy exacerbated these tensions. The bishops (who were always Irish until 1972) had difficulty harmonizing these tensions and did not always succeed. Under Bishop Matthew Harkins (1887–1921) some of these tensions were mollified by the establishment of ethnic parishes where people of similar national background were served by priests who shared their languages. Nevertheless, even within nationalities, there were conflicts. For example, the Italians in Providence came mostly from southern Italy and Sicily and did not share the views of Catholic priests (notably the Scalabrini fathers) from northern Italy.

The first Italian parish in the state was Holy Ghost Parish in 1889 in Providence. Between 1890, (when there were only 2,500 foreign-born Italians in Rhode Island), and 1920, (when there were 32,585), three Italians parishes were formed in Prov-

idence and nine elsewhere in the state. If those of Italian parent-
age are included in this ethnic group, one out of nine Rhode
Islanders was an Italo-American by 1920. This large Italian
influx caused problems for the church: in Italy the men seldom
attended mass and, because of state financial support, gave little
money to aid parish activities. As late as 1929, only 10 percent
of Saint Ann's parish received the sacraments in a year and 80
percent of these were women. Many Italians brought with them
an anticlerical bias because the church in Italy had usually sided
with the aristocratic, wealthy landlords against the peasants, and
most of the immigrants were peasants. Some Italians carried
with them superstitions that the church frowned upon in
America—fears of "the evil eye," magic folk rituals and po-
tions for sickness, witchcraft, good fortune, or love.

To non-Catholics in Rhode Island, the church seemed such a
solid phalanx of power and belief that they did not notice how
difficult its path was. Saint Ann's parish (formed in 1895), the
second Italian parish in Providence, was given a priest from
northern Italy, Father Anthony Bove. Despite his best efforts,
Father Bove aroused considerable hostility because of his dislike
of the local feast days and folk customs of his parishoners. In
1907 he prohibited them from collecting funds to provide fireworks for their feast days because he thought the money would
be better spent for the church, the school, and the Saint Vincent
de Paul Society. In 1918, Bove generated even more antagonism by his attacks on the fraternal society called the Sons of
Italy. He denounced its leaders as enemies of the church. But he
failed to prevent his parishioners from joining it.

Father Domenico Bellotti of Holy Ghost parish antagonized
his parishioners by opposing a feast-day celebration in which
the image of the Blessed Virgin was carried into the church
against his wishes. Hundreds of Holy Ghost parishioners petitioned Co-adjutor Bishop William Hickey in 1920 asking for
Bellotti's removal. They also accused him of refusing to perform baptisms without payment of a fixed fee. Father Angelo
Strazzoni, who succeeded Bellotti, fared no better and had to
call in the civil authorities to arrest seven of his parishioners for
interrupting mass in November 1920, because they objected to

the Scalabrini Order to which he belonged. Father Strazzoni left in February 1922. Protestant nativists who claimed that Catholic immigrants were completely under the thumbs of their priests somehow never saw these incidents. They could not, however, ignore the major dispute that took place between the French Canadians and Bishop Hickey in the 1920s.

The Sentinellist Controversy, as it came to be known, pitted the intense loyalty of French Canadians to local control over the parish against the conviction of Bishop Hickey that efficient administration of the diocese required more centralized control. The first French Canadian parish, Precious Blood, was organized in Woonsocket in 1872. The great bulk of French Canadian immigration came to the Blackstone valley between 1865 and 1910. They were predominantly farm families forced to emigrate because of the farm depression in Quebec. Many French Canadians moved back to Quebec Province whenever a depression hit the textile industry, and family connections with those in Canada always remained strong. The French were particularly concerned with the retention of their French heritage and language: *la langue et la foi* seemed irrevocably linked because of French subjection to English Protestant rule in Canada after 1763. Like the Italians, they were used to state support for the church and found the constant demands for voluntary contributions by their pastors a great burden upon their small incomes. The lack of French Canadian priests was another bone of contention. In addition, the Irish workers saw the French Canadians as "scabs" and Republicans (especially after the election of Aram Pothier in 1909). Bishop Hickey was Irish.

The hardships caused by the textile strike of 1922 and the animosity aroused over the nativist-inspired Peck Education Act that year (which required parochial school teachers to give instruction in English only) further increased tensions where the French were most numerous. The Peck Act was part of the great antiforeign upsurge in America in the 1920s, leading to the renascence of the Ku Klux Klan (which in Rhode Island was more anti-Catholic than antiblack) and the passage of the nation's first immigration restriction laws. The Peck Act was ruled unconstitutional and dropped a year later, but many Catholics held Governor Pothier partly responsible for its passage because it had strong Republican support and Pothier had failed to veto it. In some communities, such as Woonsocket, probably half the children or more attended parochial schools.

The Sentinellist Controversy arose in 1922, when the bishop started a fund-raising drive for schools and assigned Irishmen to obtain the quota of one million dollars levied on the Woonsocket parishes. A similar crisis began that year in the French Canadian parishes in Central Falls, when the bishop incorporated as a diocesan hospital an institution for which the French had raised money as part of the parish of Notre Dame du Sacré Coeur. Monseigneur J. H. Béland, the pastor at Notre Dame, sided with his people against this assertion of central control. The bishop reacted by withdrawing his support for the hospital. When the bishop tried to enforce the instruction of the National Catholic Welfare Committee that parochial schools should be taught in English, he further heightened the tensions with French Canadians. He also decided that a French-speaking Catholic high school for which the Central Falls people had raised money would not be opened because it did not fit into the diocesan educational pattern.

Throughout these conflicts, the French-language newspaper, *La Sentinelle,* in Woonsocket, attacked the bishop's centralization policy and called vigorously for local parishes to defend their rights and privileges. The editors received indirect support from Cardinal Bégin, Archbishop of Quebec. *La Tribune,* another French-language newspaper, sided with the bishop. At that point, a secret society, *Les Croisés* (the Crusaders) was founded by Catholic laymen to preserve the French language in Woonsocket and Central Falls. The whole issue became increasingly complex, as canon law and civil law became intertwined. In 1927 sixty-three laymen in Central Falls sued the bishop in a civil court for the return of funds raised by them to build their high school. The bishop ultimately suspended two priests who abetted the lawsuit, and the Holy See in Rome excommunicated the sixty-three laymen who brought it. The Holy See also placed *La Sentinelle* under interdict, making it a sin for any Catholic to subscribe to or read it. The issue aroused national attention

when nativists, in other parts of the country, like Senator James
Heflin of Alabama and various KKK leaders, took the side of
the "persecuted" French Canadians against the Pope and his
"tyrannical" bishop in Providence. A year later, when Alfred
E. Smith ran for president as the first Roman Catholic ever
nominated for that post, fiery crosses were seen burning on the
rural hills of Roger Williams's state. However, the controversy
ended in 1929, when the leaders of *La Sentinelle* and *Les Croisés* yielded their submission to the bishop's authority. After
Bishop Hickey died in 1933, his successor, Bishop Keough,
pursued a conciliatory course that ended the smoldering feud.

National attention focused unsympathetically on Rhode Island
in two other controversies in the 1920s: the great textile strike of
1922 and the famous "stink bomb" episode in the state legislature. The textile strike resulted from wage cuts and increased
working hours, as Rhode Island manufacturers, like those elsewhere in New England, began to feel the competition of southern textile mills. Traditionally, Rhode Island labor unions had
been weak and ineffective. They had failed, in the 1830s, to obtain the ten-hour day or to curtail child labor. From 1873 to
1876, they had tried again with the formation of the New England Ten-Hour Association and failed again. Some small
unions among skilled workers managed to improve the conditions for typesetters, stonecutters, cigar makers, carpenters,
bricklayers, plasterers. But the great mass of Rhode Island
workers were unskilled and unorganized. Among the textile operatives, the Mule Spinners Union (centering in Fall River) had
some success, and later organizations of the more skilled workers (loom-fixers, carders, dyers, bleachers, and finishers) were
able, because of their key positions, to obtain higher wages for
themselves. Most of these were led by English immigrants who
had had previous union experience. In 1884 the Rhode Island
Central Trades and Labor Union (later affiliated with the American Federation of Labor) claimed a membership of three thousand skilled workers. But these constituted less than 10 percent
of the industrial workers.

The first major union organizing among the unskilled workers
was undertaken by the Knights of Labor. District Assembly 99

of this national union was organized in Rhode Island in 1882 and by 1886 claimed to have almost 12,000 members in sixty-four locals. But the tactics of the K of L proved unsuccessful, and the membership dwindled away by 1890 to a few hundred. In 1891 the AFL chartered the United Textile Workers of America, but most of its locals were made up of the skilled operatives. Out of 47,600 operatives in 188 cotton and woollen mills in 1900, less than 10 percent belonged to the UTW. Total union membership of all kinds in the state was less than 18,000 in 1904, and these were almost wholly skilled craft workers.

Prior to 1920 the most serious labor trouble was not in the textile mills or metal factories, but among the streetcar workers. In January 1902, reformers had got through the legislature a law restricting streetcar workers to a ten-hour day in the interest of safety. But Marsden J. Perry and the streetcar managers considered the law an unconstitutional infringement on their right to manage their own business. They refused to obey it. Consequently on June 3, 1902, the Amalgamated Association of Street Railway Employees (organized in 1894) went on strike. They were led by John W. Arno and Albert C. Vetter. Despite public sympathy for the strikers, the Republican governor, Charles Kimball, at Perry's request, declared martial law in Providence on June 12. It was the first time that had happened since the Dorr War. Seven hundred militiamen were called out and kept the streetcars running with scab labor. The company threatened to fire any worker who did not return to work immediately. Within two weeks, the strike was broken. Shortly thereafter, Brayton and Kimball prodded the legislature into repealing the ten-hour law.

Between 1908 and 1914, the Industrial Workers of the World tried to organize the textile workers into more militant unions, but they never matched in Rhode Island the success they achieved in Lawrence, Massachusetts, and Paterson, New Jersey, in these years. Rhode Islanders, including the operatives, accepted the stereotyped image of the IWW as a violent, anarchistic movement. Workers not only refused to co-operate with their organizers but, in 1914, in Pawtucket, asked the town officials to expel them from the city as outside agitators. Nevertheless, labor's influence at the polls continued to grow. It was claimed that Peter Gerry, a Democrat, defeated Henry Lippitt, a Republican, for the United States Senate in 1916 because Lippitt, related to a wealthy textile family, openly opposed the union shop. He was alleged to have also said that a dollar a day was sufficient wages for a millworker, though in fact it was Lippitt's father who had said that, some years earlier.

In 1919 the National India Rubber Company workers in Bristol went on strike in April over a severe wage cut. The company hired private detectives, and violence broke out in May. Governor R. L. Beekman called out the militia to protect those who had been hired to take the strikers' places. The strike was broken in June. But this short-lived strike did not attain anything like the notoriety of the eight-month strike in 1922—the first successful statewide textile strike by rank-and-file operatives in the state's history.

Although World War I had given a temporary boost to Rhode Island industry and enabled the textile mills to make large profits, despite growing southern competition, the years 1921 and 1922 brought a severe recession. Early in 1921, textile wages were cut 22.5 percent. Some mills closed; others increased the hours of work to increase their slim margin of profit. The workers grumbled but did not strike. In January 1922, the textile companies announced another 20 percent cut in wages, and an increase to a fifty-four-hour work week. Twenty-one locals of the United Textile Workers Union met and unanimously voted to strike. In addition, the Amalgamated Textile Workers Union, founded in Paterson, New Jersey, voted to join the strike. Thomas F. McMahon and John Powers, who led the UTWU, were not happy over the presence of the ATWU because they considered it too radical, but the workers were sufficiently desperate to accept organized assistance from wherever they could get it. Both unions organized "flying squadrons" that marched or drove from mill to mill to call out the workers, man the picket lines, and get the operatives to join the union. The millowners called the police, claiming harassment of scabs by labor agitators. Violence took place on the picket lines outside the Natick Mill in West Warwick. The millowners turned to Governor Emery J. San Souci, who antagonized many French Canadian strikers who had voted for him when he declared a state of emergency and called out the National Guard. But this time the militia could not break the strike.

Many of the mills were forced to close; twenty thousand workers were out on strike at the peak. It dragged on through the whole summer, and after eight months it was finally settled in September by the agreement of the millowners not to make the 20 percent cut and to return to the old hours of work. Their willingness to agree was in part dictated by the end of the recession and the upsurge of production orders. But the workers had at last learned that they could succeed. The difficulty was that, as northern millowners were forced to pay better wages and improve working conditions, they steadily lost ground to the cheaper labor and production costs of southern millowners. Employers claimed that the unions were cutting the throats of the workers by cutting the profits of the owners. But in truth, the days of New England's supremacy in the textile industry were over.

By 1923 Rhode Island was a bitterly divided state, socially, economically, and politically. The unions, having tasted victory, continued to wage sporadic strikes, while more and more mills closed rather than meet their demands. The Democrats, after being a minority party for almost a century, suddenly discovered that they were able to win almost as many votes from second- and third-generation immigrant families as the Republicans could win from the old Yankee constituency. Even many Yankee operatives in the mills were persuaded by the unions to vote for the Democrats as "the party of the people" against the party that supported the bosses. The Republicans, although they had made some concessions to the immigrants by helping French Canadians to win high office, still remained the party of the business elite, the middle class, and the Protestant small-town folk. By repeated efforts, the Democrats had, over the years, won grudging increases in the electorate by small changes in the constitutionally defined suffrage requirements, but the urban areas were still underrepresented in the general assembly and the propertyless were still unable to vote for city councilmen.

As the party of the middle and upper classes, the Republicans stood for efficiency and civic improvement. The party's progressive wing after 1905 was strong on social uplift and constantly worked at improving police and fire departments, obtaining better playgrounds, street lighting, and parks; they built better hospitals, schools, and insane asylums. Through the effort of Dr. Charles V. Chapin, the state had done much to improve public health and sanitation. Life for the middle class was pleasant in the years 1865 to 1930. They lived in well-appointed Victorian homes surrounded by lawns and gardens on wide boulevards; they were waited on by Irish servants. Their parks were well kept, their taxes low, their cultural enjoyments inexpensive. The city of Providence at the turn of the century had five theaters, several stock companies, a professional baseball team (which at one time had Babe Ruth on its roster). While the middle class knew that there was poverty in the slums and mill towns, it did not feel that much needed to be done about it. The hard-working, deserving poor would eventually rise in status, and the rest got what they deserved. Hence they saw no need to pass laws to improve working conditions. The effort to obtain an eight-hour day was consistently defeated in the legislature. Child labor continued. Yet the labor strikes and the mill closings in the 1920s indicated that the easy, prosperous pattern of life was changing.

In the fall election of 1922, the Democrats won the governorship, the lieutenant governorship, and strong minorities in both houses. Because a bill vetoed by the governor had to receive a 60 percent majority to pass over his veto, the Democrats found themselves with the power to frustrate all Republican bills; they had more than 40 percent of the votes to prevent the overriding of a veto. Since Lieutenant Governor Felix Toupin presided over the senate, the Democrats decided to use their negative power to force the Republicans to pass the amendments to end the property qualification for urban elections and reapportion the seats in the legislature so as finally to end rural domination. To do that, Toupin recognized from the chair only Democrats who wished to speak; in effect, the Democrats filibustered the Republican majority to a standstill. Days, weeks, months went by, and the Republicans could not even get their annual appropriation bill passed. Finally, after five months, the Republicans conceded the right of the Democrats to bring their bills for constitutional amendments to the floor. The bills were duly voted down, but the Democrats thought they had made their point; they were no longer going to be pushed around. Unfortunately, the Republicans were not yet ready to concede.

At the 1924 session of the legislature, the Democrats demanded that the Republicans call a constitutional convention. They refused, and the filibustering began again. This time it lasted six months, until, on June 19, 1924, the exasperated Republicans hired a Boston thug to set off a stink bomb of bromine gas behind the senate rostrum. The fumes forced the evacuation of the chamber. All the Republican members of the senate then left the state and went to live in a hotel in Rutland, Massachusetts. Their absence prevented a quorum, and the session ended with no legislation bill, not even an appropriation to pay the salaries of government employees and sustain state institutions. Twenty-three banks in the state joined to lend money to the state to cover these expenses till the next session.

But the filibuster effort backfired against the Democrats, as Rhode Island became the laughing stock of the Jazz Age. In the fall of 1924, the Republicans made a clean sweep of all state and federal offices and won overwhelming control of the legislature. Yet, four years later, the Democrats forced two constitutional amendments through, marking the beginning of the end of Republican dominance. They first reapportioned the senate (though not very radically) by allowing towns or cities with more than 25,000 voters to elect one senator for every 25,000 voters or any fraction thereof up to a total of six. The second amendment ended the real-property qualification for urban voting and made the payment of any tax, real or personal, sufficient to qualify a vote. Not until 1973 was this qualification eliminated, finally giving Rhode Island universal suffrage. The second amendment at last gave the Democrats control of all the major city governments, enabling them to build up their machines and patronage; the first helped considerably to equalize the urban vote in the state senate. However, the continued requirement that every town have at least one senator and one representative kept the Republicans in control of the legislature for another seven years.

The demise of one-party Republican rule in Rhode Island was hastened by the coming of the Great Depression. With it came a great loss of confidence in the party of American business and many of the principles for which it stood: the belief in rugged individualism, the opposition to labor unions, the dislike of social welfare legislation, the fear of government regulation of business, the distrust of ethnic voters. In Rhode Island the tide finally turned with the election of November 1934. When the Democratic majority took charge on January 1, 1935, it engineered a "bloodless revolution" that started a new era in the state's history.

6

Changing, Surviving, Hoping

*T*HE handwriting was on the wall for Rhode Island long before the stockmarket crash of October 1929. Sooner or later, the Yankees had to yield their power to the ethnics, and the textile prosperity of New England had to succumb to the developing enterprise of the South. Rhode Island paid the price for its loss of economic flexibility, its overreliance upon the textile industry, its unwillingness to plow its profits back into modernizing its plants. New England industrialists argued that the textile crisis after 1920 stemmed essentially from the wage differential between the North and the South. They could think of no solution but to keep wages low. That meant using the Republican party to help fight unionism, which in turn meant losing more and more votes to the Democrats.

The "New South" that arose after the Civil War turned rapidly to industrialization to find jobs for its people as its farm crisis deepened. Willing to work for almost any wage, these farmers—like those in Rhode Island a century earlier—offered a large, docile supply of labor to an area rich in cotton, needing only investment capital to capture the textile market from New England. Ironically, much of that capital came from the North. In 1880 the southern states produced only one-sixteenth of the nation's cotton goods; in 1910 they produced almost one-third; by 1923 they produced 47 percent, and New England manufacturers were suddenly fighting for their lives. They lost. From

1926 to 1933, expenditures exceeded earnings in New England's mills. Between 1923 and 1938, Rhode Island textile production fell by two-thirds, and the number of workers in the industry dropped from 33,993 to about 12,000. Yet the South, despite the crash and the depression, was actually increasing its production of cotton goods from 1923 to 1938.

The South gained considerable advantage in the contest from the absence of an effective labor-union movement, just as the union movement in New England gathered strength. After 1920 Rhode Island workers refused to accept the low pay and bad working conditions that their parents and grandparents had put up with. Between 1924 and 1934, New England hourly wages in the textile industry were 16 percent to 60 percent higher than those in the South. In Rhode Island, the average hourly wage for a cotton operative in 1920 was 18.6 cents an hour; in 1930 it was 40.6 cents; in 1937 it was 46.2 cents. Such was the price of union progress. In the South, the unions made no progress.

Rhode Island had become so heavily engrossed in textiles that it could find no quick or easy solution to its crisis. Those who sought other sources of investment did so outside the state. That left the workers with no new sources of income. In 1920, 55 percent of the state's work force was engaged in one aspect or another of the textile industry. By 1930, 27 percent of the state's cotton workers were unemployed and so were 24 percent of the workers in woolen and worsted. Many of those who were working were on a half- or quarter-time schedule, bringing home less than nine dollars a week. After 1920 textile owners had two choices: to close the mills or to make increasing demands on their workers. First they tried the latter, applying the new techniques of "scientific management" and "efficiency experts" so skillfully satirized in Charlie Chaplin's popular movie of the 1930s, *Modern Times*. Millowners utilized both the "speed-up" system (running the machines faster and requiring the workers to work faster) and the "stretch-out" system (cutting back the work force and requiring those who remained to tend not only their own machines but the machines of those who had been fired). As workers saw the mills closing and antiunionism increasing in the 1920s, they became intimidated. Many who went on strike saw their mill permanently closed; the owner invested his money in southern mills or in some other non-Rhode Island enterprise. There was no other work for the operatives to go into. Erstwhile busy communities became ghost towns all over the state, with large, empty mills and workers' deserted tenements. By 1934, seventeen thousand operatives were on relief.

Millowners pleaded with their workers to "co-operate" to keep the textile industry alive, but co-operation meant longer hours, faster work, lower wages, and the open shop. By 1934 the labor force was desperate and decided that only unionization could help them survive. In the end, it was not the success of the unons so much as the inception of massive federal aid and the passage of new social welfare laws that rescued them.

The great textile strike of 1934, which caused more damage and bloodshed than any other strike in the state's history, was not the result of a wage cut, but of a unionizing effort. The leaders of the United Textile Workers Union who called the strike on September 1, 1934, did so on a nationwide basis to protest the wage differential between the northern and southern mills. As an effort to raise the wages of southern operatives (and help equalize labor costs, north and south), it could be described as a way of helping the northern mills survive. In addition, of course, the strike sought to unionize all the mills in the country. Textile owners North and South considered that a dangerous threat to free enterprise. In 1934 the Providence Chamber of Commerce opposed the Wagner-Connery bill then in Congress as "un-American," "class legislation," and a "direct interference with the operations of business."[1] (The bill was designed to help unions attain collective bargaining power.) But the strike originated from the fact that guidelines for the textile industry established under President Franklin Roosevelt's National Recovery Act (the NRA) were not being followed by southern millowners. Under that act, all textile workers in the nation were to receive a minimum wage of thirteen dollars a week. The New England millowners were already paying that,

1. Brock, *Collective Bargaining in the Cotton Industry in Rhode Island*, p. 46.

but the southern millowners were not, and they refused to raise their wages. Francis Gorman, president of the UTWU, therefore called upon all union workers to come to the aid of their exploited fellow operatives in the South and force those millowners to comply with the law of the land. Gorman also hoped that a strike would break the open-shop policy of the textile owners' associations and compel New England millowners to accept the UTWU as the bargaining agent for their workers.

Under Section 7-*a* of the NRA, union-breaking policies had been declared illegal, but the textile owners, north and south, had failed to follow that aspect of the law. At the time of the strike, only about 5 percent of the textile operators in Rhode Island were unionized. That left them helpless against the "speed-up" and the "stretch-out" systems. If the strike could enlist a majority of the workers in the union, it would have the power to remedy these abuses. Joseph Sylvia headed the UTW forces in Rhode Island during the strike; the Independent Textile Workers Union and the National Textile Workers Union also supported the strike. On September 1, 500,000 workers in the northern and southern mills went out on strike. Union leaders claimed that 90 percent of the textile workers in Rhode Island left the mills, though it was probably less. The millowners in New England were determined to continue their fight against unionization.

As the strike gained support, stories were spread in the newspaper, saying that the union "agitators" (especially those in the National Textile Workers Union) were Communists. On the day the strike started, the *Pawtucket Times* (which spoke for the millowners) printed on its front page a picture of one of these radicals—a handsome, red-haired young woman named Ann Burlak—whom it described as "the Red Flame of Communism." Burlak lived in New Bedford, Massachusetts. Twenty-five years old, she had been active among the millworkers there and elsewhere in New England for several years. "Authorities everywhere," said the paper, "consider her dangerous"; her "inspired oratory can turn the average merely curious crowd into something approaching a revolutionary mob." Anti-Communist vigilantes from the American Legion and Ku Klux

Klan announced that they would take care of any outside agitator who entered the state. Female leadership was important, because so many of the textile workers were women. Other leading women in the strike were Stella Moskwa of Pawtucket, whom the newspapers called "the strikers' 'Joan of Arc,' " and Elizabeth Nord, also of Pawtucket, chairman of the New England Silk and Rayon Workers Union.[2]

The millowners hired deputies to prevent pickets from stopping "scabs" who crossed picket lines, and soon violence broke out between the pickets and the deputies, many of whom were off-duty policemen. Governor Theodore F. Green finally called out the National Guard to preserve order. He blamed outside Communist agitators, rather than respectable AFL labor leaders for the violence and took care to retain the respect of labor by placing responsibility for the strike on the refusal of the millowners to bargain with the union. Green was a Democrat. More fighting followed, after the Guardsmen arrived, and in several days of rioting in Saylesville and Woonsocket, fourteen persons were wounded by gunfire, many injured by clubs and rocks, and three killed. The strike ended on September 22, when President Roosevelt appointed a national arbitration board. There were no gains for the workers in Rhode Island, and the union lost rather than added members. Some who had been most active in the strike were fired as troublemakers.

Not until after the passage of the Wagner Act in 1935 and the formation of the Textile Workers Organizing Committee of the CIO (Congress of Industrial Organizations) in 1937 was there a successful drive to unionize the rank-and-file textile workers in Rhode Island. Unfortunately, the UTWU leaders in the state could not work harmoniously with the new CIO leaders; and in 1938 the CIO formed the Textile Workers Union, which for years competed with the UTWU for members within the state. Not until the 1950s were most industrial workers members of unions in Rhode Island. Meanwhile, the textile industry went into further decline and the millowners continued to oppose

---

2. The *Pawtucket Times* (Pawtucket, Rhode Island), September 1 and September 5, 1934.

workers' efforts to improve their conditions on the theory that they could not do so without losing more ground to their southern competitors.

Finding unionization ineffective, the workers turned more ardently to political reform. Inspired by the prolabor policies of the New Deal, the Democratic party in Rhode Island made a concerted effort to appeal to the working class. The man who led the Democrats to their "bloodless revolution" in 1935 was Theodore Francis Green. He succeeded in large part because he taught the Irish members of his party that they would have to include the other ethnic groups in their party organization if they were to weld the political union that would accomplish what labor unions could not. Among those who worked closely with Green in engineering this movement were Robert E. Quinn, Thomas P. McCoy, and J. Howard McGrath.

Green and the Democrats capitalized on more than the antiunionism of the millowners. Many factors led to the downfall of the Republican party. Among them were the growing distaste of many normally Republican voters for the corruption and ineptitude of their leaders, the gradual reforms of the state constitution, the increasing number of immigrants and their children. In addition, World War I produced many ethnic veterans who returned to the state determined to assert their roles as citizens. The career of Al Smith inspired Roman Catholics with the potential power of their vote and the thought that someday a Catholic could be president. And finally, the intense nativist movement of the 1920s served to weld the ethnic groups together behind the Democrats. The immigrants became champions of pluralism against those old Yankees who demanded "100 percent Americanism" and conformity. They began slowly to alter the old melting-pot notion of Americanization as assimilation and to replace it with the new salad-bowl concept. Hyphenated they might be, but Irish-Americans, Italo-Americans, Franco-Americans, Luzo-Americans and the rest considered themselves more true to certain basic American ideals than many who thought America belonged only to Anglo-Saxon Protestants.

As a result of the election of 1934, the Democrats were within two senate seats of political domination, and these two seats, they were convinced, had been "stolen" from them by election frauds in two small Republican towns. Led by Governor-elect Green, the party decided to undertake a political coup. Green, a millionaire lawyer of impeccable Yankee background, had been active in Democratic politics since 1906, when he was elected to the state senate on a fusion ticket of progressive Republicans and Democrats disgusted with Brayton's bossism. In the 1920s, with the help of other old Yankees (Peter Gerry and John Nicholas Brown, in particular) he persuaded the Irish party regulars to open their ranks to other ethnic groups. In 1934 that had paid off.

Green had met Franklin D. Roosevelt in 1916 and remained close friends with him as Roosevelt rose to leadership in the Democratic party. When most of the Rhode Island delegation to the Democratic party convention in 1932 supported Al Smith's nomination, Green had supported Roosevelt's. His close ties with Roosevelt were to prove of great importance. When Green was elected governor in 1932, Roosevelt chose to channel federal relief funds and patronage to Rhode Island through him rather than through the state's Republican delegation in Congress, who were opposing the New Deal's reform programs. But for his party to gain the full benefit of this "pipeline" to Washington, Green had to win control of the state legislature. With his re-election in 1934, he stood ready to support the coup that became known as "the Green revolution." It was all carefully plotted out between November and January by Green, Quinn, McCoy, and McGrath.

According to the state constitution, each house in the legislature was entitled to judge the elections of its own members. So, when the senate assembled on January 1, 1935, Lieutenant Governor Quinn as presiding officer refused to allow the two Republican senators from Portsmouth and South Kingstown to be sworn in until a recount was taken of the votes in those towns. That left the senate tied, with twenty Republicans and twenty Democrats, and Quinn had the tie-breaking vote. With that vote, the Democrats appointed a committee to recount the votes—and sure enough, they discovered that the Democrats had really won those two seats. For the first time in a century, the Democrats were in control of the whole Rhode Island legislative and executive branches. But they did not yet control the judiciary; and that Republican body, to which the election count was sure to be brought for adjudication, might well nullify the whole effort. The next act in the coup was to replace all five judges of the State Supreme Court (which had been made up of Republicans since the 1850s). That was perfectly legal, because the constitution stated that the judges served at the will of the legislature (which they still do). Although there was some quarreling among the various factions of the Democratic party as to who should have the honor of replacing these judges, Green persuaded his colleagues to let him appoint at least two Republicans, one a Yankee, one an Italo-American; two of the Democratic appointments were Irish, and one was a Yankee. One of the Irishmen demanded, and got, the promise of the chief justiceship. With Democrats in control of the court, the Republicans had no way to appeal against the "revolution."

The coup went on to abolish the office of State Commissioner of Finance, where Frederick S. Peck, Brayton's successor as Republican party chief, held sway over the budget and all expenditure bills. Then the Democrats removed the Republican-dominated Providence Safety Board and the High Sheriff of Providence County, who had been appointed by the Republicans to control the Providence city police and fire departments: that patronage was returned to the Democratic-controlled city. Following that, an omnibus bill with eighty closely integrated parts reorganized the entire state government, abolishing various intricate mechanisms the Republicans had established to check and balance Democratic governors and growing Democratic power in the legislature. The bill created the various bureaus and departments of the state that have continued ever since. The Brayton Act was abolished, returning the power of appointment to the governor after thirty-four years. These and other actions cementing Democratic control could be undertaken by legislative action, but the more important steps in reapportioning the legislature required constitutional amendment. Green's next step was to be the calling of a constitutional convention, but that part of his plan went awry.

Most of this action was taken by voice vote and became law within twenty-four hours after Green had started his second term on January 1, 1935. Green made a special radio broadcast after the coup (following the example of Roosevelt's "fireside chats") to explain to the people of the state why these actions were necessary. Citing the ideals of Roger Williams and Thomas W. Dorr, Green explained that he was merely returning the power usurped by a minority to the rightful hands of the majority; it was simple republicanism. The Republicans in the state and throughout the nation complained bitterly about Green's high-handed despotism. Colonel Robert McCormick, editor of the Republican *Daily Tribune* in Chicago, declared that Rhode Island was a state of rogues and that Green's action was unconstitutional. McCormick ordered one star cut out of the flag that flew from the *Tribune*'s building, to represent his ostracism of the state. (He had to restore it when his lawyers informed him it was against the law to desecrate the flag.) The *New York Times*, however, lauded the overthrow of Rhode Island's ramshackle old political system. The great mass of voters in Rhode Island agreed that the bloodless revolution was long overdue.

The most significant political differences arising from the shift from Republican to Democratic dominance in the state, apart from the strengthening of the executive branch, were in tone and temper. The Democrats talked of helping "the people," where the Republicans had talked of "efficient business administration." The locus of power under the Democrats shifted from the rural to the metropolitan centers, where ethnic voters outnumbered Yankees, and Catholics outnumbered Protestants; hence much of the old nativism faded or took cover. The governor and his party took over responsibility for the actions of his administration; no longer did some nonelected "boss" manipulate the legislature from behind the scenes. If machine politics remained, it was much clearer to the general public where the responsibility for legislative action (or inaction) lay; as head of the party, the governor bore the brunt.

Much of the 1935 session was devoted to removing Republicans from administrative positions and replacing them with Democrats. Green did his best to see that various ethnic groups and party factions were fairly represented in these selections, but he generally favored the Providence wing of the party. Under Green's leadership, and with continued federal support from Roosevelt, the Democrats cemented their affiliation with the working class. In 1935 and 1936, a series of reforms (which Republican legislatures had blocked and which labor union bargaining and strikes could not achieve) were enacted by the Democrats to improve working conditions. These included state minimum wages for women and children; an old-age pension system; a forty-eight-hour work week; an anti-injunction law, and various laws to provide unemployment compensation and insurance. The working man had at last become influential, not through economic power but through political power. The close working relationship between the party and the labor unions led to the appointment of union men to important administrative posts dealing with labor. In return, the unions worked to turn out votes for the party. That relationship lasted until 1960.

In 1936 Green was elected to the United States Senate, where he served with distinction on the Foreign Relations Committee until his retirement in 1960. In 1936 the Democrats also won both congressional seats, one of them going to a Franco-American, Aimé J. Forand. In 1940, John F. Fogarty, a union bricklayer, was elected to Congress. Forand and Fogarty were immensely popular because of their successful support of legislation on behalf of the working class and the aged, particularly in the area of health care.

Although, in 1936, the Republicans won six more seats in the state senate than the Democrats, seven Republicans agreed to co-operate with the Democrats, thereby enabling them to retain control of the legislature. That happened in several other elections prior to 1958, because the Democrats were unable to agree on the best way to get the constitution amended to reapportion the rural districts. (That was not accomplished until the United States Supreme Court's "one man, one vote" decision in 1962.) It was Green's most serious failure. Because Democratic control was thus precarious in the early years of their dominance, any strong faction of Democrats was able to wield undue pressure on the party by threatening to withhold its votes. Typical of the factionalism preventing the consistency and long-range planning that might have helped the state out of its economic decline was a quarrel centering around the political ambitions of Thomas P. McCoy of Pawtucket. The history of Rhode Island politics since 1935 has been a series of such intraparty struggles for office, often with damaging effect to the general prosperity of the state as well as of the party.

Thomas P. McCoy was born in Pawtucket in an Irish working-class family. He quit school at fourteen to work in the textile mills. Later he was a conductor on the trolley cars of the United Electric Company and joined the carmen's union. Entering politics in 1906 under the aegis of James H. Higgins, he worked with the Democrats to try to win control of the city of Pawtucket from the Republicans. In 1920 McCoy was the first Democrat elected to the state legislature from Pawtucket, though the city was predominantly working-class and ethnic in its inhabitants. In 1922 he supported the textile strikes against Governor San Souci and introduced a bill for a forty-eight-hour week without wage reductions. He also introduced the first old-age pension bill and the first bill for a state inheritance tax. But none of his reforms stood a chance against the Republican majority. McCoy helped to engineer the repeal of the Bourn Amendment in 1928 and thus freed his city and others from Republican domination.

McCoy ran unsuccessfully for lieutenant governor with Green in 1930 and seemed destined to rise high in the party after the Green revolution. From 1933 to 1936, he was city auditor of Pawtucket, and from that powerful position he controlled the city's ten seats in the legislature. Closely allied with Albert J. Lamarre and Harry C. Curvin, he quarreled with Mayor John F. Quinn of Pawtucket and his nephew, Robert E. Quinn, Green's lieutenant governor from 1932 to 1934, thus alienating himself from some of Green's closest supporters. But because McCoy's ten Pawtucket votes were so crucial to Green after 1934, Green chose McCoy as state budget director, one of the major patronage jobs under the reorganized state system.

Green and McCoy fell out over who should be chosen director of public works and director of taxation for the state. The patronage from those posts and their budget power would give major political strength to the faction that controlled them. McCoy wanted to reward his loyal supporters, Lamarre and Ernest Santingini, by giving them these posts. But Green had plans to appoint Irishmen from the Providence and Cranston wings of the party. That contest became embroiled with McCoy's fight against the Blackstone Gas and Electric Company, which he accused of gouging the consumers in Pawtucket. Green had campaigned on a platform calling for municipal ownership of public utilities, and McCoy was determined to create a public power plant in Pawtucket to serve as a "yardstick" (like Roosevelt's TVA) to measure the rates of the Blackstone Gas and Electric Company. To do so, he needed state legislation and Green's help. But the lobbyists for the company appealed to Green for assistance and made a deal with him to lower their rates voluntarily by 10 percent. Green used that to argue that he had accomplished more to help the people of the Blackstone valley than McCoy. He then refused to back McCoy's plan for municipally owned utilities. As a wealthy Yankee Protestant, Green was never as radical on economic questions as some of the working-class reformers in his party.

After a difficult intraparty fight in 1935, in which McCoy successfully blocked much of Green's legislation, Green blocked the appointments of Lamarre and Santingini. McCoy thereupon used his balance of power in the legislature to join the Republicans in preventing passage of Green's budget. Green responded by firing McCoy from the directorship of the state budget. Then, by offering other political plums to some of McCoy's supporters, he managed to break the opposition of the Pawtucket machine and get his budget passed in a special session.

McCoy's later career as mayor of Pawtucket pitted him against Green's successor as governor, Robert E. Quinn, and highlighted the involvement of the Democrats with organized gambling in the state. Green had signed the bill creating the first horse-racing track in Rhode Island in 1934, but he did so reluctantly, because he feared it would attract a criminal element. The Narragansett race track was located in Pawtucket, and

McCoy, as mayor there, became closely associated with Walter J. O'Hara, the Fall River textile manufacturer who was the head of the Narragansett Race Track Association. O'Hara was eminently successful in his post and pari-mutuel betting netted the state four million dollars in revenue between 1934 and 1937. Somehow, during the depths of the depression, Rhode Islanders and other horse-racing fans from nearby states managed to find thirty to forty million dollars a year to expend during the sixty-day track season. With his profits, O'Hara expanded his textile business and bought the failing Manville-Jenckes factory in Pawtucket. He planned to sell the large power-generating plant of that mill to McCoy or to the city of Pawtucket to serve as the basis for a municipal yardstick and competitor to the Blackstone Gas and Electric Company. It was said that the McCoy family expected to make considerable money from that deal; and in exchange, McCoy would back O'Hara in his bid for the governorship against the Green-Quinn machine. O'Hara had already won considerable support from important legislators and other politicians by liberally distributing stock in the track and free season passes to its activities.

Governor Quinn claimed that O'Hara had broken some of the regulations of the state Racing Commission, which regulated the track, and when O'Hara refused to accept the ruling of the commission on the matter, bitter words passed between Quinn and O'Hara in the public press. Quinn brought a libel suit against O'Hara and, claiming that the race track was a gathering place for gangsters and hoodlums, called out the state militia to prevent the opening of the track in October 1937. What was worse, he declared a state of martial law around the track, on the grounds that McCoy, as mayor of Pawtucket, had refused to do anything about the criminal element in that town. The grand jury indicted O'Hara, and, though the United States District Court later quashed the indictment, O'Hara resigned as president of the track's corporation and withdrew from politics. Unfortunately, the whole episode hurt Quinn and the Democratic machine as much as it did McCoy and O'Hara. In 1938 William Vanderbilt was elected governor on the Republican ticket. And while McCoy remained "the Prince of Pawtucket" until his death in 1945, he never won high state office nor overcame the reputation of harboring a shady criminal element in his city.

That kind of intraparty feud, though often less colorful and dramatic than the race track episode, has continued to hurt the Democratic party to the present. As its various factions fought among themselves, the public often became disgusted with the party's ineptitude. The *Providence Journal-Bulletin,* which published the state's largest paper and the only one circulated statewide, remained in Republican hands and constantly headlined the more unsavory aspects of these feuds. Leading lobbyists for the manufacturers, insurance companies, banks, and public utilities were able to forestall regulatory legislation by pitting one faction against another. Ethnic divisions, exemplified by Green's appointment of Irishmen instead of Lamarre and Santingini, have also kept the Democrats in a constant state of disarray. Ethnic cohesion declined rapidly after the victory in 1935. Clearly, Anthony, Aldrich, and Brayton ran a much tighter ship than the Democratic machine was able to do. But then they had only one ethnic group to pacify, and the predominant business elements were on their side. The preference of the Democrats for a code of personal loyalty (and feuding) and the alleged willingness of Democrats to tolerate gambling and criminal elements served to continue the old nativist tensions between Protestant Yankees and Catholic ethnics. Furthermore, the Democrats had learned much about machine politics from their predecessors, and while their strong majorities did not require the same amount of petty bribery and voting fraud against the Republicans as was true earlier, internal, factional feuds often produced similar tactics within the party. It began to appear, after the first spate of social reform legislation was passed in the 1930s, that the state had simply exchanged one unattractive machine for another.

None could deny, however, that at last the state was run by its majority. The changing membership of the legislature reveals not only the sharp decline of the Republican-Yankee control, but also the fact that the political revolution reflected the demographic revolution. In 1900, three out of four legislators were of Yankee stock; by 1950, one out of every two were non-

Yankees. The change was particularly evident among the Democrats. In 1900, two-thirds of the Democratic legislators were Yankees, but by 1950 only one-fifth were. The remainders were 33.8 percent Irish, 22.1 percent Franco-American, 13.2 percent Italo-American, 4.4 percent Portuguese-American, and 4.4 percent Jewish-American. Naturally, the proportion of Democrats also constantly increased over the years. In 1900, the lower house contained only twelve Democrats to sixty Republicans; by 1950, there were sixty-eight Democrats and thirty-two Republicans; as of 1976, there were eighty-six Democrats and only fourteen Republicans. A similar but less rapid decline in Republicans took place in the senate. One reason the Republicans remained predominantly Yankee and Protestant was that they held their power in the rural areas and among the wealthy urban groups. To open their ranks to ethnics would be to alienate many loyal party members who identified with the older image. But just as the Irish hated to yield to other ethnic Democrats, so Yankees in the Republican party resented sharing power within their party.

While the Democrats were eager to redress the socio-economic balance in the state by passing social legislation and levying heavier taxes upon business, their actions were not ideologically motivated. They were simply responding to old ethnic animosities and working-class needs that had long been dammed up. At heart, they were no more opposed to free enterprise capitalism than the New Dealers in Washington. They simply wished to spread its benefits more evenly and widely, to open up the system to new men. The philosophy of the poor upon which the Democrats acted was "deal us in," not "do them in." It did not take labor union leaders long to see that the Democrats were as fearful of driving business out of the state as the Republicans. Business meant jobs. Increasingly, after 1945, labor leaders protested that their party caved in far too easily to complaints of the business community that it could not survive higher taxes and that more regulation of industry, more social welfare legislation, and more workers' benefits would only compound the state's shaky economic situation.

Analysis of the declining harmony between union leaders and

the Democratic party after World War II reveals several factors at work. The feeling grew among party leaders that they had done enough for "the labor vote" and were in danger of alienating other constituencies. There was growing awareness among working people that the labor unions represented only one aspect of their lives as citizens; they were also taxpayers and consumers. There was recognition by the party that, while union leaders might endorse their candidates, they could not regularly deliver the votes to elect them; on the other hand, union leaders came to realize that the party could not, or would not, always live up to its platform promises for prolabor legislation. Behind this loss of mutual support lay the fact that, as workers gained in income and economic security, they moved out of the cities and into the suburbs. With that shift in milieu, workers began to adopt white-collar attitudes, ceasing to think of themselves primarily as working-class or as an underprivileged, exploited group. What had seemed in the 1930s like a long-range harmony of interest between the Democratic party and the rising labor union movement was in fact a temporary conjunction of mutual needs. The relationship was bound to weaken as labor unions achieved many of their primary goals and as the party sought to widen its base of support. The Democrats began to say that they represented "*all* the people" not just "the [little] people." Unionism redressed America's social balance, but its function was never to alter its economic structure.

Differences over labor's political function were reflected in the continuing feuds between the more conservative, pragmatic AFL leaders in Rhode Island and the more radical, ideologically oriented CIO leaders, even after the groups entered an uneasy merger in 1958. The AFL found it easier to go along with the Democrats' effort to co-operate with business, to see labor and capital as partners, while the CIO resisted claims that increasing benefits to workers would drive old businesses out of the state and frighten off potential new businesses. Furthermore, in these years, the CIO often claimed that the Democrats were more favorable toward AFL leaders and gave them an undue share of offices in the state department of labor, the department of employment security, or on various commissions and review boards dealing with labor questions. But during the second great red scare, the era of McCarthyism, the CIO was often put on the defensive by claims that some of its national affiliates were infiltrated with Communists. During the Eisenhower years, as public opinion grew more critical of labor unions and as Rhode Island's unemployment rate rose to be the highest in the nation, the Democrats felt they lost more than they gained by being too friendly toward labor. The public began to associate "Big Labor" with "Big Business" as enemies of the consumer and to resist labor's continual demands for special-interest legislation, particularly when it appeared that better labor benefits were simply passed on to the consumer in the form of higher prices. Was that what was meant by the partnership between labor and capital?

In Rhode Island, Republicans and the Republican-dominated press, radio, and television, continually argued that the high unemployment rate resulted primarily from the state's heavy tax burdens upon industry, placing it at a grave disadvantage with competitors, not only in textiles, but in all industries. In their desire to curb labor costs and overcome cheap competition from abroad, the manufacturers conveniently failed to stress other competitive disadvantages the state faced.

When the Republicans elected, in 1958, their first governor since 1938, labor leaders in the state discovered that by tying themselves too closely to the Democatic party they had made it very difficult to work effectively with a non-Democratic administration. Although the Democrats returned to power in 1960, the new governor was not so eager to co-operate with labor because part of the party's understanding of its failure in 1958 was that it had been too prolabor. By 1962 the AFL-CIO's legislative report on the poor response of the Democrats to labor's concerns stated that both parties were reactionary and that the Democrats were more sympathetic to "the interest of the race tracks, insurance companies, medical lobbies, liquor dealers, and self-seeking political hacks" [3] than to the general

3. Jay S. Goodman, *The Democrats and Labor in Rhode Island, 1952–1962* (Providence: Brown University Press, 1967), p. 36.

welfare. When a Republican governor elected in 1962 signed into law an antistrikebreaking bill that the previous Democratic governor had vetoed (in order to prove that his party was not simply the tool of labor leaders), the unions decided to rethink their affiliation. Since 1962 there have been repeated official statements from the AFL-CIO, claiming that it is independent of all party ties and will endorse its friends regardless of what party they represent. Clearly, that gave the unions and the Democrats more freedom of action, but it was a dramatic shift from the 1930s. Though most voters remained Democrats, they were no longer automatically prolabor.

Meanwhile, the Republican party learned, after 1956, that it too must broaden its base of support if it was to survive. That meant it had to become less Yankee and more prolabor, and that in turn meant it had to break with some of its old party stalwarts in the rural areas and begin to appeal to the rising middle-class ethnic voters in the suburbs. That coincided with the gradual break-up of the cohesive ethnic coalition that had given the Democratic party its great strength in the 1930s and 1940s. The internal change in the Republican party was not quite so pronounced prior to 1950. In 1900, 94 percent of the Republicans in the lower house were of Yankee stock; fifteen years after the Green coup, 84 percent of them were still of that stock. However, while the only ethnic group represented among Republican legislators in 1900 was the French Canadian, by 1950 party members in the lower house were 9.4 percent Irish, 3.1 percent French Canadian, and 3.1 percent Italo-American. When the Republican party nominated Christopher Del Sesto, a former Democrat at odds with his party, as its gubernatorial candidate in 1956, many Italo-Americans switched parties to vote for him. But his nomination required a major change in the strategy and power within the Republican party. The "liberal-urban" wing of the party had wrested control from the conservative-rural-Yankee wing. When the Democrats "cheated" Del Sesto out of a victory by a technical ruling that invalidated the absentee ballots (which would have clinched his victory), many other voters became disgusted with the incumbent, Dennis J. Roberts. In 1958 a Franco-American Democrat, Armand J. Coté, challenged Roberts in the primary campaign. When Roberts's Irish-dominated Providence machine beat Coté's supporters in a bitter intraparty fight and then went on to lose the election to Del Sesto, analysis of the votes showed that many Franco-Americans had joined Italo-Americans in switching parties. The Democrats regained the governorship in 1960 by electing John A. Notte, Jr., to woo back the Italo-American vote, but two years later many voters switched sides again to elect as Republican governor a Yankee with enormous charismatic power —John H. Chafee.

The break-up of ethnic cohesion, like the breakdown of trade-union affiliation with the Democrats, owed much to the heavy demographic shifts that occurred in the state after World War II. Providence lost more inhabitants to the suburbs in the 1950s than any other major city in the nation. The move "out of the ghetto" by ethnic people of working-class background was enormous. And like the earlier "lace-curtain Irish," the "Levitt-town Italians" and French Canadians and other ethnic groups began to take a different perspective on who they were and what they wanted from their government. They began to think of themselves primarily as consumers who wanted enough income to improve their new standard of living. This migration to the suburbs fragmented the party structure and discipline, traditionally geared to the tightly packed urban ward vote. Suddenly, new political leaders began to appear as mayors or state legislators elected from outside the city of Providence with no help from the old urban machine and no particular ties to its leaders. Like McCoy's machine in Pawtucket, new Democratic factions appeared in Warwick, Cranston, and North Providence with machines of their own. These outlying Democrats demanded advancement in the political structure for their chiefs and loyal workers. That forced the party to hold primary campaigns to determine which potential candidates would be the best vote-getters. However, primary campaigns (the stepping-stones to major statewide influence) were far more bitterly fought than the final fall campaigns when, in most areas, the Democratic candidates had little opposition from the fading Republicans. Sometimes as many as six or seven Democrats campaigned against each other in the primaries for statewide office, often leaving lasting scars that prevented statewide harmony afterward.

In 1960, when Theodore F. Green finally retired from the United States Senate, a three-way primary took place for his seat. The party officially endorsed Dennis Roberts in the primary, but Claiborne Pell, an unknown Yankee Episcopalian of wealth and prestige from Newport, not only won the primary but went on to win the election; Pell had never held elective office and had no ties to the machine. In 1967 when John Fogarty died, the party faced a difficult choice between a Providence-based candidate and a Warwick candidate. It settled upon Robert O. Tiernan of Warwick, who moved from state senator to Congress after the election.

The Republicans suffered similar intraparty conflicts before the urban-liberals consolidated control over the rural conservatives. In 1962 Louis V. Jackvony, an Italo-American, challenged John H. Chafee, an old Protestant Yankee, for the Republican nomination for governor. Jackvony claimed to speak for the ethnic voters in his party, but Chafee successfully captured both the rural Protestant and the urban Catholic vote to win his party's nomination. Campaigning as a new "liberal Republican" interested in the general welfare of all the people, Chafee successfully defeated the badly divided Democrats in three gubernatorial elections, though his party never won control of the legislature. He then lost in 1968 to a Democrat, Frank A. Licht, the state's first Jewish governor. Licht cut into Chafee's urban-liberal constituency. In 1976, when eight primary candidates made havoc of the Democratic party's primary, Chafee went on to become the state's junior senator in Washington. Now a state with one of the most heavily ethnic populations in the nation is represented by two Protestant Yankees in the Senate. The Yankees in effect have benefited by remaining outside the internal ethnic feuds.

Although that kind of seesawing occurs in gubernatorial (and occasionally senatorial) races, Rhode Island can still be considered a one-party state. The Democrats have controlled most cities and have never lost control of the legislature since 1935.

Though the constitution of 1843 was not amended to overcome the rural malapportionment in the state senate, the United States Supreme Court's decisions in *Baker* v. *Carr* (1962) and *Reynolds* v. *Sims* (1964) forced the state to pass a reapportionment bill ending the requirements that each of the thirty-nine towns have at least one senator and that Providence could have no more than six. Redistricting, with Democrats drawing the district lines, meant even fewer Republican legislators. In 1976 only 19 of 150 legislators were Republicans, and the Republicans did not even bother to run candidates for 32 of these seats. Still, the voters often defeat the endorsed candidates of the Democrats, especially in the primaries. In 1974 an almost totally unknown house painter, Edward A. Beard of Cranston, was elected to Congress against the wishes of the party chiefs; he claimed to represent "the people, not the party." That same year, popular rebellion against the Democratic machine in Providence and a four-way contest among the Democrats led to the election of the city's first Republican mayor in almost half a century. Vincent A. Cianci was also the city's first Italo-American mayor. In some respects, the very strength of the Democrats has become a liability, for they can blame only themselves when things go wrong. The voters use their power to hold them accountable. That keeps politics frothing in a small state where every action is highly visible and every politician personally known. However, being able to have close personal contact with all officeholders from dogcatcher to United States senator is one of the great virtues of living in Rhode Island. In fact, it is easier to know and to get help from your congressman, senator, or governor than from your dogcatcher.

Yet Rhode Island is, like the rest of the nation, very conservative today; it wants a lot changed, but it also wants to preserve the social gains its majority has made since 1932. The major problem for liberal reformers is that the expense of the welfare state (which has carried the heavy burden of unemployment and poverty since 1935) has become so burdensome and the state's local resources so limited that the middle class is fearful that its standard of living is declining. For the Yankee upper-middle class, undoubtedly the standard has declined since the turn of the century, when Providence was not only a very comfortable, pleasant place to live, but had an active social life and a rich cultural milieu in terms of theater, opera, vaudeville, and musical concerts. Today Boston is the cultural center for Providence people, and the city's local cultural life struggles along in subordination to that; a visit from the Boston Symphony is a big occasion. The inner city has suffered a long, steady decline despite constant efforts to revive it. Similarly, the public schools have deteriorated, and today's public parks, beaches, and amusement centers throughout the state, while more widely used than ever before, lack the amenities, the care, the great charm and beauty they used to have when fewer people had the leisure to enjoy them. They are run-down.

Many middle-class people whose scale of living has been lowered or who are just beginning to enjoy an income that provides disposable wealth for leisure can scarcely manage suburban living with both husband and wife holding full-time jobs. They fear that inflation and increasing taxes (which provide more and more services to the poor) are discriminatory and out of proportion. Yet they know there is poverty, and they are sympathetic toward those who suffer from it. The weekly wage of the average factory worker in Rhode Island in 1976 was 20 percent below the national average. It just seems that there is not enough to go around. New minorities that still lack political leverage—the blacks, the more recent Portuguese immigrants, the Hispanic-speaking from Puerto Rico and Colombia, the Vietnamese refugees—are viewed bleakly by those who have "made it" out of the ghetto. In 1946 the state budget was only $20 million a year and the sales tax only 1 percent; today the state budget is well over $500 million, the sales tax is 6 percent, and on top of it, there is now a state income tax. Taxation of business and poperty taxes in the cities have virtually reached their feasible limits without business expansion. The state's corporate income tax is 2 to 3 percent above the national average. The constant effort to find new sources of revenue recently has led to a state lottery, dog racing, jai alai, and other forms of gambling. Past experience with horse racing, however, does not raise high expectations for that form of revenue. Both state horse tracks became so run-down that they were closed in 1976. And constant publicity about Mafia influence in the state has aroused cynicism about even the best-run forms of gambling.

Since 1929 Rhode Island has consistently had one of the highest unemployment rates in the country. In 1975 unemployment figures rose above 15 percent. Although the state's population increased by 17 percent from 1950 to 1975, manufacturing jobs in that period declined from 125,000 to 109,000 and all jobs from 240,700 to 233,900. No new industry has arisen to take up the slack in textiles, though jewelry manufacturing is increasing slightly, and tourism is a major source of income during the summers. Service jobs, state and federal agencies, and education have provided most new employment since 1932. But since that date, the economy has been increasingly dependent on large and regular grants of assistance from the federal government. With long tenure common among its congressional delegates, as happens in any one-party state, Rhode Island has managed to get a goodly share of that federal income. One of the most important sources of federal aid has always been the United States Navy, whose bases in Newport, Middletown, Portsmouth, Quonset (where the Quonset hut was invented), and Davisville made the navy the state's largest single employer from 1945 to 1973. But when President Richard M. Nixon closed the bases in 1973, except for training purposes, the state suffered its most severe economic blow since 1929. Every political leader since 1930 has campaigned on the promise of bringing new industries to the state and more jobs for the people; but despite earnest effort, none of them has succeeded. There is plenty of highly skilled labor, and excellent industrial parks are available, but except for tax rebates, there is little the state can do to cut labor and manufacturing costs.

While high corporate taxes and high union wages and benefits are frequently cited as the principal reasons that the state is unable to attract new industry, there are equally pressing problems in other respects: the high cost of gas, oil, and electricity; lack of good rail transportation or port facilities; the inability to provide export cargoes for ships that might bring in imports. So long as the state's chief imports remain oil and coal, and so long as it produces no "heavy bottom" product for export, there is no possibility that its magnificent harbor can be useful to anything but naval and pleasure craft, though some see a future in building pleasure boats. The major use for the old naval docks and warehouse left by the navy may well be to provide staging areas for off-shore oil drilling. The fisheries (fin-fishing and shellfishing) around the bay and offshore have dwindled steadily, partly from pollution but more from overfishing, both foreign and domestic. The building of condominiums, ocean-view apartments, and motels around the shores have spoiled much of the state's beautiful coastline, as have the constantly expanding "tank farms" used to store oil and gas.

If there is oil near the coast and if oil companies asked to build refineries in the state (both of which seem less than likely in the near future), the people would have to measure the cost of possible pollution and possible damage to beaches and tourist income. A major fight has long been under way over the building of a nuclear power plant along the bay. So far, that has been thwarted by local fears of safety and pollution that pit ecologists against labor unions. The conservation efforts of "Save the Bay" forces are on a head-on collision course with the state's energy needs. Only a federal experiment with windpower on Block Island seems to have met universal approval as a possible source of energy. Solar heat in this cloudy, northern clime does not seem feasible. While new and sizable coal deposits have just been discovered in the Narragansett basin, the cost of digging it appears to be prohibitive. No one mentions hydroelectric power; that would mean damming up the rivers.

Now that the harbor and railroads no longer function effectively, the highways and truckers monopolize the state's transportation. But resistance to continued highway expansion across such a small area of land has caused mounting opposition to bond issues for that purpose, even though the federal government pays for 90 percent of new road-building. Not even the expansion of the mill towns and cities in the nineteenth century caused so much devastation as road-building, suburban developments, shopping malls, naval installations, power lines, tank farms, and reservoirs in the twentieth century. There has been more environmental change in this state from 1920 to 1976 than in the three centuries preceding. Today it is difficult to find a hamlet that retains its old rural charm unless it has been artificially "restored" to attract tourists. But the rise of urban property taxes and the decline of the city school systems has yet to attract people back from the suburbs, despite the gasoline shortage and the highway traffic problems.

The state has a well-earned national reputation for its many local preservation societies, which have restored scores of old homes and public buildings, mostly by private donations supplemented occasionally by government grants. These efforts have made the state a mecca for lovers of colonial and nineteenth-century architecture. Efforts are even being made to preserve some of the more interesting old mills and mill villages; Slater's Mill in Pawtucket has so far been the most successful of these efforts to preserve something of the state's technological and industrial history. Preservationists are only beginning to save some of the state's elegant Victorian homes and early factories. Providence, which has more colonial buildings standing in its midst than any large city in the nation, has preserved the buildings' exteriors but allowed interiors to be modernized for present city-dwellers. Today this industrial city rivals Newport as a tourist center.

Although the state's crime rate has risen, racial tensions have been minimal. The rising tide of ethnic pluralism has benefited two submerged minorities in recent years—the Indians and the blacks. Like every other northern city, Providence developed a system of de facto segregation of blacks in the nineteenth century; but the number of blacks in the state is today proportionately smaller than in the days when one out of nine in the population of Newport (and more in King's County) was black. Today the figure is closer to 3 or 4 percent, or a total of 30,000 to 35,000. The great majority of these live in Providence. Some are descendants of former slaves, but they have been steadily augmented by migration from the South since 1865. Some Portuguese-speaking immigrants from the Cape Verde Islands have associated themselves with Afro-Americans, but most have not. (Cape Verdeans are mostly Roman Catholic, while Afro-

Americans are predominantly Protestant.) After the state officially de-tribalized the last of the Narragansetts in 1880, it identified them in the census as black—many had intermarried with blacks—regardless of their own sense of ethnic origin. Recent census questionnaires have allowed people to define their own identities.

Providence proved to be the state's test case for desegregation in the public schools in 1967. Despite a minor riot in South Providence and a six-week boycott of public schools by black parents in that area when they discovered that the total burden of involuntary busing would fall on them, the process has continued fairly smoothly, so far. Today, however, the city and state find it difficult, because of heavy population shifts, to sustain the racial and linguistic balances that federal guidelines require. A continued influx of Hispanic-speaking groups from Puerto Rico and Colombia, plus the continued immigration of Portuguese, has complicated the definition of minorities within the public school system and increased bilingual teaching problems. Today the state is in a quandary over how to define minorities officially and whether it is educationally sound to reshuffle students from one school to another as ethnic populations shift from place to place. Resistance to forced busing is clearly mounting.

The civil rights movement brought a new Fair-Housing Law to the state in 1965, after considerable petitioning, picketing, and a sit-in at the State House. While unemployment is higher among blacks, and tension is sometimes high in the secondary schools, racial difficulties in the state have been minimal. Solid backing for integration at every level was found in virtually all churches and civic groups. There has been as little militant radicalism in this conflict as there was among the trade unionists. While the superintendent of schools in Providence is black and the city has had black members of its city council and school committee, there have been few black legislators. Past experience indicates, however, that minority representation will increase when voting power is politically directed.

The Narragansett and Wampanoag Indians, though legally declared "extinct" in 1880, never gave up their claims to ancestral lands in the state and recently have joined many other tribes in New England in asserting their case in court. In 1833 there were officially only 133 Indians in the state, most of them living on the old Narragansett reserve in Charlestown. The state offered them the rights of citizenship if they would agree to yield their identity as a tribe and sell off all their land except those parcels on which they actually lived. They refused. Finally, in 1880, the tribe did vote to accept citizenship, in the hope that that would give them better legal title to the land they lived on, permit them to use the courts to defend themselves against lawsuits, and enable them to sue those who defrauded them. In exchange for citizenship, they sold all the vacant tribal land for $5,000. That sum, divided among 324 members of the tribe at the time, gave each $15.43 for the last of their sovereignty. Thereafter, the state denied their existence as a tribal entity.

By 1897 many of the Narragansetts believed they had made a mistake in accepting citizenship on these terms. Not being informed of their obligations to pay local and state taxes, many of them lost what little land they had left at sheriffs' sales for unpaid taxes. But their protests were ignored. In 1921 and 1931, efforts were made by the Reverend Daniel Sekater, pastor of the nondenominational Indian church and chief of the tribe, to have the federal government declare the sale of 1880 null and void. Sekater demanded back 130,000 acres, which he said was illegally taken, or its equivalent, which he valued at $4 million. However, the federal government said it was a state matter. Then, in 1934, the Indian Reorganization Act of the federal government permitted the Narragansetts to reassert their tribal identity. Since that date, their annual powwows, which had been intermittent since 1830, drew an increasing number of Narragansetts from different parts of New England to reassert their traditions. Based on the tribal roll of 1880, the tribe claimed 440 members in 1934; in 1960 there were 932.

On January 8, 1975, the Narragansett tribe brought suit in the federal court in Rhode Island to regain 3,000 acres of tribal land that they say was wrongly taken from them under the act of 1880. Although the tribe at that time agreed to the sale, they argue, that sale was not approved by the federal government, which, under the Indian Intercourse Act of 1790, specified that no Indian land could be sold by any state without approval of the federal government. Land claimed by the Narragansetts is now owned by many individuals and groups, including the YMCA and the Boy's Club of America. The case is still pending. Like the rest of the state, the Indians have proved that they can survive.

It is no accident that an Irish-American, George M. Cohan, the great popular song writer from Providence, wrote "I'm a Yankee Doodle Dandy" and "It's a Grand Old Flag." Rhode Islanders still sing these songs at their Fourth of July band concerts in Roger Williams Park, left to the city by one of Williams's descendants in 1871. Rhode Islanders believe the words in Cohan's songs, because they have learned not only to identify with the best ideals of the state but also with the nation's success myth and its ability, as Walt Whitman put it, to "encompass multitudes." [4] There may be a greater gap today between the poorest and the richest inhabitants than there was in 1636 or 1776, but there is more genuine equality, more mutual respect, more personal dignity than there was throughout most of the nineteenth century. There are no slaves nor heathens to be despised; foreigners are not made scapegoats nor is the old friction between religious groups so strong. In that sense, the state has lived up to Williams's ideals.

The state stands today as a model for the concept of religious and ethnic pluralism. It has had to work hard to achieve that. Sociologists have recently discovered what Rhode Islanders were long aware of: the melting-pot theory never worked, and class consciousness has never existed. Like most Americans, Rhode Islanders think of themselves as self-reliant, self-made Americans, and they are proud of it. Political scientists say that an immigrant group has "arrived" or been accepted when it is able to field candidates for high office capable of drawing support from beyond the specific voters of the candidate's own eth-

4. Walt Whitman, "Song of Myself," in *Leaves of Grass* (New York: Random House, Modern Library Edition, 1921), p. 102.

nic group. The rise of Italian immigrants and their children to prominence since 1930 has been an excellent example. For Italo-Americans, "arrival" came with the election of John Orlando Pastore as governor in 1946.

Immigration from Italy became increasingly heavy after 1890, and in 1911 the French steamship company, the Fabre Line, began direct trips from Italy to Providence, including stops at Portugal and the Portuguese Islands for additional passengers. By 1920 there were more foreign-born Italians in Rhode Island than foreign-born Irish. In 1930, 53,635 of the 252,981 persons in Providence—more than one out of five—were Italo-Americans. Yet little effort was made at first by the two parties to appeal to these newcomers. The Republicans had made the first gesture when they appointed Antonio Capotosto as an assistant attorney general in 1912, a post he held until 1922. But the party declined to run him for any state office and instead appointed him to the state's supreme court. In 1918 the Democrats ran the first Italo-American for Congress, Luigi De Pasquale; and in 1926, they made him Democratic state chairman. In 1932 they ran Louis Capelli for lieutenant governor, but neither was elected. In 1938 the Democrats recognized the importance of Italian voters when they declared Columbus Day an official state holiday. But the first Italo-American governor took the state by surprise.

John Pastore had been elected lieutenant governor under J. Howard McGrath in 1944. When McGrath resigned as governor in 1945 to become Solicitor General of the United States, the Democrats found themselves with the first such governor in any state in the Union. Then, in 1946 and 1948, Pastore was elected on his own popularity and in 1950 went to the United States Senate, where he remained until 1976, serving with distinction on committees dealing with atomic energy and federal communications. The Irish dominance of the party cannot be said to have been broken until Joseph Bevilacqua became leader of the state's house of representatives in 1966.

John Pastore was the son of an immigrant tailor. In 1916, when he was nine, his father died, and he went to work to help support his mother, his three brothers, and two sisters. He worked while he finished high school, then worked his way through night law school. He entered the state legislature with the Green revolution in 1935, and within his mother's lifetime rose to govern the state and help rule the country from its most powerful elective body. Upon retirement from the senate after twenty-five years, he said, "To understand me and what motivates me you must understand my background. I was born on the third floor, rear, of a six-family house. We were a very poor but a very happy family. We learned to respect our elders. We learned to obey the law. We were taught from the beginning that if we worked long enough and hard enough our dreams would come true." [5] You cannot tell Rhode Islanders that the American Dream doesn't work. They have seen it work—not for all, but for enough; not always to the top, but a long way up, compared to life in the Old Country. The success story of Pastore in politics has been matched by other immigrants in business, law, and medicine.

Rhode Island is as much an immigrant state now as it was when the first immigrants arrived with Roger Williams. The immigrant has altered "American" institutions as the Yankees knew them as much as these institutions have molded him. Today the Roman Catholic Church (which the Puritans and ultra-Puritans sought to reform) is not only the dominant church numerically in the state, but the wealthiest, most prestigious, most influential. Its bishops wield more influence than the leaders of any other religious group. For many years, a Catholic priest was chairman of the state board of education. Today 90 percent of the legislators are Roman Catholic. They see their church not as an enemy of Americanism (as the Know-Nothings did in Thomas Dorr's day), but as its greatest bulwark. The fierce opposition of Catholicism to the spread of Communism since 1920 has greatly aided the immigrant in proving his loyalty to the American way of life. Today fundamentalist and Catholic patriots find they have much in common. Rhode Island's legislators see no reason why the state should not give assistance to the church in its mission, since that mission seems

5. *Providence Journal* (Providence, R. I.), September 23, 1976.

identical with America's mission. They find it hard to understand why the American Civil Liberties Union and the courts constantly claim they are breaking Roger Williams's line between church and state. Aid to parochial schools is certainly what the majority in the state wants. It may seem to infringe constitutional guarantees of separation between church and state to those who argue for the letter of the law, but ethnic legislators believe they better understand its spirit.

In 1976 John Cardinal Dearden, the first Rhode Island-born "Prince of the Church," gave an address at a bicentennial meeting sponsored by a Catholic alumni association in Providence. He praised the American principle of separation of church and state, but no one understood him to speak against state aid to parochial schools.

Catholic priests and nuns have in many ways become the social conscience of the state. They were active in the civil-rights movement. They worked for the passage of the Fair-Housing Law. They helped to integrate the schools. They joined the protests against the Vietnam War, organized on behalf of Chicano grape pickers, supported the claims of welfare mothers. Catholic prominence has raised some friction over birth control, censorship, and the Supreme Court's decision on abortion, but the legislature passed the Equal Rights Amendment. Had not Catholics come to respect the state's tradition of religous equality, the plight of non-Catholics might be more difficult today. They have not returned the bigotry they suffered, but accept the ideal of religious liberty as Roger Williams expressed it. Williams would find that very providential.

Rhode Island in its bicentennial year struggles into a fuzzy future, partly viewing itself in terms of New England's regional problems, partly seeing itself as belonging to that northeastern quadrant of the nation that has lost industrial dominance to the new "Southern rim." Most believe that it can solve its problems in energy, jobs, "stagflation," and foreign competition only through nationally directed and funded programs. Rhode Island and New England act on the national scene as a beleaguered minority pressure group. The state needs and wants help to keep up its hopes. Its internal affairs are a series of interlocking dilemmas: a solution to one problem seems only to exacerbate another.

To gain more jobs, the state needs more industry; to gain more industry, it may have to lower workers' benefits and give tax breaks to business, which will raise problems for consumers. Employers want to lower labor costs, but workers are fearful of losing hard-won labor benefits.

To increase tourism is an attractive alternative to those who want to conserve the state's natural beauty. But if limited resources go into that, they cannot go into helping industry and fisheries. Tourism may be at odds with the search for oil, with local housing development along the coast, with conservation efforts; it may mean more highways and public campsites. Conservationists generally favor tourism over new heavy industry, if the tourist sites don't harm the woods, the beaches, and the waterways—in short, if there aren't too many tourists. However, conservationists also fight against highways, which construction workers want, and nuclear power, with its promise of more jobs.

New ethnic groups, some of them aliens without visas, most of them nonunion, are welcomed by employers; but they compete with older immigrants who want union wage scales maintained. New immigrants provide cheap labor, but often increase welfare costs. Unions, though led by ethnics who worked their way up, want the new, illegal, "alien laborers" sent back. The middle class wants taxes cut, but the poor (with more votes) clamor for more aid. With limited revenues, the legislators have to take from one needy group to aid another. To cut expenditures, the state lets schools, parks, and public services slide, further annoying the voters and making the state less attractive. Recent efforts to obtain new revenue from legalized gambling aroused strong objections from the police, who said that would only increase organized crime, mobster violence, and business corruption. Yet, one legislator told the police, "We've always had organized crime, and there's no reason the state shouldn't have a piece of the action." [6] The state is torn between those

6. *Providence Journal,* February 21, 1976.

who want more police action against crime, with stiffer jail sentences, and those who insist that the penal system is itself a major source of continuing crime and injustice.

A recent editorial in the *Providence Journal* seems to touch a fundamental issue in this confusion and perhaps point to the future. Entitled "The Urgency of Preserving Rhode Island's Shoreline," it praised the work of the state Coastal Resources Management Council and the Coastal Resources Center for their efforts "to develop management policies and specific regulations." Warning of the "proliferation of residential housebuilding which is threatening one of the principal reasons for living along the south shore" and of the burgeoning "waste systems" that "threaten to disrupt the balance of nature," the editorial called for increasing co-operative effort by individuals and for increasing state management: "Substituting planned development for free-for-all coastal exploitation is the only way to ensure that one of the nation's most beautiful shorelines and one of Rhode Island's most prized assets" will survive. If the people of Rhode Island conclude that "free-for-all" individualism must give way to more co-operation, more balance and sharing, more planning in economic, political, and social affairs, the state may be on the brink of a major shift in its patterns of thought and behavior. In that breakthrough may lie Rhode Island's, and the nation's, real "Hope." [7]

7. *Providence Journal,* February 26, 1977.

Suggestions for Further Reading

Because this is only an interpretive essay, much has been condensed or omitted that is worth knowing about Rhode Island. Much of the most fascinating material is at present available only in magazine articles or unpublished theses written by students at the various colleges and universities in the state. Without trying to be all-inclusive, I will list chronologically here some of the best reading that I have found in books, articles, and theses.

The Colonial Period: 1636–1790. The most readable and up-to-date history of colonial Rhode Island is Sydney V. James's *Colonial Rhode Island* (N.Y.: Charles Scribner's Sons, 1975). James provides a lively, accurate, well-balanced treatment of the whole colonial period and a detailed critical bibliography. Of the numerous studies of Roger Williams, I find his intellectual position best stated in E. S. Morgan's *Roger Williams, the Church and the State* (N.Y.: Harcourt, Brace & World, 1967). The best study of his lively experiment in democracy is still S. H. Brockunier, *The Irrepressible Democrat, Roger Williams* (N.Y.: Ronald Press, 1940). The best general biography is Ola E. Winslow's *Master Roger Williams* (N.Y.: Geo. S. Ferguson Co., 1957). The early aspect of Anne Hutchinson's career is admirably described in Emery J. Battis, *Saints and Sectaries in the Massachusetts Bay Colony* (Chapel Hill, N.C.: U. of N.C. Press, 1962); there is no really adequate biography, but the best popular one is W. K. Rugg, *Unafraid: A Life of Anne Hutchinson* (Boston: Houghton-Mifflin, 1930). The fascinating careers of John Clarke and Samuel Gorton are available only in highly eulogistic accounts by ardent admirers: Thomas W. Bicknell, *The Story of Dr. John Clarke* (Providence: Published by the author, 1915) and Adelos Gorton, *The Life and Times of Samuel Gorton* (Philadelphia: G. S. Ferguson Co., 1907). For the early Quaker movement, there are many references to Rhode Island in Rufus M. Jones, *The Quakers in the American Colonies* (London: Macmillan Co., 1911) and Sydney V. James, *A People Among Peo-*

ples (Cambridge: Harvard, 1963). Carl Bridenbaugh has provided a sprightly account of the economic life of seventeenth-century Rhode Island in *Fat Mutton and Liberty of Conscience* (Providence: Brown U. Press, 1964). For variant views of the Rhode Island Indians and King Philip's War, see Francis Jennings, *The Invasion of America* (Chapel Hill, N.C.: U. North Carolina Press, 1975), Alden T. Vaughn, *New England Frontier* (Boston: Little, Brown, 1965), and Douglas E. Leach, *Flintlock and Tomahawk* (N.Y.: Macmillan, 1958).

Eighteenth-century Rhode Island is most succinctly described in William B. Weeden's *Early Rhode Island* (New York: Grafton Press, 1910) and Irving B. Richman, *Rhode Island, A Study in Separatism* (Boston: Houghton-Mifflin, 1905). But these older books need to be supplemented by more up-to-date studies, such as David S. Lovejoy's lively account of *Rhode Island Politics and the American Revolution* (Providence: Brown Univ., 1958), Irwin H. Polishook's scholarly *Rhode Island and the Union, 1774–1795* (Evanston, Illinois: Northwestern U., 1969), and Bruce M. Bigelow, "The Commerce of Rhode Island with the West Indies before the American Revolution," (Ph.D. diss., Brown University, 1930). The history of slavery in this era is well told in Lorenzo Greene's *The Negro in Colonial New England* (N.Y.: Columbia U. Press, 1942); the history of the Jews is thoroughly described in Jacob R. Marcus, *The Colonial American Jew* (Detroit: Wayne State U. Press, 1970). The standard history of the state's Ivy League college is Walter C. Bronson, *The History of Brown University* (Providence; Brown U. Press, 1914), and Arthur E. Wilson has provided a colorful account of the Great Awakening in the colony in *Weybosset Bridge* (Boston: Pilgrim Press, 1947). Antoinette F. Downing's *Early Homes of Rhode Island* (Richmond, Va.: Garrett & Massie Co., 1937) is a fine architectural study and should be complemented with Henry R. Hitchcock's *Rhode Island Architecture* (N.Y.: Da Capo Press, 1968) and with Ralph E. Carpenter, *The Arts and Crafts of Newport* (Newport: Newport Preservation Society, 1954) and Carl Bridenbaugh's *Peter Harrison, First American Architect* (Chapel Hill, N.C.: U. of North Carolina Press, 1949). Rhode Island's maritime and shipping history has been admirably described in James B. Hedges' two-volume study, *The Browns of Providence* (Providence: Brown U. Press, 1952, 1968) which carries the story into the early nineteenth century. Many excellent biographies are available on leading figures in eighteenth-century Rhode Island; they provide a wealth of detail about the social and intellectual life of the era: Mack E. Thompson, *Moses Brown* (Chapel Hill, N.C.: U. of North Carolina, 1962); E. S. Morgan, *Ezra Stiles* (New Haven: Yale Press, 1962); Theodore Thayer, *Nathanael Greene* (N.Y.: Twayne, 1960); Herbert A. Wisbey, *Pioneer Prophetess, Jemima Wilkinson* (Ithaca: Cornell U. Press, 1964); Stanley F. Chyet, *Lopez of Newport* (Detroit: Wayne State U. Press, 1970); and Joseph E. Conforti, "Samuel Hopkins" (Ph.D. diss., Brown University, 1975).

The Nineteenth Century. The most authoritative political and constitutional history of the state from the Revolution to the Dorr War is Patrick T. Conley, *Democracy in Decline: Rhode Island's Constitutional Development, 1776–1841* (Providence: Rhode Island Historical Society, 1977). While there are several multivolume histories of the state written at the end of the nineteenth century or early in the twentieth century that cover the period of industrial growth, they are very dull reading. Perhaps the most useful is Charles C. Carroll, *Rhode Island, Three Centuries of Democracy,* 4 vols. (N.Y.: Lewis Publishing Co., 1932). There is no good political history of that century, but two old books provide some coverage: Irving B. Richman, *Rhode Island* (N.Y.: G. P. Putnam Co., 1905) and Edward Field, *The State of Rhode Island,* 3 vols. (Boston: Mason Publishing Co., 1902). Narrower but more up-to-date studies of industrial growth are Peter J. Coleman, *The Transformation of Rhode Island, 1790–1861* (Providence: Brown U. Press, 1969), by far the best study of the rise of the textile industry; and Kurt B. Mayer, *Economic Development and Population Growth in Rhode Island* (Providence: Brown U. Press, 1953), which is statistical and demographic and goes into the first half of the twentieth century. Donald Fleming provides a short, readable account of *Science and Technology in Providence, 1760–1914* (Providence: Brown U. Press, 1952), and James V. Cassedy's excellent biography of Charles V. Chapin (Cambridge: Harvard, 1962) describes the public health movement after the Civil War. There is no good history of education in the state; so Charles Carroll's *Public Education in Rhode Island* (Providence: E. L. Freeman Co., 1918) has to suffice. Irving H. Bartlett has provided a brief, readable study of black history in the state, *From Slave to Citizen* (Providence: Urban League, 1954). This should be supplemented by Arline R. Kiven's "The Nature and Course of the Anti-Slavery Movement in Rhode Island" (M.A. thesis, Brown U., 1965). The early history of labor in Rhode Island can be traced in Editha Hadcock's Ph.D. dissertation (Brown University, 1945), "Labor Problems in Rhode Island Cotton Mills, 1790–1840" and Carl Gersuny, "Seth Luther," *Rhode Island History* 33, no. 2 (May 1974): 47–56. Also useful is Joseph Brennan's *Social Conditions in Industrial Rhode Island, 1820–1860* (Washington: Catholic U. Press, 1940). There is no good study of Irish or other immigrant groups in the state in this century, but John M. Ray discusses nativism in "Anti-Catholicism and Know-Nothingism in Rhode Island," *American Ecclesiastical Review* 148 (January 1963): 27–36. However, there is a great deal of social and immigrant history in the excellent diocesan study by Patrick T. Conley and Matthew J. Smith, *Catholicism in Rhode Island* (Providence: Diocese of R.I., 1976) and in the older volume, Thomas F. Cullen, *The Catholic Church in Rhode Island* (No. Providence: Franciscan Missionaries of Mary, 1936). Four volumes on the Dorr War deserve reading for their varying viewpoints: Arthur M. Mowry, *The Dorr War* (Providence: Preston & Rounds Co., 1901) is essentially unsympathetic; Marvin E. Gettleman, *The Dorr Rebellion* (N.Y.: Random House, 1973) portrays him as a radical; George M. Dennison, *The Dorr War, 1831–1861* (Lexington, Ky.: University Press of Kentucky, 1976) deals with broad constitutional issues; Patrick T. Conley, "Rhode Island Constitutional Development" (Ph.D. diss., Notre Dame, 1970), portrays him favorably as a liberal Democrat. Politics in the middle of the century is analyzed in William B. Thompson's M.A. thesis on "Henry Bowen Anthony," (University of Rhode Island, 1960) and Robert C. Powers's "Rhode Island Republicans in the Gilded Age" (Honors thesis, Brown University, 1972). Politics at the end of the century is carefully analyzed in Jerome B. Sternstein's "Nelson Wilmarth Aldrich" (Ph.D. diss., Brown University, 1968). The leading feminist, antislavery crusader, and suffrage reformer Elizabeth Buffum Chace is ably presented in a biography, *Elizabeth Buffum Chace*, by Lillie B. Chace Wyman and Arthur Wyman (Boston: W. B. Clarke Co., 1914). A biography of Paulina Wright Davis is badly needed. There is no adequate study of Newport society in the years 1880–1935, though it is treated in journalistic fashion in Cleveland Amory's *The Last Resorts* (N.Y.: Harper & Bros., 1948) and in Bertram Lippincott, *Indians, Privateers, and High Society* (Philadelphia: Lippincott Co., 1961). For an insider's view of Newport high society, see Maud Howe Elliott, *This Was My Newport* (Cambridge, Mass.: The Mythology Co., 1944). Newport's architecture is magnificently portrayed in A. F. Downing and V. J. Scully, Jr., *The Architectural Heritage of Newport, Rhode Island, 1640–1915*, 2d ed. (N.Y.: C. N. Potter, 1967).

    The Twentieth Century. Unfortunately, little has been done to study the important economic, political, social, and ethnographic history of Rhode Island in this century. Here the interested reader must turn to historical journals and scholarly theses. The corruption under "Boss" Brayton during the Progressive Era is sardonically told by Lincoln Steffens in "Rhode Island, a State for Sale," *McClure's Magazine* 24, no. 4 (February 1905): 330–353. The rise of public utilities is analyzed in Robert F. Falb, "Marsden J. Perry, the Man Who Owned Rhode Island" (Brown University, Honors thesis, 1964). The career of Senator Greene and his Bloodless Revolution in 1935 is traced in Erwin L. Levine's *Theodore Francis Greene*, 2 vols. (Providence: Brown U. Press, 1963 and 1971). Politics since 1920 have been studied by Matthew J. Smith in "The Real McCoy" and "Rhode Island Politics, 1956–1964" in *Rhode Island History* 32, no. 3 (August 1973): 67–86 and *Rhode Island History* 35, no. 2 (May 1976): 49–62. David Patten has provided colorful journalistic accounts of the political machinations of the 1920s in *Rhode Island Story* (Providence: Providence Journal Co., 1954). Elmer E. Cornwell traced the relationship between politics and ethnicity in "Party Absorption of Ethnic Groups, the Case of Providence, R.I." in *Social Forces* 38, no. 3 (March 1960): 205–210. Duane Lockard has a chapter on Rhode Island politics in the years 1935–1959 in *New England State Politics* (Princeton: Princeton Press, 1959) as does Samuel Lubell in *The Future of American Politics* (London: Hamish Hamilton, 1952). Neal R. Pierce, *The New England States* (New York: W. W. Norton & Company, Inc.) has, on pp. 141–181, a good summary of the recent political and economic history of the state. Interesting reflections on progressive-era politics are in John D. Buenker, *Urban Liberalism and Progressive Reform* (N.Y.: Scribners, 1973). A short but useful sketch by Murray S. Stedman and Susan W. Stedman traces "The Rise of the Democratic Party in Rhode Island," in the *New England Quarterly* 24 (September 1951): 329–41.

The rise of organized labor and its alliance with the Democratic party in the state is traced in Jay S. Goodman, *The Democrats and Labor in Rhode Island, 1952–1962* (Providence: Brown U. Press, 1967) and Edmund J. Brock, *The Background and Recent Status of Collective Bargaining in the Cotton Industry of Rhode Island* (Washington, D.C.: Catholic University Press, 1942). Valuable demographic and economic data are provided in Kurt B. Mayer and Sidney Goldstein, *Migration and Economic Development in Rhode Island* (Providence: Brown University Press, 1958).

The only book on the woman suffrage movement in Rhode Island is the autobiography of Sara Algeo, *The Story of a Sub-Pioneer* (Providence: Snow & Farnham Co., 1925); however, there are two chapters on the movement in the six-volume *History of Woman Suffrage* edited by S. B. Anthony and Ida H. Harper (Rochester, N.Y.: n.p., 1902–1922). The first is by Anna G. Spencer and the second by Elizabeth U. Yates. The famous controversy between the French Canadians and Bishop Hickey is thoroughly treated in Richard S. Sorrell's "The Sentinelle Affair" (Ph.D. diss., State University of New York at Buffalo, 1976). See also Mason Wade's broad-ranging study, *The French-Canadians, 1760–1967*, 2 vols. (N.Y.: St. Martin's Press, 1968). Leo F. Carroll has a short sketch on "Irish and Italians in Providence, R.I., 1880–1960," in *Rhode Island History* 28, no. 3 (August 1969): 67–75, and Peter Bardoglio traces Italian controversies with the diocese in "Italian Immigrants and the Catholic Church in Providence, 1890–1930," *Rhode Island History* 34, no. 2 (May 1975): 47–57. Portuguese immigrants have been studied in two Brown University theses: Susan Sharf, "The Cape Verdeans in Providence" (Honors thesis, Brown University, 1965) and Susan Ferst, "The Immigration and Settlement of the Portuguese in Providence, 1890–1924" (Master's thesis, Brown University, 1972).

Index

235

CPSIA information can be obtained
at www.ICGtesting.com
Printed in the USA
BVHW070344260821
615084BV00001B/25